TEACHING SPELLING

to English Language Learners

Johanna Stirling

PUBLISHED BY LULU
RALEIGH, USA

©Johanna Stirling 2011
ISBN: 978-1-4476-0678-9

For any other permission, queries or further copies, please email johanna.stirling@gmail.com

First published 2011

V6

Contents

About the author

Johanna Stirling works as a freelance English Language Teaching Consultant. She is based in the United Kingdom. She worked for over twenty years for Bell International as a teacher and teacher trainer. There, one of her specialisations was teaching those who struggled with spelling. She has an MA (Distinction) in Professional Development for Language Education, for which she wrote a dissertation on *The Need for an Integrated and Diverse Approach to the Teaching of English Spelling to Adult EFL Learners*.

Nowadays, much of Johanna's work is at NILE (Norwich Institute for Language Education) where she is an Associate Trainer. She also works for Cambridge University Press, writing teaching materials and giving presentations and workshops to teachers around the world. She is the webmistress of The English Language Garden at www.elgweb.net. She also has a blog dedicated to all things related to spelling:

The Spelling Blog at http://thespellingblog.blogspot.com

For more details about Johanna please see http://www.elgweb.net/cv.html
She is available to give workshops and courses. Contact: **johanna.stirling@gmail.com**

Acknowledgements

from the author

I owe a great deal to a great many people. Two who have been of invaluable direct help with editing are Carole Robinson and Sharon Whittaker. They have been truly generous friends. Daryl Fraser (www.darylfraser.com) has not only helped with text and advice, but has been the rock solid support that has allowed this book to finally reach completion. His tolerance and encouragement have been remarkable and deeply appreciated.

Thanks also to Sandra Escursell for the cover design and Luke Tuddenham for his generously lent eagle eyes.

Many other people have contributed less directly, not least the many learners who inspired my interest in the subject and ultimately this book. I would also like to thank colleagues over the years and I hope I haven't unwittingly stolen any of their ideas and presented them as my own.

This book is dedicated to the memory of Jean Mary Stirling 1920 – 2002.

Johanna Stirling

Introduction

Aim of the book

The overall aim of this book is to present a fresh and effective methodology for spelling improvement along with activities to help students who struggle with English spelling. To implement this methodology, teachers need an understanding of the problems that their students face in terms of the language, the learning process and the tuition they may receive.

Who is the book for?

This book is written primarily with teachers of English language learners (teens and adults) in mind.

However, English is English and learning is learning. So very much of the book will be relevant to teachers of:

- young learners of English as a foreign language;

- native-speaker adults who struggle with English spelling, due to lack of appropriate education or learning strategies, or perhaps a condition such as dyslexia;

- native-speaker children (although this is the one group for which there is already extensive literature on spelling, teachers and parents are sure to find some new ideas and invaluable background information here too).

Many factors are common to all of the groups above and I have researched literature from them all. Here I have collected ideas from these different sources and attempted to join up the dots to make a coherent picture of how we can most successfully deal with the business of spelling.

Note: British English spelling is used throughout the book, but US English variations are addressed when analysing the language system.

Finding your way around

The book is divided into three parts.

Part A outlines the issues involved in teaching and learning spelling. This is approached by looking at the importance of spelling, and the challenges related to the language itself, the learners and the teachers.

Part B attempts to deal with these issues by presenting a fresh, new approach to the teaching of spelling to English language learners. It takes into account what English spelling is really like, what learners are really like and what teachers are really like.

Part C offers tools in the form of activities, techniques and resources for implementing the approach outlined in Part B.

If you like, Part A tells us *why* we have a problem, Part B tells us *what* we can do about it and Part C shows *how*.

There is no need to work through the book from beginning to end but a much clearer picture will emerge if you do. Many teachers will not have time to do this, so start with what you need or what interests you. There is extensive cross-referencing, so if you prefer, you can 'surf' through it. References inform you of the page number and which part of the book it is found in so that you know whether it refers to background knowledge (A), the approach (B), or activities (C). A reference to B:130 means page 130 which is in Part B of the book.

The Spelling Blog

The Spelling Blog at **http://thespellingblog.blogspot.com** is a valuable companion to this book. There you will not only find worksheets from this book to download in colour and sound files for many of the activities, but also discussion of many of the issues raised in the book. There is also an up-to-date list of available resources related to spelling and some PowerPoint presentations that can be used in class.

Glossary and Abbreviations

Affix	Letters added to a word to change the meaning or function. See **Prefix, Suffix, Morpheme.**
AmE	American English.
Automaticity	The ability to do something, such as spell, without conscious thought about the process.
Base element	A **morpheme** that carries the main meaning in a word. Also called Root or Base word.
BrE	British English.
C	Consonant. In writing, the letters *b, c, d, f, g, h, j, k, l, m, n, p, q, r, s, t, v, w, x, y, z*.
Concordancer	A computer program which contains a large corpus of text and enables the user to search for examples of language.
CVC words	Words ending with a consonant-vowel-consonant pattern.
Digraph	Two letters used together to make one sound, such as *ch* or *ir*. (Three letters together for one sound make a trigraph.)
Diphthong	Two vowel sounds that glide together to make one sound, such as /a/ + /ɪ/ which make /aɪ/.
Dyslexia	An inherited condition which makes reading, writing and spelling very difficult.
EFL	English as a Foreign Language.
ELL	English language learner.
ESOL	English for Speakers of Other Languages (term used in the UK for classes of learners who are already resident there).
Etymology	The study of the origin of words.
Grapheme	A letter or combination of letters that make one **phoneme.**
Homophone	A word that sounds the same as another which has different spelling and meaning.
Humane dictation	A dictation in which learners have the opportunity to see the text and learn difficult spellings before having to write.
IELTS	International English Language Testing System (language test for university entrance, migration and some jobs)
Inflection	Letters added to the end of a word to change the grammar, such as *-ed, -s.*
In-line letters	Letters without **sticks** or **tails**: *a, c, e, i, m, n, o, r, s, u, v, w, x, z.* (Author's own terminology.)
Kinaesthetic	To describe activities which involve physical movement.
L1 /L2	L1 is the mother tongue, L2 is the target language
Letter string	A sequence of letters commonly found in words, e.g. *ough*
Mnemonic	A trick for remembering something.
Morpheme	The smallest part of a word that carries meaning — **base elements, prefixes** and **suffixes** are all types of morpheme.
Morphology	The study of **morphemes** and how they combine.
NLP	Neuro-Linguistic Programming: A study of human behaviour which leads to the creation of models of excellence in different fields. Informs some humanistic teaching methods.
Orthography	The spelling and punctuation of a language.

Outlining	Drawing around the shape of a word.
Overwriting	Writing over the top of certain letters with a different colour to highlight them.
Phoneme	The smallest unit of sound that carries meaning.
Phonics	A system for teaching spelling by relating sounds and letters.
Prefix	Letters added to the beginning of a word to change its meaning, such as *un*- or *anti*-.
Rhotic/ Non-rhotic accent	In a rhotic accent the letter *r* is pronounced after a vowel in words such as *car* (most **AmE** accents); this *r* is not pronounced in non-rhotic accents (e.g. most southern British accents).
Schwa	A short unstressed **vowel** sound made with the mouth and tongue in a neutral position; the final sound in *teacher*.
Shallow/deep orthography	If a language is spelled phonetically, it is described as having a shallow **orthography**. If it is deep, there is not strict correlation between sound and spelling.
Sticks	Tall parts of letters *b, d, f, h, k, l, t*.
Suffix	Letters added to the end of a word that usually change the word class, or occasionally the meaning, such as -*ment*, -*ion*, -*ful*.
Syllable	In pronunciation, a part of a word that includes one vowel sound and possibly one or more consonant sounds.
Synonym/Antonym	Two words with the same or very similar meanings are synonyms. Antonyms are opposites.
Tails	Parts of letters *g, j, p, q, y*, that fall below the writing line.
V	Vowel. In writing, the letters *a, e, i, o, u*.
VAK	Visual, Auditory, **Kinaesthetic**.
Verb 1 (V1)	The infinitive without *to*. For example, *work*, *see*.
Verb 2 (V2)	Also called past form. Regular verbs have -*ed* ending. For example, *worked*, *saw*.
Verb 3 (V3)	Also called past participle. Regular verbs have -*ed* ending. For example, *worked*, *seen* .

Throughout the book the following styles have been used:

- Examples of letters, combinations of letters, and words are in ***bold italic*** to distinguish them from the rest of the text.

- Examples of errors are in ~~***bold italic strikethrough***~~. Seeing misspellings, especially commonly confused ones, can cause them to stick in the reader's mind or cause doubt where there previously was none. The ~~strikethrough~~ hopefully disrupts the visual sense of the word, so it won't be remembered.

- Examples of foreign words (not used in English) are in *italic*.

Key to Pronunciation (British)

(International Phonetic Alphabet)

Consonants

IPA symbol	Key word
b	ball
d	day
ð	then
dʒ	joke
f	for
g	gate
h	hill
j	yes
k	key
l	long
m	man
n	not
ŋ	sing
p	pot
r	rat
s	soon
ʃ	shop
t	tell
tʃ	chip
θ	thing
v	van
w	win
z	zero
ʒ	television

Vowels

IPA Symbol	Key word
Short vowels	
æ	add
e	egg
ə	again
ɪ	ill
ɒ	hot
ʌ	up
ʊ	book
Long vowels	
ɑː	car
ɜː	her
iː	green
ɔː	door
uː	blue
Diphthongs	
aɪ	eye
aʊ	now
eə	air
eɪ	say
əʊ	know
ɪə	ear
ɔɪ	boy
ʊə	pure

PART A
Issues in Spelling

Introduction to Part A: Issues in Spelling

The first part of the book describes the ways in which spelling is an issue, and then what some of the obstacles to spelling accuracy are. These relate to the language itself, the learners and the teaching of it. Below is a brief description of each chapter.

- We start by considering why good spelling is important for learners (Chapter 1)

The Language

- An overview of attitudes towards English orthography, the systems that construct it and some variations that exist (Chapter 2).
- A brief history of English spelling — quite a story! (Chapter 3). This is where we see there is some method in the apparent madness, but also some madness in the attempt to make method.
- A description of the etymological system within English spelling (Chapter 4). Here we explore more specifically how historical influences can really inform our spelling choices.
- The section on the phonological aspects of English spelling (Chapter 5) is detailed and should provide useful future reference. It helps us to see to just what extent English spelling is or isn't based on sound — a crucial question.
- The chapter on graphemic patterns looks at common letter strings and conventions in spelling that are not directly related to sound (Chapter 6).
- Exploring the morphological system next (Chapter 7) comes as rather a relief, as there is much more regularity and predictability here.
- And looking at the lexical system is revelatory and, dare I say it, fun (Chapter 8).

Throughout these chapters we see why some 'rules' need to be questioned and we question why some useful patterns are usually ignored. All this knowledge allows us to recognise and appreciate a sense of system that we can pass on to our learners rather than agreeing with them that English spelling is a completely chaotic mess (it certainly isn't).

The learners

- How we spell, both when reading and when writing. And why some people find it much easier than others (Chapter 9).
- How we learn successfully. What we know about learning in general that we must consider when thinking about learning spelling (Chapter 10).
- The kind of errors that different types of learners make and why (Chapter 11).

The teaching

- How spelling is currently taught in different contexts (Chapter 12).
- What English language teachers say about teaching spelling (Chapter 13).

Chapter One:

Why Teach Spelling?

Why should we bother teaching English spelling?

Is good spelling necessary in this technological age?

Does spelling affect other writing skills?

Does spelling affect general language learning?

Is spelling caught or taught?

Why should we bother teaching English spelling?

Remembering spellings is no problem when it is not a problem and a considerable problem when it is.

(Smith, 1982)

Spelling matters

For many people spelling is just not an issue. They write what they want to write and the spelling seems to flow from the tips of their fingers or pen onto the screen or paper. They occasionally hesitate over a word but are soon back into full flow, enjoying being able to choose just the right words to express themselves accurately. Or, perhaps more likely, not actually enjoying it but taking it for granted that all of those words are there for them to pick and choose from at will.

For others however, writing is a painful and frustrating process. Letters are not their friends. Letters are part of a code they can't break, but everyone else, it seems, can. Letters and words make a language they can't use properly, where they hesitate, can't say what they really mean, come across as less intelligent, less witty or less careful than they really are.

Poor spelling can cost people their jobs (or potential jobs), can deny them educational opportunities and can lose them business. Whether we like it or not, many people do judge others on their spelling (*See C:250*). It seems that even people who are not good spellers themselves look down on those whose spelling is worse than their own.

English language learners

Many English language learners (ELLs) pick up English spelling remarkably well, but others find it a tremendous struggle. Why?

Some possible reasons:

- Their first language may use the same alphabet but be spelled just as it sounds, like Italian or Finnish, so they can't understand why English isn't like that too.
- Their mother tongue is written in an entirely different script, like Chinese, which makes the work load so much heavier.
- Maybe vowels are less important in their own language, say Arabic, and they see them as optional in English too.
- They may find it difficult to discriminate between sounds.
- Perhaps they just haven't seen enough written text in English.
- They may not have been taught spelling properly.

In fact, a few years ago I was worried that I was one of those teachers who were failing to help her students who were struggling with spelling. I would watch learners who were communicative, intelligent and hard-working repeatedly missing their goals because spelling was such an obstacle. I was frustrated that I had no useful and appropriate advice for such learners. That frustration, incidentally, led to this book!

For some language learners, writing is not important; effective oral communication is the main aim, and spelling is not a matter of concern. On the other hand, there are some students who need a reasonable proficiency in writing to be able to continue their academic or professional careers. They may need to pass public examinations which are required by their employers, potential employers or academic institutions. They may be taking an IELTS or TOEFL test to enter English-speaking higher education, or maybe they just need to be able to write clear and accurate letters, reports, essays, etc.

Young learners also need help to achieve a good, solid base of spelling ability. It is easier to teach it well when children are just starting to learn to write in English, rather than many years later trying to correct errors that have become fossilised.

Is good spelling necessary in this technological age?

Writing is in!

The most stunning effect that the growth of ICT (Information and Communication Technology) has had is that writing is re-emerging as a widely used skill. It's estimated that about 200 billion emails are sent a day, which is about 2 million every second. There are more than 500 million active users of Facebook worldwide, with more than 4 billion minutes spent on the site per day. We send text messages (SMS), 'chat' online, join discussion groups, 'tweet' on Twitter, write blogs, comment on blogs and even publish our own books! Some of these require less accurate spelling (or, as in the case of SMS, even *different* spelling), but this makes it even more important for learners to know what is 'correct' or acceptable when they are in a situation that does demand accuracy.

"Texting is ruining spelling"

Complaints are often voiced that 'chatting' online and texting are ruining young people's spelling, as they carry over shortened forms into more formal writing. However, according to extensive research by Stanford University this is not the case. The Stanford Study of Writing collected and analysed 14,672 pieces of writing from US college students and found that there was no evidence of this. Furthermore, the organiser of the study, Professor Andrea Lansford, said,

> I think we're in the midst of a literacy revolution the likes of which
> we haven't seen since Greek civilization.

(Lunsford, 2009)

She found that students were enjoying writing (out of class) because they had a real audience and a real purpose. They also had an acute awareness of who they were writing for and an ability to adjust their writing to suit that context. In other words, they were fully aware of when shortened forms were appropriate and when they were not.

David Crystal, in his book *Txtng: The gr8 db8*, argues that the very people who use a lot of abbreviations in their text messages are the ones with good literacy skills:

> Children could not be good at texting if they had not already developed
> considerable literacy awareness. Before you can write abbreviated forms
> effectively and play with them, you need to have a sense of how the sounds
> of your language relate to letters. You need to know that there are such
> things as alternative spellings. You need to have a good visual memory and
> good motor skills.

(Crystal, 2008, p. 162)

Spell-checkers

Some may argue that computer spell-checkers make it unnecessary to learn spelling nowadays. They are certainly very useful tools, but the misspelling of a word has to be reasonably similar to the real word to prompt the correct spelling to be shown.

Also, for many learners, some training is needed in how to use spell-checkers effectively (*See B:150, C:256*). I have witnessed learners in my class automatically choosing the suggestion given at the top of the list without looking at the others, sometimes with nonsensical results. One who wanted to start a sentence with "The main thing is..." produced "The main thighbone is..."!

The other serious drawback to spell-checkers is that they only recognise whether a spelling exists, not whether it is correct in its context. So homophones (and words which may sound homophonous to a language learner's ear), such as the ones in this poem, are not marked as errors by a spell-checker:

Eye halve a spelling chequer,
It came with my pea sea
It plainly marques four my revue
Miss steaks eye kin knot sea

Eye have run this poem threw it,
I'm shore your pleased two no,
Its letter perfect in it's weigh;
My chequer tolled me sew.[1]

For learners whose first language is not English or who struggle with spelling, we can see that a spell-checker is not a reliable replacement for spelling skills and knowledge, only a tool that becomes increasingly useful as spelling improves.

Computers demand accuracy

In fact, far from making us lazy with our spelling, computers are very demanding of accuracy. If you misspell the URL (web address) of a website by even one letter you will not find the correct page. An email with a tiny mistake in the address, such as a space, will bounce back to you. If a computer game requires you to write anything, the smallest error will lose you the same points as a completely wrong answer. (*See B:158, C:250*)

Does spelling affect other writing skills?

Spelling is, of course, only one skill within writing, but a vitally important one if learners are to make further progress with other writing skills. As Scott points out,

> *Cognitive resources directed to spelling compete with those needed for generating content, with attendant rate and quality implications.*

(Scott, 2000, p. 67)

In other words, if you are too busy concentrating on spelling letter by letter, your brain is unlikely to be at its creative or intellectual best.

Another detrimental effect of poor spelling is that the learners may severely limit their lexical range, rejecting more appropriate or precise words for those that are easier to spell.

Research and experience suggest that poor spelling (and handwriting) can negatively affect teacher evaluations of writing, even if other considerations such as content and structure are of a good standard (Chase, 1986). It may not be fair, but it's a fact.

Does spelling affect general language learning?

An awareness of one's own spelling deficiencies can also lead to a lack of self-confidence, which can impact on other areas of language improvement. Written answers to grammar exercises can suffer, not because the learner has failed to grasp the structural point, but because poor spelling masks the correct answer or distracts the reader from it.

---

[1] There are many versions of this poem that illustrate the point. This is a shortened version of one found at http://en.wikipedia.org/wiki/Spell-checker .

Working in a private language school in the UK, my colleagues and I had numerous conversations about students who spoke and understood English well, knew a wide range of vocabulary and grammatical structure, could use English appropriately, and so on, but when their pens hit paper they were highly inaccurate. What do you do with the student who can't spell well but who can answer all the questions confidently in class, who is getting frustrated by classmates who are functionally weaker at the language, and who is working hard to improve. Do they move up to a higher group, where they will not get any help with spelling? Or should they go down to a lower one, where their motivation and self-esteem are likely to flag?

Future consequences

Holding learners back because of their weak spelling can have negative consequences on their future plans. They may need English to study at an English-speaking university, or for business purposes, but be obstructed by the level of their spelling. Alternatively, the weak spelling itself may be the hindrance if it prevents students succeeding at examinations. For example, in the IELTS examinations[2] candidates are penalised for spelling errors in their answers in the listening paper (although, perversely it seems, there is more tolerance of errors in the writing paper). If the learner does manage to secure a place on an undergraduate or post-graduate course, there will be assignments, reports and dissertations to write and students will want to produce error-free work that does not detract from the content.

Is spelling caught or taught?

There has been much discussion about whether spelling is 'taught' or 'caught' in the mother tongue. As Peters writes,

> *... although it is generally agreed that children must be taught to read, it has long been assumed that spelling is caught, that it occurs incidentally, and if it doesn't there's very little teachers can do about it.*

(Peters, 1985)

The fact that most ELLs manage to spell reasonably well with little instruction certainly seems to suggest that for the majority of them spelling is largely 'caught'. However, many others have certain areas of difficulty in spelling and some learners struggle far more to spell English accurately and need help. In other words they need to be taught.

Looking through most English language learning coursebooks, it seems that the assumption is that spelling is caught. There is usually very scant attention paid to this area of language learning. Even quite advanced students are often surprised and grateful to learn about certain spelling patterns, frequently responding with "Why hasn't anyone told me this before?"

---

[2] IELTS (English Language Testing System) is an examination which many students need to take to enter English-speaking higher education institutions, especially in the UK and Australia.

Summary of Chapter 1

- Accurate spelling is needed to succeed in many areas of life. Those who find it difficult because of their mother tongue or other reasons, can be disadvantaged if their problems persist.

- Living in a wired world actually demands higher spelling abilities as we have to write more, abbreviate language, use spell-checkers wisely and type accurately to get the required results.

- Learners who struggle with spelling may produce less sophisticated writing as they avoid words they can't spell, or focus so much on spelling that they have little time left for the content.

- Weak spelling skills can hold learners back in their general language development as they can't cope with written work at the level of the rest of their English, and this may also affect their future plans.

- While some learners 'catch' or acquire spelling from reading, others need much more instruction

TEACHING SPELLING

Chapter Two:

Descriptions of English Spelling

How has English orthography been described?

Are these descriptions fair?

Is English orthography unsystematic?

What about other varieties of English spelling?

How has English orthography been described?

Harsh words

English spelling comes in for a great deal of criticism. Some see it as a chaotic mess, others as a very faulty system based on phonology. Its irregularities and exceptions are often highlighted and laughed about. Here is more defamation of its character:

> In regard to the acquisition of our language by foreigners, the evil of our irregular orthography is extensive, beyond what is generally known or conceived. While the French and Italians have had the wisdom and the policy to refine and improve their respective languages, and render them almost the common languages of all well-bred people in Europe; the English language, clothed in a barbarous orthography, is never learned by a foreigner but from necessity; and the most copious language to Europe, embodying an uncommon mass of science and erudition, is thus very limited in its usefulness.
>
> (Webster, An American Dictionary of the English Language, 1884, p. 95)

> ... the English alphabet is pure insanity... It can hardly spell any word in the language with any degree of certainty.
>
> (Twain, undated)

18

Ours is a mongrel language which started with a child's vocabulary of three hundred words, and now consists of two hundred and twenty-five thousand; the whole lot, with the exception of the original and legitimate three hundred, borrowed, stolen, smouched from every unwatched language under the sun, the spelling of each individual word of the lot locating the source of the theft and preserving the memory of the revered crime.

(Twain, undated)

Our language is a rich verbal tapestry woven together from the tongues of the Greeks, the Latins, the Angles, the Klaxtons, the Celtics, the 76'ers and many other people, all of whom had severe drinking problems.

(Barry, undated)

The English have no respect for their language, and will not teach their children to speak it. They spell it so abominably that no man can teach himself what it sounds like. It is impossible for an Englishman to open his mouth without making some other Englishman hate or despise him. German and Spanish are accessible to foreigners: English is not accessible even to Englishmen.

(Shaw, 1916)

Are these descriptions fair?

But others have a different view:

The use of English, even by foreigners, doesn't seem to have been halted by difficulties in reading and writing it. This is because the spelling system, no less than the grammar and vocabulary, is sensitive, systematic, economical, and able both to resist and to accommodate change.

(Visser, 1994)

Conventional orthography is ... a near optimal system for the lexical representation of English words

(Chomsky N. H., 1968)

In order to come to the defence of English spelling, we need to assess just how regular or irregular it really is.

Who is more accurate, Noah Webster, in calling it "a barbarous orthography" or, at the other extreme, Noam Chomsky, who described it as "a near optimal system" (Chomsky & Halle, The Sound Pattern of English, 1968, p. 49)?

One thing we can agree on is that English spelling is complex. A language can be described as having a 'shallow' orthography, that is, a spelling system which correlates closely with the pronunciation of the words. Finnish and Italian are examples of this; English obviously is not — in other words, the orthography is 'deep'. However, spelling doesn't necessarily have to be based on sound. Most Chinese writing, for example, is logographic — that is the strokes or 'radicals' in the characters represent meaning rather than sound. This is an example of a deep orthography.

So is English more like Finnish or Chinese? It is usually assumed that it is based on sound like Finnish, but that it's very defective. Perhaps by looking at it as halfway between Chinese and Finnish we don't need to label it as defective after all. So it is often the *perception* that is at fault, not the language itself.

Is English spelling unsystematic?

If English is clearly not *completely* logographic, nor reliably based on sound, which system does it use? The answer is several different ones, and this is what makes it so complex. Ken Albrow describes it as "polysystemic". He explains,

> *Many of the so-called irregularities of our writing system can be regarded as regular, provided it is not assumed beforehand that everything must of necessity be forced into one framework.*

(Albrow 1972, p. 7)

So while even Chomsky would not argue that it is phonologically regular, we can see a much higher degree of regularity if we consider five different systems.

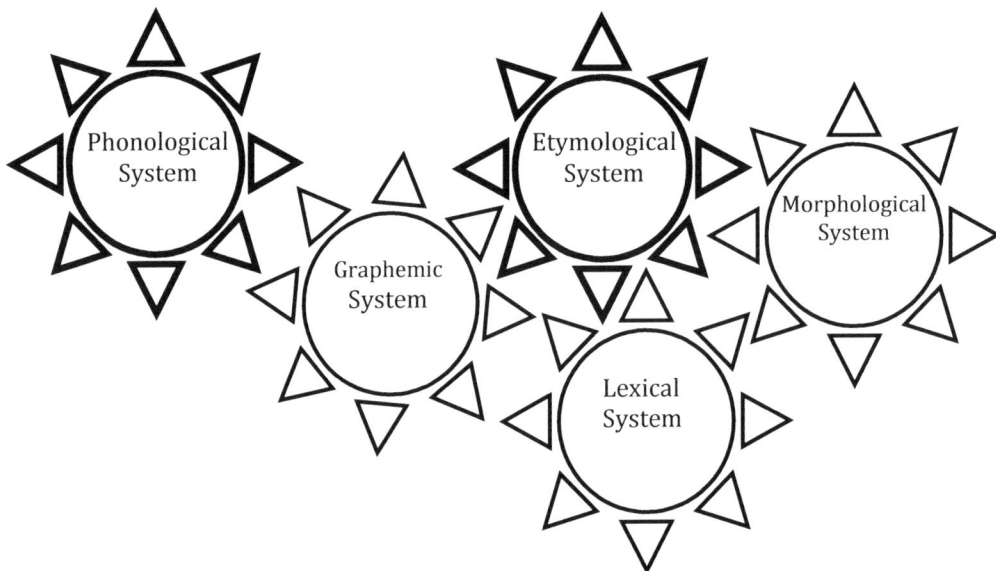

Figure 1: *Systems in English Orthography*

There is, of course, the **phonological** system, which is what most people first try to relate English spelling to. English writing is alphabetic so spelling must be based, at least partially, on sound. However, as we will see, several other systems not only exist but also sometimes over-ride this phonological system.

People also learn **graphemic** rules (for example, "*i* before *e* except after *c*"). These can be helpful guides but are also very often plagued by exceptions, so we cannot entirely rely on the graphemic system either.

Much more regular and reliable is the **morphological** system. The spelling of prefixes, suffixes and the rules for adding these to words are remarkably predictable, although of course they do not help with all words.

Most people are aware that words that have been imported from other languages may have different spelling conventions (e.g. *cello*, *chef*), but may not be aware how critical **etymological** systems are, and that they in fact have primacy over most other systems.

Another consideration, one that is largely overlooked but very important is the **lexical** system. Spelling relates to meaning far more than people generally believe.

What about other varieties of English spelling?

In describing English spelling, we also have to take into account that there isn't just one variety in use.

Spelling has been described as 'a unifying force in world English' (Quirk, Greenbaum, Leech, & J, 1985). In other words, pronunciation varies widely but spelling is much more consistent. There are, however, some differences. The most obvious are those between British English and American English.

How did US spelling come to be different from English spelling? The big mover and shaker was Noah Webster, who said,

> *It has been observed by all writers, on the English language, that the orthography or spelling of words is very irregular ... The question now occurs; ought the Americans to retain these faults which produce innumerable inconveniencies in the acquisition and use of the language, or ought they at once to reform these abuses, and introduce order and regularity into the orthography of the AMERICAN TONGUE?*

(Webster, 1789)

Mr Webster thought reform was definitely needed. And he proposed the following changes:

- "*The omission of all superfluous or silent letters.*" So he wanted **bread** to be **bred**, **friend** to be **frend** and **give** to be **giv**.

- "*A substitution of a character that has a certain definite sound, for one that is more vague and indeterminate.*" This would give us **neer** for **near**, **laf** for **laugh**, **blud** for **blood**, **wimmin** for **women** and **korus** for **chorus**.

- "... *ch in French derivatives should be changed into sh*". So you would do your washing in a **masheen** and a **shef** would work in a restaurant. Other French spellings would also go, leaving us with **toor** (**tour**) and **obleek** (**oblique**).

- *"A trifling alteration in a character, or the addition of a point would distinguish different sounds, without the substitution of a new character."* So here he proposed putting a little line across **th** to distinguish the voiced and unvoiced sounds. And he suggested using some dots over vowel letters to differentiate them.

Some of these suggestions were adopted, at least in part, but many of them the public just refused to use:

- The string **our** got changed to **or**, so **colour** became **color**, but it never got as far as ~~culor~~.

- The letters **re** at the end of a word became **er**, so the British **theatre** became the US **theater** but for some reason not always (**American National Theatre**) and **acre** didn't become ~~acer~~ (because it would change the pronunciation).

- **Cheque** got shortened to **check**, but **unique** didn't ever make it to ~~uneek~~ (or ~~yooneek~~).

But nit-picking aside, on the next page is a list of the most common differences between British English (BrE) and American English (AmE). Australia and New Zealand generally use BrE spellings and Canada largely uses it too except where noted below.

There are also some individual words that have spelling variants. There is a good list at http://en.wikipedia.org/wiki/American_and_British_English_spelling_differences.

Differences between British English and American English

SPELLING PATTERN BrE/AmE	British English (BrE) spellings	American English (AmE) spellings	Notes
-our/-or	*colour* *favourite* *neighbour*	*color* *favorite* *neighbor*	
-re/-er	*theatre* *centre* *litre*	*theater* or *theatre* *center* *liter*	There are also many words that end in -er in BrE. *theatre* is sometimes used in AmE for names of particular establishments.
-ise /-ize	*categorise* or *categorize* *apologise* or *apologize*	*categorize* *apologize*	In BrE, the -*ize* endings are actually older and preferred by some, but the -*ise* endings are more widely used. Canada uses AmE spelling.
-yse/-yze	*analyse* *paralyse*	*analyze* *paralyze*	Canada prefers -*yze*.
-ence / -ense	*licence* *defence*	*license* *defense*	Some nouns ending in -*ence* in BrE use -*ense* in AmE.
-ogue/-og	*catalogue* *analogue* *dialogue*	*catalog* or *catalogue* *analog* or *analogue* *dialogue* or *dialog*	AmE uses both forms, but *catalog* and *analog* are more common. However, *dialogue* is more common than *dialog*.
-l/-ll	*traveller* *modelling*	*traveler* *modeling*	Generally, a one-syllable word that ends CVC doubles the final C before a vowel suffix or inflection. So does a word of more than one syllable, but only if the stress is on the final syllable. In BrE this doesn't apply to words ending in *l* — the *l* is always doubled.
oe or ae/e	*oestrogen* *encyclopaedia* or *encyclopedia* *mediaeval* or *medieval*	*estrogen* *encyclopedia* *medieval*	BrE sometimes keeps vowel digraphs from Greek whereas AmE has replaced them with a single *e*. In many words the single *e* is becoming common in BrE spelling too. Canada uses AmE.
silent *e* before suffixes	*judgement* *ageing*	*judgment* *aging*	BrE is more likely to retain a final silent *e* before a suffix. AmE only retains the *e* if dropping it would affect the pronunciation: *noticeable* (to keep the *e* soft before *a*).

Summary of Chapter 2

- English orthography certainly gets some bad press. It is usually criticised for lacking sound-to-letter correspondence.

- Although it cannot be labelled as regular in phonological terms, there are other, non-phonological, systems that make it much more regular. In fact, these may well take precedence over the phonological system.

- Spelling reform in the USA led to some minor spelling variations in American English. Some of these are used by Canadians too.

Chapter Three:

A Brief History of English Spelling

Why do teachers need to know about the history of English spelling?

What was English spelling like before the 12th century?

How did it change in the following 500 years?

How have developments in the past 500 years led to the spelling we use now?

How might English spelling change in the future?

Why do teachers need to know about the history of English spelling?

We saw in the last chapter that English spelling is a complex 'system of systems'. Before taking a more detailed look at these different systems in the next few chapters, it helps to have some understanding of how this complexity came about. Teachers will find this background knowledge helpful:

- It will inform their teaching as they will be able to help learners make links between words and make educated guesses about unknown spellings.
- It helps them to see English spelling in a more positive light. They will see reasons for what may have previously seemed illogical. There are historical explanations for many of the apparently irrational and complex forms of English spelling. If this positive attitude can be passed on to learners it can make the task of learning English spelling seem more manageable.
- It may even help teachers with their own spelling, if they need it!

The following brief history of Old English (OE), Middle English (ME) and Modern English also happens to be a compelling tale of invasions, power struggles, snobbery, bad timing, and a few well-intentioned mistakes.

What was English spelling like before the 12th century?

Celtic

Until the 5th century AD, several languages were spoken by the Celtic[3] inhabitants of different regions of Britain (or rather, what we now call Britain). A very few examples of Celtic writing, known as Ogham, still exist and from this we can see that it was mainly written on wood or occasionally stone. The writing started at the bottom of the 'page' and worked its way up. The characters were alphabetic (that is, they were linked to sounds) and their designs were said to represent different sacred trees. Here is an example:

Anglo-Saxon

From about 450 AD, German tribes — the Angles, Saxons and Jutes — invaded Britain and brought over their languages, which spread to most parts of the country. Strangely, almost all of the old Celtic language was eradicated and hardly any of it survives now[4]. This mixture of Germanic languages became Old English (sometimes known as Anglo Saxon). There were also other overseas influences on the language, as the invading Danes and Vikings added some Old Norse into the mixture. The writing of the time was in the form of ancient Runes, which again were alphabetic.

The alphabet

In the 7th century however, the Christian missionaries in England favoured the Latin alphabet, as they objected to some pagan elements in the runes. So this started to be used in England, although the ancient runes continued to be used for several hundred years too. At that time, the Latin alphabet did not include some letters we use now, such as *j*, *q*, *v*, *x* and *z*. However, there were also some characters used in the English of that time that we do not use today, which came from the Runes:

- þ, known as 'thorn', which represented the *th* sounds;
- ƿ, called 'wynn', for present-day *w*;
- æ, called 'ash', for the vowel sound /æ/ as in *cat*.

---

[3] Celtic is pronounced with an initial hard /k/ sound — /'keltɪk/.
[4] A few surviving words of Celtic origin: *bog*, *slug*, *trousers*, *whiskey*.

These letters were retained because the Latin alphabet could not spell all the sounds that existed in the language.

Pronunciation

The pronunciation at that time was very different from now and the spelling was reasonably shallow — there was much more sound-to-letter correspondence than we have now. Each vowel letter (which included *y* as well as *a*, *e*, *i*, *o*, *u*) had one long and one short pronunciation. Every letter was articulated, even in the case of double letters; nothing was silent. The letter *r* was always pronounced too — in other words, the accent was rhotic[5]. So words like **knight** would have started with the /k/ sound and would have also included a guttural sound represented by the *gh*.

Vocabulary

Many of the words we use today that concern our basic needs and everyday life, such as **woman**, **man**, **child**, **sleep**, **tree**, **house**, and **land**, are derived from Old English (OE). They also include many of our common function words: **for**, **from**, **him**, **the**, **was**. When we look at Modern English we can recognise words that originate from Old English by certain letter strings: **igh**, **gh**, **wh**, **ch** for /tʃ/, **aw**, **ow** and **ew**.

Words derived from Old Norse often begin with the letters: **sk**-: **skin**, **sky**, **skip**; but there are other common examples too, such as **window**, **bag**, **anger**.

The Latin words introduced by the Roman Christian missionaries were often related to religion, government, learning and medicine and so give us, for example, **altar**, **rule**, **master** and **cancer**.

So before the 11th century we had a basic stock of Germanic Anglo-Saxon, seasoned liberally with Old Norse and some Latin. It was written with a modified Latin alphabet, but this was not entirely suitable for the sounds that were in the language at that time. This is perhaps where the problems began ... but not where they finished.

How did English spelling change in the next 500 years?

The Norman Invasion

In 1066 the Normans invaded from Northern France allowing William the Conqueror to rule England. This brought about huge changes in the language. The ruling classes started to use French for written literature, in court, and at public events and they preferred Latin for academic and religious purposes. English was still spoken by the rest of the people for everyday life. This meant that not much English was actually written down at that time as most text was in French and Latin, and the majority of the common people would have been illiterate.

---

[5] See Glossary page 7.

Middle English

Gradually a kind of fusion between French, Latin and Old English took place which led to what we now call Middle English. This brought about fundamental changes in grammar, vocabulary, pronunciation and spelling.

Grammar and inflections

Old English grammar had been based on inflections, but most of these were dropped, leaving us with just the Middle English equivalents of *-s*, *-ed*, *-est* and *-ing* (Crystal, 1995, p.32).   To replace inflections as conveyors of meaning, word order became more important and we see the consistent use of the subject-verb-object sentence structure.

Vocabulary

In terms of vocabulary, there was a huge influx of words from French during this period. Many of these that we use now illustrate French spelling conventions that did not apply to OE, for example, *castle* (hard *c* before *a*), *palace* (soft *c* before *e*) ; and new letter strings appeared in words like *honour* (*our*), *beauty* (*eau*), *pleasure* (*ure*).

English and French words were used side by side. For example, animals retained their Old English names, such as *cow*, *sheep*, *pig* — perhaps because they were the names used by the English farmers — but meat from these animals took names derived from Norman French: *beef*, *mutton*, *pork* — perhaps because this was the food served to the French-speaking nobles. (Beason, 2006)

Pronunciation

Pronunciation changed considerably too over this period, especially the quality of vowel sounds. The letter *e* at the end of words was no longer sounded. The pronunciation of double consonants was also dropped.

New spelling rules

However, our main concern here is with spelling, which was also dramatically affected. Many Old English words changed their spelling to follow French orthographical conventions. For example, some sounds were written differently:

Sound	Old English	Middle English
/kw/	cw	qu
/tʃ/	c	ch
/s/	s	sometimes c (before *e*)
/ʃ/	sc	sh
/dʒ/	cg/gg	dg
/v/ /ʌ/	u	v (beginning of word) u (middle of word)

It was also at this time that long vowel sounds became marked by an extra vowel letter and short vowels were followed by double consonants to distinguish them from long ones.

Silent *e*

Silent final *e* was 'discovered' and was used as a marker for certain pronunciation features. However, it was used so enthusiastically that it ended up with too many different roles, causing us some confusion in spelling today. It started to be used to:

- indicate a long preceding vowel: ***dome, make*** *(See A:47, B:134, C:229, C:231)*;
- show where *u* was a consonant: ***have***, ***give***. At that time *u* and *v* were interchangeable. So the *e* here does not make the preceding vowel long, it merely clarifies a confusion which is no longer relevant (thus causing more present-day confusion!);
- mark a soft *g* /dʒ/ (as opposed to /g/): ***wage*** (***wag***);
- distinguish between homophones and similar words: ***be/bee***; ***to/toe***;
- show that a word that ended with /s/ was not plural: ***horse***, ***please***
- make certain final consonants voiced rather than unvoiced: ***bath / bathe***.

How handwriting affected spelling

Have you ever wondered why ***love*** is spelled with an ***o*** rather than a ***u***? An interesting change, and one that accounts for several spelling irregularities nowadays, was due to the handwriting of the time. Letters in this period were written with more vertical strokes (known as minims) than we use in our more rounded writing today. This meant that letters such as ***u, v, n*** and ***m*** all looked very similar. Where these letters appeared in sequence in a word they were difficult to read, so the ***u*** was often replaced with ***o***. That is why we spell words such as ***love***, ***above***, ***oven***, ***cover***, ***dove***, ***glove***, ***some***, ***come***, ***done***, ***none***, ***wonder*** etc., as we do. This change was surely made with good intentions, but nowadays nobody is thankful for it, as the script has changed and the old solution has only caused new confusion — again! (Crystal, The Cambridge Encyclopedia of the English Language, 1995, p. 41)

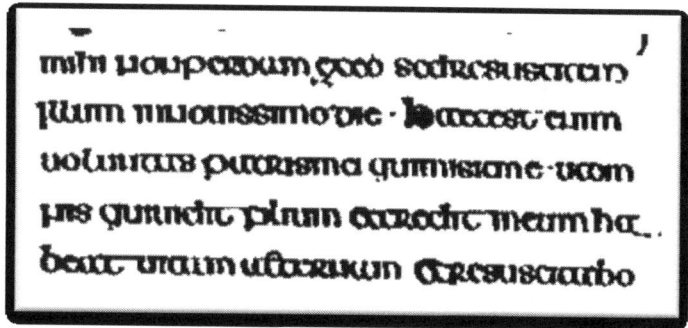

So now added to the problem of words from different languages, we have the further complication that the spelling system was interfered with.

However, Middle English was still a relatively shallow system — it was largely based on sound-to-letter correspondence. There were no silent letters, for instance. But because there were great regional differences in pronunciation, there was also extraordinary variance in spelling. The word ***between***, for example, was spelled ***between***, ***bytuene*** and ***bytwene***. David Crystal lists 20 different spelling of ***might*** found in one anthology. (Crystal, The Cambridge Encyclopedia of the English Language, 1995, p. 40)

How have developments in the past 500 years led to the spelling we use now?

Printing

It was in the late 15th century that a single invention changed the face of English spelling. William Caxton set up the first printing press in England in 1476. This not only meant that writing was more readily available, but it also eventually led to a need for more consistency in spelling.

In the 16th century, spelling was still remarkably inconsistent, sometimes even within the same text. Printers were often blamed for this — many were foreigners and were accused of using spellings from their own languages. It is said that if they ran out of one particular letter for printing they would just substitute it for another and that they would fiddle with spelling to make words fit on a line. But since spelling was also inconsistent before the printing press was conceived, maybe they shouldn't take all the blame.

Dictionaries

The first English dictionary appeared in the early 1600s. Finally there were reference books that prescribed what the spelling should be for the whole nation.

Pronunciation changes

The aim of these dictionaries may have been to provide some consistency but there was a major problem. Unfortunately these dictionaries were published during a period of great change in the spoken language. The so-called Great Vowel Shift, which took place between about 1450 and 1750, saw the pronunciation of many vowels change considerably. Consonant sounds also underwent great changes. Some disappeared altogether in spoken language, for example:

- a guttural sound written as *gh* in words like *right*

- the /g/ and /k/ sounds in words like *gnat* and *know*

- the /l/ in words such as *half*

- the /w/ in *write* .

However, because printing had already started to dictate and prescribe fixed spellings of words, the orthography no longer reflected this new pronunciation. In other words, the spelling was set in stone while the pronunciation was evolving. This is the source of many of the 'irregularities' we find in English today *(See B:134, C:227)*. Vivian Cook explains,

> *Present-day English in a sense has a Middle English letter to sound correspondence system and Modern English pronunciation system.*
>
> Cook (quoted in White, 2004)

Spelling changes

As well as changes in pronunciation that were not reflected in spelling, there were some changes in spelling that were not reflected in pronunciation! This arose from a move in this period to make English spelling more systematic. So, for example:

- the Old English spelling of 'coude' was changed to **could** to resemble **would** and **should**;
- **wh-** was used more at the beginning of words;
- **-ed** was consistently used to show most Verb 2 (past simple) and Verb 3 (past participle) endings.

So, many of our orthographical rules date from this period.

In the name of consistency, there was also an attempt to follow orthographical rules from the source language of loan words. For example, a **b** was added to the English spelling to make the word **doubt**, so that it would reflect its Latin root from *dubitare*. This was never pronounced and so has always been a silent letter. Nowadays it's tempting to wonder why they bothered doing this. Unfortunately, they also made some mistakes with this reform that we still have to live with. **Island** gained its **s** because it was, understandably, thought to come from the French word *isle*, but in fact it was from an Old English word without an **s**. Similarly, the **c** in **scissors** was added to make it resemble the Latin word *scindere* which means to **split**. But in fact it was not the root of the word at all. The silent letters are our legacy.

More new words

From the beginning of the 18th century English was commonly used in the universities and so many polysyllabic words entered the language from Greek as well as many additional Latin words.

The Greek words tended to be not only long but also technical or scientific. They included certain spelling conventions which we still use today and account for 'difficult' words such as **ache**, **rhythm** and **psychology**.

A large number of new words based on modern French appeared, also bequeathing us with modern-day letter strings found in such words as **ballet**, **beauty** and **unique**.

Other new words have entered English from languages spoken in the British Empire as well as some from other parts of the world: **umbrella** came from Italian, **coffee** from Turkish and, perhaps surprisingly, **alcohol** from Arabic. In fact English is made up of words from a hundred different languages. Here is a breakdown of the origin of the words we use nowadays.

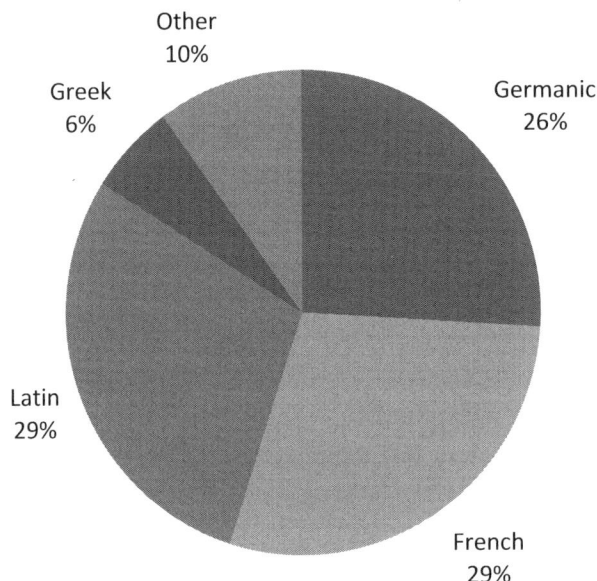

Figure 2: *Where current English words come from.*

How might English spelling change in the future?

Loanwords

Language is constantly changing and new words are being imported daily from many sources. Many other languages change the spelling of imported words to make them follow the orthographical rules of that new language. In English, we rarely alter the spelling from the original, even if it doesn't accord with English spelling-pronunciation patterns, such as **buffet** from French, **sauerkraut** form German, **cappuccino** from Italian, **tsunami** from Japanese. So if globalisation continues on its present course, we will see English become even more phonologically irregular. We are also finding that variations between different Englishes are getting progressively more blurred. American spellings such as **thru** are increasingly used in the UK for example, but at present are still not recognised as standard.

There is talk of English spelling changing due to 'texting' or SMS language. Some think that **you** will eventually be spelled **u** as standard in all situations. Other candidates for this type of change might be **2** for **to**, **4** for **for**, **cos/coz** for **because**, **ur** for **your/you're**, **l8r** for **later** etc.

Summary of Chapter 3

This chapter can most neatly be summed up by the following diagram which shows the recipe for English Orthographical Soup. Add all ingredients and stir gently!

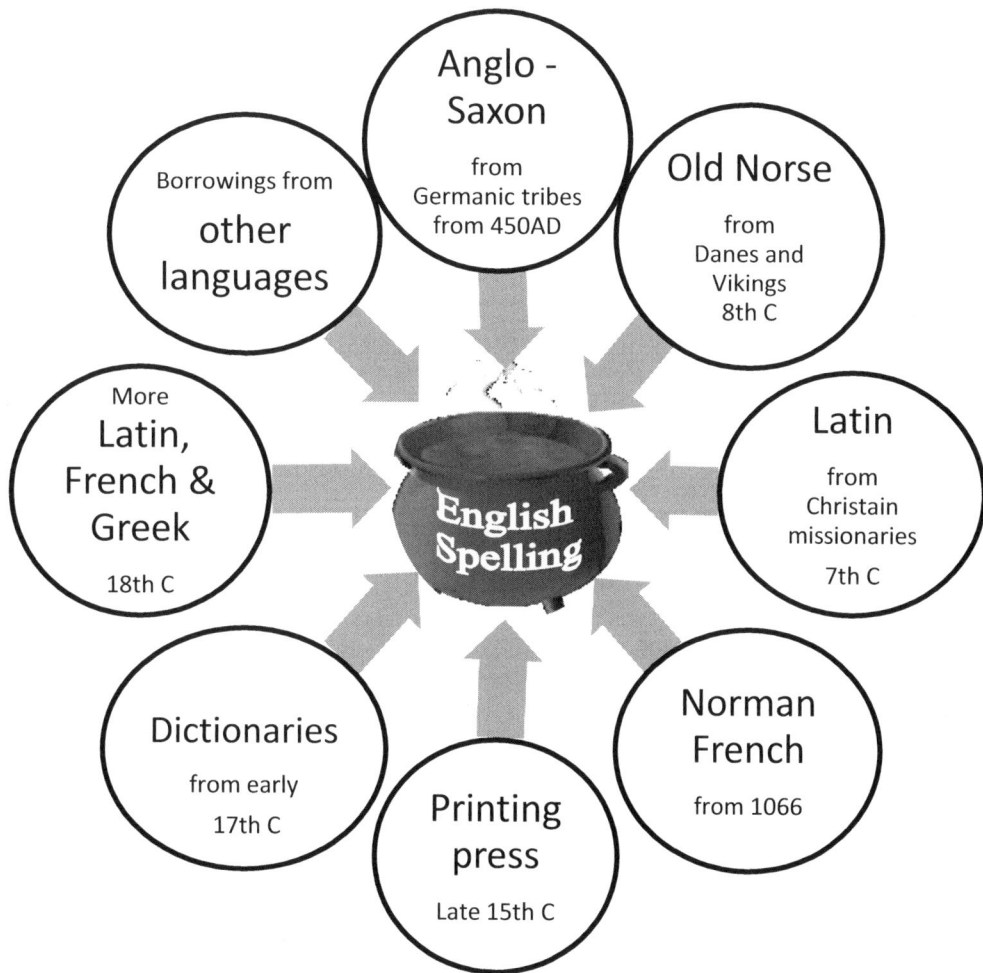

Figure 3: *English Orthographical Soup*

Chapter Four:

Etymological System

How is present-day English spelling influenced by:

>   Old English?

>   Latin?

>   French?

>   Greek?

>   Other languages?

How does that knowledge help us to spell?

How is present-day English spelling influenced by etymological factors?

Every word has a story and the stories are often enshrined in the spelling.

(Palmer, 2000)

We have seen from the last chapter that English spelling is by no means a pure-breed! Etymological factors often take precedence over all the other systems of English orthography. In this section we will explore in more detail some of these factors that affect present-day English.

Old English

Many words that derive from Old English are vital for communication because they include the most common everyday words in the language. Almost all of the 100 most frequently used words in modern English do have Old English roots (See Appendix A 267).

Also, unfortunately, these words that derive from Old English are often the least regularly spelled, in phonological and graphemic terms, because, as we have seen, so many changes have taken place in English since these ancient words appeared.

34

Some Old English words[6], arranged by topic:

Function words	Everyday verbs	People	Body parts	Agriculture
he, him, his	eat	man, woman	finger	milk
in	drink	child	chin	horse
for	sleep	father	arm	land
from	sing	queen	head	field
to	teach	monk	nose	harvest
was	fight	knight	foot	crop

Some common Old English orthographical patterns

Whenever we see words with the following patterns we can guess that they come from Old English. Just a few examples that have derived from Old English are given in this table.

wh-	kn-	-gh	-igh	aw	ow
when	knife	through	right	law	cow
who	know	brought	eight	drawer	show
whether	knock	daughter	frighten	saw	shadow
white	knee	enough	high	raw	below
wheel	knight	laugh	neighbour	straw	bowl

How this helps

Learning a few of these common patterns means that fewer of the most common words have to be learned by sight letter-by-letter. Learners who expect to see -*gh* in a word are less likely to write -*hg* by mistake *(See B:140)*.

Knowing *why* some words start with an unpronounced *k* or *w* — because they used to be pronounced — helps learners to understand that they are not just there to trip them up!

The list above is a good illustration of the fact that there are many patterns, but they are not necessarily related to pronunciation.

Latin

Latin words were introduced in several different periods. They started to arrive with the Christian missionaries in 597 AD. These were largely words related to religion, government, medicine and nature. But, in fact, Latin words continued to find their way into English, either directly or through French for many hundreds of years. Now more than half of Modern English comes from Latin or French.

---

[6] Note: the spelling is not identical to Old English as the alphabet itself has changed since then.

Some ways to recognise Latin words

- They generally do not contain the letters **k**, **w**, **th**, **sh** or **gh**.
- They may end with the suffix **-ion** or be related to a word that does.
- They might have a negative prefix **in-** or be related to one that does.
- They may be scientific or technical words ending -**us** (plural: -**i**), -**a** (plural: -**ae**), or -**um** (plural: -**a**).

Examples of Latin words

Note that some of these have come into English via French.

Those which have a related word ending in -*ion*	Those with a related word with negative prefix *in-*	Those which end in -*us*, -*a* or -*um*
convict (conviction)	conclude (inconclusive)	cactus (cacti)
admit (admission)	form (informal)	nucleus (nuclei)
educate (education)	depend (independent)	formula (formulae)
discuss (discussion)	direction (indirect)	larva (larvae)
magnify (magnification)	decide (indecisive)	medium (media)
collect (collection)	frequency (infrequent)	bacterium (bacteria)

How this helps

Probably the first two clues are the most helpful. If a word ends in the suffix **-ion**, or has a 'relative' that does, it means it has a Latin origin. And then that tells us that the word is very unlikely to contain the letters **k**, **w**, **th**, **sh** or **gh**. The third clue is of limited use because the **un—** negative prefix is also added to some words from Latin. And the words in the final column above are lower frequency and more technical.

French

French has also had a huge effect on present-day English. This came in two waves: the first one following the Norman invasion in 1066 and the second around the 16th and 17th centuries. The earlier words came from a northern French dialect while the later ones were mainly Parisian. This accounts for some strange pairs of words, such as **gaol** (Norman) and **jail** (Parisian).

Here are some examples of words from French, arranged by topic:

Administration	Law	Food/drink	Fashion	Arts	General
court		fruit	boots	colour	substance
crown	convict	salad	dress	dance	marriage
government	prison	beef	button	literature	large
palace	blame	olive	collar	music	poor
peasant	judge	sugar	lace	romance	continue
tax	jury	lemon	wardrobe	preface	travel

Some ways to recognise French words

French is firmly based on Latin so at times it is difficult to categorise words as French or Latin in origin. The French introduced some letter strings that were new to English, many of which remain today. In some, such as *ch* and final *et*, the pronunciation has remained similar to the French but others, such as *ure* have become more anglicised.

Here are some common patterns found in French-derived words:

- -*et* (*ballet*, *buffet*)
- *ch* pronounced /ʃ/ (*chef*, *machine*)
- -*ure* (*picture*, *leisure*)
- *eur* (*chauffeur*, *masseur*)
- *eau* (*beauty*, *plateau*)
- -*que* (*unique*, *cheque*).

Words with these prefixes and suffixes are also generally from French:

- *con-*
- *trans-*
- *pre-*

- -*ance*
- -*ment*.

How this helps

Knowledge of some common letter strings from French is useful. Rather than trying to remember the three consecutive vowels individually in *beauty*, it is much more efficient to remember *eau* as a 'chunk' or common letter string. This etymological knowledge also provides a 'reason' for apparent irregularities, such as the pronunciation of *ch* in *chef* and it is easier to remember if you are aware of these origins.

By checking if the word or a related one includes the affixes above we can get other clues to the spelling. If we have a word ending in –*ance,* we are very unlikely to find a letter string like -*igh* in the same word.

Greek

Many Greek words entered English during the 16th century. During this Renaissance period, as new concepts and inventions appeared, vocabulary was needed to be able to discuss them. The words stemming from Greek tend to be abstract, technical or scientific terms such as:

Science & medicine	Mathematics	Education and knowledge	Language
microscope	diagram	school	orthography
geology	polyhedron	technical	grammar
diagnosis	pyramid	analysis	dialect
symptom	geometry	encyclopaedia	lexis
schizophrenia	diagonal	symbolise	phonetics

Some ways to identify Greek words

Greek-influenced words are often easy to identify because of certain spelling features:

- *ch* representing the sound /k/ (***chemistry, anarchy, ache***)
- a middle *y* (not following a vowel) (***analyse, rhythm, hymn***)
- initial silent *p* (***psychology, pneumonia, pterodactyl***)
- *ph* for /f/ (***telephone, photograph, graph***)
- these endings: *-ology* (***biology***), *-gm* (***paradigm***), *-graph(y)* (***paragraph, geography***), *gram* (***epigram***), *scope* (***telescope***)
- these beginnings: *dia-* (***diameter***), *tele-* (***telescope***), *auto-* (***automatic***), *poly-* (***polygon***), *syn-*(***synthetic***), *sym-* (***symbol***), *rh-* (***rhyme***).

How this helps

Again, some knowledge of predictable letter strings helps people spell these long 'difficult' words. For example, with a word such as ***rhythm***, knowing that ***rh*** is a common beginning helps the writer know that the spelling is not ~~***ryhthm***~~.

Other loanwords

Within the last few centuries there has also been a great influx of loanwords from other languages:

- Italian: ***balcony, cartoon, gallery***
- Spanish: ***alligator, potato, tobacco***
- Arabic: ***admiral, alcohol, algebra, sofa***
- Chinese: ***ketchup, tea***
- Japanese: ***karaoke, Sudoku, tsunami***
- Hindi and Urdu: ***avatar, bungalow, guru, jungle, khaki, pyjamas, shampoo***.

Spanish and Italian

But it is particularly from Italian and, to a lesser extent, Spanish that we can find many words which retain their original spelling and therefore may not follow English orthographic conventions.

Older English words rarely end with a vowel other than *e*, but Spanish and Italian words often finish with *o*, *a* and *i*. (This explains perhaps why native speakers sometimes wrongly add an *e* to some words such as ~~***potatoe***~~ and ~~***tomatoe***~~.)

Here are some examples of loanwords words from Italian and Spanish in which the spelling reflects the source language:

Italian	Spanish
broccoli	avocado
cappuccino	guerrilla
cello	mosquito
graffiti	patio
influenza	tango
malaria	
pizza	
opera	
spaghetti	

Italian plurals:

In Italian, if a singular noun ends in *o*, the plural is made by changing the last letter to *i*, *a* changes to *e*, and *e* also changes to *i*. So **graffiti** is actually the plural of an Italian word *graffito* which means a **scribbling**, and **broccoli** comes from the Italian *broccolo*, meaning a **sprout**, because it consists of a collection of little sprouts. In English we never use the words *graffito* or *broccolo*. Similarly, the plural of **pizza** in English is **pizzas**, whereas the Italian is *pizze*. In other words, the lexical item has been taken into English but not the inflections.

Soft and hard *c* and *g* in Italian

In Italian:

- the letter *c* is pronounced as /k/ when followed by *a*, *o* or *u* (as is usually the case in English words) and as /tʃ/ when followed by *e* or *i*. So in **cappuccino**, the first *c* is pronounced as /k/ as it's followed by *a* and the *cc* is pronounced as a (long) /tʃ/ sound because it's followed by *i*;
- An *h* is inserted after the *c* to give it a hard /k/ sound before *e* or *i*, as in **macchiato**;
- The same pattern is followed for *g*. If *a*, *o* or *u* follows *g*, it produces a hard /g/ sound, but *e* and *i* give a preceding *g* a softer /dʒ/. Compare **gondola** with a /g/ sound with **adagio** pronounced with /dʒ/;
- Adding an *h* after the *g* keeps the sound hard even before *e* or *i*, as in **spaghetti**.

Generally English has kept these spelling and pronunciation features.

Double consonants

Double consonants in Italian and Spanish words only appear if they are sounded differently from single consonants in their native language, so in **cello**, the *ll* is a longer sound than the *l* in **broccoli** when spoken by Italian people. In the Spanish word **guerrilla**, the double *r* indicates a rolled sound which is longer than, for example, the single *r* in **Florida**. However, these single and double sounds are not differentiated in English and so it is impossible to know from the sound whether there is one consonant or two in these imported words.

How this helps

Obviously some knowledge of other languages is a great help here. If a writer knows the Spanish word *guerra* (war) he will be more likely to know that there is a double *r* in **guerrilla**. If he knows about Italian orthographical rules, he will have fewer problems spelling words like **cappuccino** and **spaghetti**.

Summary of Chapter 4

- We have seen that the etymology of a word often over-rides all other systems and clues to spelling, so we cannot afford to ignore it.

- Some of our most common words come from Old English and their antiquity may cause them to have the most irregular spelling.

- There are some letter strings and patterns in words derived from Latin that tell us that certain other letters or letter combinations are unlikely within that word. More than half of our words are originally derived from Latin.

- There are also common letter strings in words from French that we can learn as one chunk instead of perhaps three separate letters.

- Greek has given English some words that are useful for science, technology and abstract ideas. Again there are predictable patterns that are worth learning.

- There have been a great many loan words from many different languages within the past few hundred years. These account for many un-English-looking spellings, but knowing some basic features of Spanish and Italian orthography could help with English spelling.

Chapter Five:

Phonological System

How phonetically regular is English spelling?

How do letters and sounds correlate?

What is the significance of long and short vowels?

Are commonly-taught phonological spelling rules reliable?

Are there other more reliable patterns that aren't usually taught?

How phonetically regular is English spelling?

Of course at the heart of English spelling there *is* a phonological system. If English speakers see a new word, for example, 'desh' (an invented word), they can guess that the pronunciation is probably /deʃ/, and if they hear the pronunciation /deʃ/, they can make a reasonably confident attempt at the spelling. However, the big question is, what proportion of English words are phonetically spelled?

A study in 1966 (Hanna, Hanna, Hodges, & Rudorf) counted and examined every phoneme-grapheme correspondence in over 17,000 English words in order to make computer algorithms which were then used to try to spell words. About 50% of these words were correctly spelled by the computer. A one in two chance of getting the correct spelling is not a high enough ratio for people to be able to rely on sound alone. And this is particularly true for those whose native languages have 'shallow' orthographies: their expectations of sound-to-letter correspondence just won't be met.

How do letters and sounds correlate?

Letters to sounds

Sound-symbol correspondence in English is often extremely complex. Every phoneme can be represented by more than one different letter or combination of letters (See Appendix B 268 for a list of ways different sounds can be spelled in English). And almost every letter in the alphabet can correspond to more than one sound (or silence). Here are just a couple of words with different pronunciation for each letter (certainly not an exhaustive list):

A *bad*, *tasty*   J *joke* (one pronunciation only)   S *story*, *boys*
B *bird*, *debt*   K *kiss*, *knife*   T *tap*, *action*
C *ceiling*, *curtain*   L *late*, *half*   U *under*, *union*
D *tidy*, *wished*   M *meet*, *mnemonic*   V *vote*, *have to*
E *red*, *we*   N *new*, *government*   W *winter*, *law*
F *find*, *of*   O *dot*, *love*   X *exit*, *xylophone*
G *gentle*, *gate*   P *pet*, *psychology*   Y *yes*, *happy*
H *hand*, *hour*   Q *queen*, *antique*   Z *lazy* (one pronunciation only)
I *sit*, *I*   R *very*, *party*

This situation occurs because we have only 26 letters to make about 44[7] sounds. Jamieson and Jamieson (2003, p. xi) claim that all the 20 vowel sounds (including diphthongs) can be represented in 160 different ways in writing, and the 24 consonant sounds in over 100 ways. Many of these correspondences involve more than one letter, digraphs or trigraphs (two or three adjacent letters representing one sound). Moreover, we find some letters that are only included in a word to change the sound of another letter. For example, the *e* in *fine* is silent, but indicates the length of the *i*, which is not even an adjacent letter.

If about 50% of words are phonetically regular, does that mean the other 50% are irregular? Words cannot always be identified as 'regular' or 'irregular' as they are often spelled as they are sounded in some parts and not in others. It is more useful to see regularity as a scale, or as Scott (2000, p. 71) more grandly calls it, "a continuum of predictability and invariance".

Unfortunately, as we've seen, the most irregular words are also the most frequent ones (Crystal, 1987, p. 217). There is a reason for this. These common, everyday words tend to be the older ones, dating back from the 5th -11th centuries. They are the words we have always needed, like **woman**, **bread**, **although**, **right**, **said**. The pronunciation has undergone many changes but the written words have remnants of older spelling systems.

A truly phonologically regular system of English spelling would require many different spellings of words to reflect different accents, rather as it was before lexicographers attempted to standardise spelling in the eighteenth century.

If we think in terms of sound-spelling rules, they are so complex, and at times unreliable, that few people would benefit from learning them all. It has been suggested that a list of more than 600 rules would be needed to analyse English spelling phonologically. And there would still be exceptions (Wren). Life and language lessons are too short!

Sounds to letters

In some languages each phoneme corresponds to only one letter, and each letter has one pronunciation. No such luck with English! We can't say that one particular letter represents one particular sound as there are so many possibilities. At best, we can only really match sounds to *combinations* of letters.

---

[7] Different accents, even within one country such as Britain, have different numbers of phonemes.

In Appendix B (page 268) I have attempted to show the different ways each of the 44 sounds in English[8] can be spelled. In fact there are a few other spellings that are rare or found in foreign words used occasionally in English — these are not included[9]. Even in this incomplete list you will find 109 ways to spell the 24 consonant sounds and 149 ways to spell the 20 vowel phonemes. Sometimes the choice depends on the position of the letter in the word and sometimes on other letters in the word.

If you take a look now you'll see it's quite a list! But what purpose does this information serve? Should we attempt to teach it all to our learners? If we did that, there would be little time for any other learning and it would surely cause confusion and depression, not to mention terminal boredom! The list is mainly for reference and to see which are the most common spellings of a particular sound. The other purpose of the list is to illustrate the lack of one-to-one sound to letter correspondence. To base English spelling on phonology alone just cannot be done. However, can we make any generalisations from this information? We will investigate this soon. But before we can do this, we need to examine the difference between long and short vowel sounds which seem to be highly significant in English spelling.

What is the significance of long and short vowels?

In English pronunciation we can divide vowel sounds into two groups: 'long' and 'short'[10] . In British English, they are:

Long (including diphthongs)	Short
/eɪ/ day	/æ/ apple
/iː/ green	/e/ egg
/aɪ/ why	/ɪ/ list
/əʊ/ snow	/ɒ/ pot
/uː/ blue	/ʌ/ up
/ɑː/ car	/ʊ/ put
/ɜː/ bird	/ə/ teacher [11]
/eə/ hair	
/ɪə/ ear	
/ɔː/ door	
/aʊ/ how	
/ɔɪ/ boy/	
/ʊə/ tour	

[8] There are of course many different English accents. This table is based on the sounds given in the International Phonetic Alphabet (IPA) for British English. However, even within Britain, the sounds vary considerably.
[9] The most complete list I have found at the time of writing is at http://en.wikipedia.org/wiki/English_orthography (accessed 16 January 2011).
[10] Some linguists object to the terms 'long' and 'short' to refer to vowels, and prefer 'free' and 'checked'. Others do not apply the term 'long vowel' to diphthongs. I do refer to 'long' and 'short' vowels (and include diphthongs) as teachers and materials most generally use these terms.
[11] Often called 'schwa'.

The sounds /æ/, /e/, /ɪ/, /ɒ/ and /ʌ/ are the short sounds commonly represented by the letters *a*, *e*, *i*, *o* and *u*. Each of these letters also has a long sound which is like the name of the letter, so:

/eɪ/ sounds like *A*

/iː/ sounds like *E*

/aɪ/ sounds like *I*

/əʊ/ sounds like *O*

/uː/ /juː/ sounds like *U*.

Some of these, such as /iː/ and /uː/ are single vowels (monophthongs) and others, like /eɪ/ and /əʊ/, are diphthongs (two vowel sounds that glide together to form one sound).

There are also two other short vowel sounds, /ʊ/ and /ə/. The latter, sometimes known as the schwa, is an unstressed spoken form of any of the five vowel letters and many different combinations of them. Eight other long vowel sounds exist for many speakers of British English *(See table above)*.

There are a great many different ways to represent these long and short vowel sounds. We have seen *(See Appendix B on page 268)* about 150 ways to write these twenty sounds by using different combinations of letters. Some combinations are more likely to spell a long vowel and others more likely to spell a short vowel. Generally speaking, short vowel phonemes tend to be made with single vowel letters and longer vowel phonemes with two or more vowel letters[12], but there are many exceptions to this *(See B:131, C:200, C:229)*.

Are commonly-taught phonological spelling rules reliable?

In this chapter we have seen that there are a great many ways to spell our 44 English phonemes. We cannot realistically or usefully teach our learners all of these to help their spelling. So there have been attempts to make some more general rules to help them. Five common rules that are taught are:

1. "Short vowels are followed by two consonants; long vowels are followed by one consonant."
2. "A silent *e* at the end of a word makes the vowel before the preceding consonant 'say its name'."
3. "When two vowels go walking, the first one does the talking — it says its name."
4. "The letter *c* followed by *a*, *o*, *u* or a consonant, makes the 'hard' /k/ sound. The letter *c* followed by *e*, *i* or *y* makes the 'soft' *c* sound /s/."
5. "The letter *g* followed by *a*, *o*, *u* or a consonant, makes the 'hard' /g/ sound. The letter *g* followed by *e*, *i* or *y* makes the 'soft' *g* sound /dʒ/."

Now we will look at these so-called rules one by one and test their validity.

---

[12] The two vowels are not necessarily adjacent.

1. Short vowels are followed by two consonants; long vowels are followed by one consonant.

Here is the first paragraph from this book:

> The <u>overall</u> aim of this book is to **pres**ent a <u>fresh</u> **and** <u>effect</u>ive <u>meth</u>od<u>ology</u> for <u>spelling</u> <u>imp</u>rovement al**ong** <u>with</u> **act**ivities to <u>help</u> <u>students</u> who <u>struggle</u> with **Eng**l**ish** spelling. To <u>imp</u>lement this methodology, **teach**ers need an **understand**ing of the <u>problems</u> that their students face in **terms** of the <u>language</u>, the <u>learning</u> <u>process</u> and the tuition they may receive.

In this paragraph we can find 23 different words (underlined) that contain a vowel-consonant-consonant (VCC) pattern. Several words contain more than one example of VCC, so in the paragraph we can find 26 such letter strings (in **bold**). Of these, 22 do in fact represent short vowel sounds.

VCC patterns with short vowel sounds		VCC patterns with long vowel sounds
ent	ith	all
esh	act	each
and	elp	erm
eff	ugg	earn
ect	Eng	
eth	ish	
ogy	und	
ell	ers	
ing	obl	
imp	ang	
ong	ess	

There are four strings that do not seem to follow this pattern:
*over**all**, **teach**er, **term** and **learn**ing*.

- You will notice that two of these (***teach**er* and ***learn**ing*) have two vowels before the consonants. This shows that two vowel letters together are less likely to spell a short vowel.

- Also in two of them (***term*** and ***learn**ing* again) the first consonant is *r* which here is used to represent part of a long vowel sound rather than a consonant sound in its own right (in non-rhotic[13] accents). The other one, *over**all**,* illustrates that there are certain letter combinations that overrule this general pattern. ***all*** is usually pronounced /ɔːl/, as in **wall**, **ball**, **tall**, etc.

---

[13] See Glossary page 7.

There are a few more points we should take into account when dealing with VCC strings:

- Usually a long vowel is heard before words ending C+*le* or C+*re*, so **table**, **title**, **noble**, **litre**, **metre** (in British English). To make a short sound we need to add another consonant: **little**, **bottle**, **centre**. In other words, C+*re* acts like C+*er*, and C+*le* is like C+*el* or C+*al*.

- The two consonants that are used to shorten a preceding vowel may well be the same one, a double letter in other words. This gives us the difference between:
  - *diner* /ˈdaɪnə/ and *dinner* /ˈdɪnə/
  - *hoping* /ˈhəʊpɪŋ/ and *hopping* /ˈhɒpɪŋ/
  - *riding* /ˈraɪdɪŋ/ and *ridding* /ˈrɪdɪŋ/
  - *super* /ˈsuːpə/ and *supper* /ˈsʌpə/

- As double k is very rare in English, ck is usually used instead with the same effect. And this gives us *liking* /ˈlaɪkɪŋ/ and *licking* /ˈlɪkɪŋ/.

- In words of more than one syllable, things become rather more complicated. We only double a final consonant when adding a suffix, to keep the vowel short, if the stress is on the final syllable. So **reGRET** becomes **reGRETTing**, but **VISit** becomes **VISiting** (no double *t*). Similarly **SHOP** gains another *p* when it becomes **SHOPPed**, but **deVELop** does not double the *p* because the final syllable does not carry the stress: **deVELoped**.

- Unfortunately, there are many common words that do not follow the short sound VCC pattern: **find**, **mind**, **most**, **pint**. There seems to be no particular explanation for these anomalies.

VC

Does the fact that VCC strings usually result in a short vowel necessarily mean that the converse is true? We can do the same analysis with the first paragraph of this book, but this time looking at single vowels followed by single consonants.

> The **over**all aim **of** this book **is** to present a fresh and effective methodology **for** spelling improvement along with activities to help students who struggle with English spelling. To implement this methodology, teachers need **an** understanding of the problems that their students face in terms of the language, the learning process and tuition they may receive.

In this paragraph there are 23 different words (underlined) that contain a single vowel + single consonant pattern. Several words contain more than one example of VC, so in the paragraph I have highlighted 25 such letter strings. Fifteen of these correspond to short vowel sounds in these words and only nine to long vowel sounds.

VC patterns with short vowel sounds		VC patterns with long vowel sounds	
er	iv	ov(e) /əʊ/	oc
of	it	or	ey
is	em	ov(e) /uː/	ay
es(e)	an	ud(e)	ec(e)
iv(e)	at	ac(e)	
od	in		
ol	ag(e)		
al			

We can clearly see that single vowels that are only followed by one consonant are not necessarily long, in fact from this sample they look as if they are more likely to be short. Short single syllable words often have just one final consonant after a short vowel: *but*, *cat*, *dog*.

The letter after the consonant has some effect on the preceding vowel sound; we are told that an *e* makes it long. I have marked where the consonants are followed by *e* (admittedly sometimes across morphemic boundaries) and we see these are a little more likely to be pronounced with a long vowel.

The verdict
"Short vowels are followed by two consonants." This is very often true, as long as there's only one vowel before the two consonants and one of those consonants isn't *r*.

"Long vowels are followed by one consonant." This is a much less reliable guide.

2. A silent e at the end of a word makes the vowel before the preceding consonant 'say its name'.

Vowels written with one letter only are often short and adding another vowel may lengthen them. That second letter could be adjacent. Compare
- *bed* /bed/ and *bead* /biːd/,
- *ran* /ræn/ and *rain* /reɪn/,
- *spin* /spɪn/ and *Spain* /speɪn/ .

However, very often the two vowels are separated by a consonant, so, for example, compare:

- *not* /nɒt/ and *note* /nəʊt/ ,
- *mad* /mæd/ and *made* /meɪd/.

Usually adding an *e* (which is silent in itself) after the consonant makes the previous vowel 'say its name'. So the *a* in *made* sounds like the name of the letter *A*, *e* in *eve* sounds like *E*, *i* in *fine* like *I*, *o* in *note* like *O* and *u* in *use* like *U* or sometimes just without the /j/ (*rude*).

When English children are taught this, it is often introduced as the 'magic *e*'[14]. How reliable is this 'rule'?

I tested it by putting different C+*e* endings into a concordancer[15] and found some interesting results:

- Words ending in one vowel before -*be*, -*de*, -*fe*, -*ke*, -*le*, -*pe* and -*ze* are generally pronounced with the vowel that sounds like the name of the letter. Examples are ***tube***, ***fade***, ***wife***, ***like***, ***while***, ***hope***, ***amaze***.

- Words ending in -*ce* and -*ge* followed the rule if they had one syllable only (***face***, ***huge***), or on most longer words having stress on the final syllable (***advice***, ***oblige***). If there were two or more syllables, however, and the stress was not on the final one, such as in ***OFFice***, ***PALace***, ***COLLege***, ***DAMage*** and many more, they did not follow this rule.

- -*me* words generally followed the rule (***dome***, ***same***, ***assume***). Two common words, ***some*** and ***come*** are exceptions, as are any words including these, such as ***wholesome*** and ***become***.

- Many words ending in -*ne* follow the pattern (***plane***, ***alone***, ***fine***), but there are also many exceptions, such as ***one***, ***gone*** and ***done***. Longer words that have the stress on an earlier syllable, such as ***DIScipline***, ***FEMinine*** and ***MEDicine*** do not have a long vowel sound. And there is also a group of words that do have stress on the final syllable but use a different long vowel sound /iː/: ***maCHINE***, ***magaZINE***, ***margaRINE***, ***rouTINE***.

- -*se* is also an ending that has many words that follow the rule: ***wise***, ***those*** and even some longer words where the stress is not on the final syllable: ***COMpromise***, ***EXercise***. However, ***lose*** and ***whose*** are irregular, as are some longer words with earlier stress, like ***PURpose***, ***PRACtise***, ***PROmise***.

- -*te* is another complex ending. One-syllable words and longer verbs (wherever the stress is) behave according to the rule, but many adjectives and nouns do not: ***accurate***, ***favourite***, ***private***, ***climate***, ***chocolate***. Where there is a noun and verb with the same spelling we can see that the verb follows the rule while the adjective does not, for example:
  - ***separate*** (adj) /ˈsepᵊrət/ ***separate*** (vb) /ˈsepəreɪt/
  - ***moderate*** (adj) /ˈmodᵊrət/ ***moderate*** (vb) /ˈmodəreɪt/.

- Even many one-syllable words with the -*ve* ending are irregular: ***give***, ***have***, ***live***, ***love***, ***move***, ***above***, although there are regular ones too (***dive***, ***save***, ***eve***). Longer adjectives (and nouns like ***adjective***!) very often have a short vowel sound: ***active***, ***administrative***, ***supportive***.

---

[14] There is a nice video of a 'Silent e' song here: http://www.youtube.com/watch?v=EVC9TayQIh8.
[15] http://www.lextutor.ca/concordancers/concord_e.html .

All these complications may make you think that 'magic *e*' is a very poor rule. But as English phonetic rules go, it is actually one of the more reliable. There are certainly exceptions to the rule and although they are not numerous, they tend to be very common words such as ***some*** and ***give***. Words with two syllables or more which end with a silent *e* are less likely to have a long preceding vowel unless that syllable is stressed. So ***PRACTice, PURpose, PRIVate*** and ***MINute*** (60 seconds) do not follow the rules, but ***proVIDE, preCEDE, minUTE*** (tiny) do.

As we saw when examining the history of English spelling (page 28), sometimes the final silent *e* can have other uses, besides making the preceding vowel say its name. Most of these reasons are graphemic rather than phonetic and we will come back to these in the next chapter.

The verdict
"A silent *e* at the end of a word makes the vowel before the preceding consonant 'say its name' " is certainly a good rule of thumb, although there are plenty of exceptions *(See B:131, C:229, C:231).*

3. When two vowels go walking, the first one does the talking — it says its name.

This rule is often taught to children. It means in a word like ***bean***, the *e* is pronounced with the long sound like the name of the letter *E*, and the *a* is silent.[16] Here are some more examples:

> ***boat   toe   rain   tied***.

BUT ... I tested the rule out and found that it is in fact very unreliable. I entered all the possible vowel digraphs (two written vowels together that make one sound), such as ***ae, ai, ao, au, ea, ei***, etc., into a concordancer. My results showed that the rule clearly only works for a few digraphs and, even for these, not very consistently.

These are the ones that generally do work:

- ***oa*** — ***coat, load, approach, goal***, etc. Most words with ***oa*** make the letter **O** sound and the *a* is silent, except if it is followed by an *r* : ***board, coarse***;

- ***ai*** — ***rain, paint, rail, failure***, etc. This one is pretty good too, but some common words do not follow the rule: ***said, pair***, etc.);

- ***ea*** — ***sea, beans, easy, please, beach***, etc. This one sometimes behaves according to the rule, but look at all these exceptions: ***leather, already, early, appear, break, bread***, and there are many more.

---

[16] There is a video for children that illustrates it very clearly (and cutely) at http://pbskids.org/lions/videos/twovowels.html .

Some digraphs have a few examples which follow the rule, but many that do not:

- *ui — juice, fruit, suit* (but not *liquid, build, guide, biscuit* and many more);

- *ei — ceiling, receive* (but not *height, eight*);

- *oe — toe, woe, goes, potatoes* (but not in *shoes, does, poem, foetid* or *canoe*);

- *ue — blue, true* and some other words that end in *ue* (but not words that end *que* or *gue*).

And the others (*ae, ao, au, eo, eu, ia, ie, io, iu, ou, ua, ue* and *uo*) really do not follow this rule at all. At best there are two or three words that follow it, but generally none.

The verdict
"When two vowels go walking, the first one does the talking — it says its name" is commonly taught as a rule to children, although it is highly unreliable.

4. The letter *c* is used to write a hard /k/ sound before the letters *a, o, u* or consonant; before *e, i* or *y*, it has the soft sound /s/.

We can see in the table in Appendix B that there are several ways to spell the sound /k/. So how can we know which one to use? Many of the factors are etymological, for example, we often use *que* at the end of words from French and *ch* can represent the sound in words of Greek origin *(See Chapter 4)*. But most commonly we use *c* or *k*. We just need to decide which.

The pattern given above seems to be remarkably consistent. For example, we write **candle, carrot, cot, contain, customer, cup, clock** and **crisp** but **cell, city** and **cycle**. So at the beginning of a word we should use the letter ***k*** *only* when we cannot use ***c*** because it would give a soft /s/ sound. Therefore we write **kettle, keep, king, kiss**. No native words start ***ka, ko*** or ***ku***, only relatively recent imports such as **kangaroo, kohl** and **karaoke**. Similarly the only time native English words start with ***k*** followed by a consonant is when ***k*** is silent before ***n***.

In the middle or at the end of a word ***k*** or ***ck*** are often used for the sound /k/. The letter ***c*** is usually only found at the end of a word if it is part of the adjective or noun suffix *-ic* [17]. After a long vowel (usually consisting of two vowels) we generally find ***k*** (**cloak, leak, cheek**) or ***ke*** (**like, joke**). After a short vowel in a one-syllable word we are more likely to read ***ck*** — **sack, deck, sick, sock, duck**. The digraph ***oo***, pronounced as /ʊ/, is also followed by ***k*** — **book, took, look**. The letter ***k*** follows ***n, s, r, l*** too — **bank, task, bark, walk**.

---

[17] Some exceptions I could find were 'havoc', 'mollusc', 'zodiac' and 'disc'.

Adding a **k** after a **c** makes the hard /k/ sound, even if followed by an **e, i** or **y** — **trucker**, **picnicking**, **lucky**. Compare these words with **truce**, **nice** and the name **Lucy** /luːsi/ to see what effect the **k** has.

If we have a word that ends in *-ce* and we need to add a suffix that begins with **a, o** or consonant then we need to retain the final **e** before adding the suffix. Otherwise the **a, o** or consonant would make the **c** hard like /k/. So although we write **lovable** and **famous** (dropping the final **e** of **love** and **fame**), we keep the **e** in **noticeable** and **placement**.

The verdict
"The letter **c** is used to write a hard /k/ sound before the letters **a, o, u** or a consonant; before an **e, i** or **y**, it has the soft sound /s/" seems to be one of the most consistent phonological patterns we have *(See B:136, C:244, C:247).*

5. The letter *g* is used to write a hard /g/ sound before the letters *a, o, u* or consonant; before *e, i* or *y* it has the soft sound /dʒ/.

While students are learning about hard and soft **c** as discussed above, the teacher often deals with **g** in the same way. Many equivalent rules are given for **c** and **g**. While we can certainly find plenty of examples which do follow the rule, such as **gap, go, argue, glass, great, gentle, giraffe** and **biology**, these rules are much less consistent than those for **c** and **k**. There are so many exceptions, especially among common words, that they must be treated with caution: **get, younger, biggest, eager, finger, give, girl, begin, singing**.

Unreliable as they are, they do help account for the silent **u** sometimes seen after **g**. The **u** here hardens the **g** before an **e** or **i**, hence **guest, guerrilla, dialogue**[18], **guide, guilty** and **guitar**. It also helps with the spelling of confusing word pairs such as **college** and **colleague**. However, we also spell **guard** and **guarantee** with a **u** for etymological not phonological reasons.

The soft /dʒ/ sound can also be spelled with a **j**, as in **jam** and **major**, but this is never at the end of a word. When we want to spell a word that ends with the sound /dʒ/, we generally use *-ge*: **page, siege, oblige, huge**. But after a short vowel we prefer *-dge*: **badge, hedge, fridge, lodge, nudge**.

The verdict
"**g** is used to write a hard /g/ sound before the letters **a, o, u** or consonant; before an **e, i** or **y** it has the soft sound /dʒ/" is too unreliable to be of much real use.

---

[18] In AmE the **ue** on such words is dropped: **dialog, catalog**, etc.

Are there other more reliable patterns that aren't usually taught?

One phonetic element of spelling that is rarely taught, but deserves more attention, concerns words beginning with **w** followed by certain vowel sounds:

- /wɔ:/ is usually written as **war** — **warm**, **warning**, **war**, **ward**, **dwarf**, **towards**;

- /wɜ:/ is usually written **wor** — **word**, **world**, **worse**, **work**, **worm** (a notable exception is **were**);

- /wɒ/ and /kwɒ/ are usually written **wa** and **qua** — **was**, **want**, **watch**, **wash**, **swallow**, **quality**, **qualifications**, **squad**.

These words are usually taught as irregular anomalies but we can actually see a useful pattern here *(See C:242)*.

Summary of Chapter 5

- There is a phonological system at the heart of English but over the centuries it has been influenced (some would say corrupted) by other systems. It is estimated that English spelling is about 50% regular in purely phonological terms.

- There are many different ways to pronounce each letter in a word and many different spellings of each phoneme. These are often dictated by the position of the letters in a word.

- The distinction between long and short vowels is often important for spelling.

- Some spelling patterns that are often taught are generally reliable:
    - a vowel followed by two consonants is often pronounced as a short vowel;
    - a silent *e* at the end of a word following a single vowel and a consonant usually makes the preceding vowel long;
    - the letter *c* usually makes a hard sound before *a, o, u* or a consonant, but a soft sound before *e, i* or *y*.

- Some spelling patterns that are often taught but are not very reliable:
    - where there are two vowels together in a word, the first one is usually sounded (it 'says its name') and the second one is silent;
    - the letter *g* usually makes a hard sound before *a, o, u* or a consonant, but a soft sound before *e, i* or *y*.

- Some spelling patterns that are rarely taught but are generally reliable:
    - the letter *w* before a vowel often changes the vowel sound.

Chapter Six:

Graphemic System

What is a graphemic system?

Are there graphemic spelling rules in English?

What useful graphemic patterns can we find in English?

What common letter strings can we find?

What is a graphemic system?

> *The more closely one looks at that supreme, and for many people solitary,*
> *spelling rule* [i before e], *the more peculiar it seems.*
>
> (Carney, A Survey of English Spelling, 1994)

Many of the 'rules' that we are taught about spelling belong to the Graphemic system. By this I mean typical letter patterns in English words that are not related to sound. In fact, these often do cross over with phonological factors too but in this section we will focus on patterns that seem to be independent of sound. There are also certain crossovers with morphemic conventions but we will reserve those for a separate category too.

Are there graphemic spelling rules in English?

'Rule' is a rather dangerous word. It's prescriptive. It suggests that something must happen. Then people get upset if it doesn't happen. To have rules that are then followed by a long list of exceptions fosters a sense of chaos and anarchy. A school may well have a rule that children must not run in the corridors. This is probably a sensible rule to keep the environment safe. However, if the rule was "Don't run in the corridor … unless you are wearing red today or your grandparents are Greek", it becomes a stupid rule! It is not only unfair but it is also more difficult to remember. And, more to the point, it defeats the object of the rule because some children will still be running and causing accidents.

The wise English teacher avoids using the words 'always' and 'never' when teaching about language, especially spelling. There may be a few real rules, but even these can often be questioned. We could state that no word can have three of the same letters side by side, that there is no 'tripling' of letters, in other words. Certainly when we want to add *ed* to a word that ends with double *e*, like *agree*, we need to drop one *e* to avoid three *e*s in a row, ~~*agreeed*~~. So this does look like a rule (one I have never seen anyone break, incidentally), until we arrive at the ***boss's office***. Here we have three *s*s in a row, only broken by an apostrophe. To make the rule watertight we need to then add "unless there is an apostrophe". It is already starting to get more complicated.

An alternative is to only describe 'patterns'. Patterns are descriptive. They don't tell you what you *must* do ("oh, but not if..."), they show what usually happens and suggest that the writer may use this information to help guess a spelling.

What useful graphemic patterns can we find in English?

Syllables need vowels

Words and syllables contain at least one of the five vowel letters or the semi-vowel *y* (***rabbit***, ***strength***, ***table***, ***stylistic***).

The three-letter pattern

'Content' words, that is, words that carry meaning rather than grammar, have more than two letters. The only very common content words with two letters are ***go*** and ***do***, although interestingly both of these can also be used as function words[19]. A homophone that has a two-letter spelling and a three-letter spelling will use the two-letter one for a function word and the three-letter word for the content word:

- *be   bee*
- *to   too/two*
- *by   buy/bye*
- *so   sew/sow*
- *in   inn.*

Note, however, that there is no restriction on function words — they do not have to have less than three letters, it is only the content words that are limited to three or more letters: ***because***, ***their***, ***although***, ***underneath*** *(See C:249)*. (Cook, The English Writing System, 2004)

CVC doubling

One-syllable words which end with the consonant-vowel-consonant (CVC) pattern double the final consonant before a vowel suffix is added: ***running***, ***bigger***, ***reddish***. *(See C:236)*

---

[19] Scrabble players will surely know many more two-letter content words but not ones in daily use.

-ed endings

Regular verbs end with -**ed** in the Verb 2 and verb 3 forms (also called 'past' and 'past participle'), irrespective of whether the sound is /d/, /t/ or /ɪd/, as we hear in the words **allowed**, **walked**, **started**.

qu –

The letter **q** is followed by the letter **u**: **queen**, **unique**.

'Illegal' endings

Native English words do not end with **i**, **j**, **q**, **u** or **v**. So these letters or strings are often used instead:

i	>	-**y**	**hilly** (See C:238)
j	>	-**dge**	**judge**
q	>	-**que**, -**ck**	**antique**, **quick**
u	>	-**ue**	**blue**
v	>	-**ve**	**give**.

Letters that don't double

These letters are rarely or never doubled in native English words: **a**, **h**, **i**, **j**, **k**, **q**, **u**, **w**, **x**, **y**. This does not apply if one of those letters is at the end of the first part of a compound word and the beginning of the second part, **hitchhike**, (See C:258).

-ck not at the beginning

The consonant digraph **ck** can be used in the middle or at the end of a word, but never at the beginning. **ck** is sometimes described as a stand-in for **kk**, and this would suggest why we don't find it at the beginning of a word: English words don't begin with double consonants (See C:258). Other patterns that don't appear at the beginning of words include -**dge**, -**mb** and -**tion**.

-y to i

When we want to add an ending to a word that ends in C+**y**, the **y** changes to **i** before the ending is added. The ending might be -**es** for present simple third person singular or for a plural, or –**ed** Verb 2 and 3 endings, or suffixes (except ones that begin with **i**, because we don't have double **i** in native words). Some examples:

puppy > **puppies**	**heavy** > **heaviness**
lady > **ladies**	**marry** > **marriage**
apply > **applies**	**accompany** > **accompaniment**
hurry > **hurried**	**rely** > **reliable**
easy > **easily**	**rely** > **relying**.

If the word finishes V+**y** we don't change the **y** to **i**: **toys**, **obeys**, **destroyed**, **prayer**, **enjoyable** (See C:238).

10. Plurals

-f to -ves

Most words ending in CV+*fe*, VC+*f* or sometimes VV+*f,* change the ending to -*ves* when made plural:

- ***knife > knives***
- ***calf > calves***
- ***leaf > leaves***.

-o to -os/-oes

Nouns that end in *o* can make their plural by adding *s* or *es* and many of them can be either. The patterns are not very clear[20] but:

- Words ending in V+*o*, just add *s*: ***radios, patios, zoos, kangaroos***.
- Many words ending in C+*o* add *s*, especially if they are newer words to English, short forms (***kilos, photos, logos***), proper nouns (***Eskimos***) or loan words (i.e. with no change of spelling from the original language) from Spanish (***tacos, sombreros***) or Italian — especially musical terms (***concertos, solos, stilettos***).
- Some words that entered the English language long ago (and particularly if the spelling was Anglicised) end with ***oes***; the most common are ***potatoes*** and ***tomatoes***, but others are shown below.
- A large number of words ending in *o* can add either *s* or *es*:

-os	-oes	-os or -oes
albinos	echoes	buffaloes/buffalos
avocados	embargoes	ghettos/ghettoes
casinos	heroes	mangoes/mangos
kimonos	potatoes	volcanoes/volcanos
logos	tomatoes	zeros/zeroes
typos	torpedoes	tornados/tornadoes

i before e

One very commonly-taught rule is "*i* before *e*, except after *c*". Look at the Wordle below and see whether it is a good rule or not.

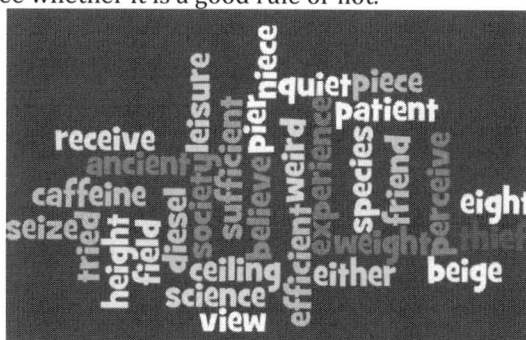

Figure 4: *Words containing* ***ie*** *and* ***ei***.
(Image made with Wordle at www.wordle.com)

---

[20] See a presentation about this at http://thespellingblog.blogspot.com/2010/01/plurals-of-words-ending-in-o-when-to.html

You will find several words that follow this rule, such as *piece*, *view*, *receive* and *ceiling*. There are also rather a lot that don't: *weight*, *beige*, *science*, *ancient*.

Some people add to the rule:

> When the sound is ee
> Use *i* before *e*
> Except after *c*

This is an improvement, but it still doesn't account for the spelling of words like *seize* and *caffeine*.

The British Government has recently advised teachers to stop teaching this rule to children, but some people still find it useful. (Department for Children, Schools and Families 2007)

12. –able and –ible

The endings *-ible* and *-able*, both usually mean that you are able to do something. They sound the same, so how do you know which to use? *(See C:240)* Here's some help:

-able	-ible
• most common ending (5:1);	• less common ending (1:5);
• usually added to a complete word (perhaps just dropping the silent *e* or changing *y* to *i*) e.g. *fashionable*, *lovable*, *deniable*;	• if the ending is removed, a complete word doesn't usually remain, e.g. *edible*, *compatible*;
• a related word may be found ending in -*ation*: *applicable* (*application*), *adorable* (*adoration*);	• a related word may be found ending in -*ition*, -*tion*, -*sion*, -*cian* or -*ion*, but NOT -*ation*: *comprehensible* (*comprehension*), *convertible* (*conversion*);
• added to new words: *offsetable*, *recession-proofable*;	• not added to new words;
• from Latin word ending -*are*.	• from Latin word ending -*ere* or -*ire*.

13. Words ending in –le, –el and –al

There are three different spellings for words that end with the /əl/ sound:
-*le* as in *table, title, stumble, deductible*
-*al* as in *critical, individual, aerial*
-*el* as in *towel, travel, camel*.

- *-le* is by far the most common of these, accounting for over 70% of /əl/ endings. The words with this ending can be nouns, verbs and adjectives, particularly those with the suffixes *-able* or *-ible*.

- *-al* is the next most common. It is used for a few nouns (***aerial***, ***funeral***), but mainly adjectives (***local***, ***educational***, ***individual***, ***critical***).

- *-el* is the least common and used mainly for nouns and verbs (***travel***, ***towel***, ***camel***).

There is also a very peculiar pattern that seems to emerge related to these endings. We can talk about some letters having a 'stick' or 'tail', that is part of the letter that rises above the main part or falls below the line *(See B:147)*. So letters with sticks are ***b***, ***d***, ***f***, ***h***, ***k***, ***l***, ***t***, and letters with tails are ***g***, ***j***, ***p***, ***q***, ***y***. By far the majority of words ending with *-le* have a letter with a stick or tail immediately before the *-le*: ***able***, ***angle***, ***ladle***, ***waffle***, ***tickle***, ***bottle***. And conversely, most of the words ending with *-el* or *-al*, have an 'in-line' letter (i.e. without a stick or tail) before this ending: ***towel***, ***camel***, ***special***, ***local***, ***animal***. Strange, but largely true![21]

What common letter strings can we find?

As we saw in the chapter on etymology, there are certain letter strings that are frequent in English and others that are not or are impossible. So within the 100 most common words[22] we can find, for example, ***ould***, ***ight***, ***st***, ***er***, ***ow***. Sometimes these strings are restricted to one part of the word, others are generally found in a particular position: ***er***, ***ing*** and ***ow*** are more likely to be found at the end or in the middle of a word than at the beginning, whereas ***st*** could be anywhere.

Other strings seem to be related to meaning or use: the three letters ***the*** are often found at the beginning of function words: ***the***, ***they***, ***then***; and ***wh*** is, of course, the beginning of many question words: ***when***, ***where***, ***why***, etc. These will be considered in Chapter 7.

Other letter strings are very common as they are prefixes and suffixes, but these will be dealt with in the next section of the book.

There are also letter strings that are usually impossible such as ***bg***, ***sr***, ***chc***, ***iu***, ***aoa***, although these may occur across morpheme boundaries: ***subgroup***, ***beachcomber***.

---

[21] See presentation at http://thespellingblog.blogspot.com/2009/02/spelling-words-ending-with-le-el-and-al.html
[22] See Appendix A page 267.

Summary of Chapter 6

- A graphemic, or orthographical, system is based on patterns in words that are not related to sound.

- In English, it is probably better to talk in terms of patterns, which are descriptive, than rules, which may be taken as prescriptive.

- There are some useful graphemic patterns which can help learners. These are related to syllables, word length, doubling, position and word endings.

- There are common letter strings and some that are rare or impossible.

Chapter Seven:

Morphological System

What is a morpheme?

How can knowledge of base elements help spelling?

How do prefixes affect spelling?

How do suffixes and inflections affect spelling?

How are compound words spelled?

Which takes precedence, the morphological or phonological system?

What's a morphological system?

A morpheme is a part of a word that carries meaning. In the word **unhelpfulness** there are four morphemes: **un** + **help** + **ful** + **ness**. In this example each morpheme is one syllable, but this isn't necessarily so: in **disconnection** there are three morphemes: **dis/connect/ion**, but four syllables: **dis/con/nec/tion**. Morphemes are related to meaning not phonology. In **disconnection** the final syllable is **-tion** /ʃən/ but the final morpheme or suffix is **-ion**, so the /ʃ/ sound is not indicated. We can tell the morpheme is **-ion** rather than **-tion** because **disconnect** ends with a **t**, which makes the **t** part of the morpheme **connect**. Think also of words like **education** (**educate**), **television** (**televise**) and **inflection** (**inflect**).

There are different types of morphemes:
- base elements,
- prefixes,
- suffixes,
- inflections.

The relationship between these is shown on the next page.

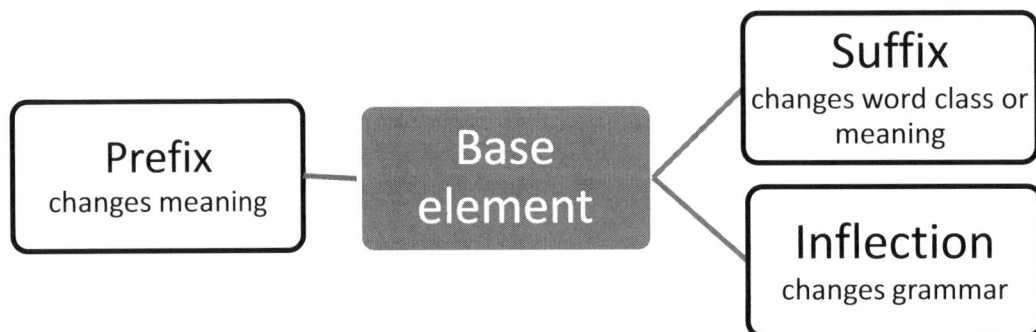

Figure 5: *Building words with morphemes*

These can also be divided into 'free' morphemes and 'bound' morphemes. In **unhelpfulness**, **help** is a free morpheme because it is a word that can be used alone without any other morphemes or it can be used with different morphemes, as in **helplessly**. On the other hand, **un**, **ful** and **ness** are bound morphemes because they have no meaning if used on their own.

So the morphological system involves constructing words with morphemes. It is the most regular and least complex of the English spelling systems, yet it helps considerably with spelling even long words. If you really wanted to write the longest (non-scientific) word in English, **antidisestablishmentarianism**, you would only need to remember six relatively easy chunks rather than 28 individual letters.

Base elements

A base element, the part that we add the prefixes and suffixes to, is sometimes called a 'base word', but it does not necessarily need to be a whole word. In the word **disturbance**, for example, **turb** is the base element but it is not a word in its own right. To put it another way, **turb** is not a free morpheme, whereas the base element in **playfully** (**play**) is also a base word, so that makes it a free morpheme.

Base elements carry the core meaning, which may be modified by the affix or inflection. So in **committee**, **mit(t)** refers to **putting**, the prefix **com-** adds the **together** element of meaning, and the suffix -**ee** tells us it's a noun referring to a person or body of people. Knowing the meaning of a wide range of base elements helps considerably with spelling and general vocabulary development.

The spelling of the base element often stays largely unchanged when adding prefixes and suffixes, even if the stress or other elements of pronunciation change. A clear example of this is the family of words based on the base element **dict**; the **c** is silent in the word **indictment**, but pronounced in others such as **dictation** and **contradict**. The spelling of **dict**, however, remains consistent.

On the other hand, sometimes the ending of the base is modified to accommodate the suffix. In the last sentence, for example, we read **modified** rather than ~~**modifyed**~~. And in **committee** we had to add an extra **t** before the suffix. More specific details about this are in the section on suffixes below.

A few base elements do let the side down though, by making internal changes depending on the suffixes added: **pron_ounce** becomes **pron_unciation**, **prev_ail** becomes **prev_alent** and **f_our** becomes **f_orty**. There are, thankfully, few of these.

Prefixes

Prefixes are placed before the base element. They change the meaning of the word, often, for example, making it negative.

One of the learner-friendly aspects of prefixes is that they are added to the whole word, that is, nothing has to change between the prefix and the beginning of the word. That is why **misspell** has two **s**s, one for **mis-** and one for **spell**, but **misunderstand** only has one **s** *(See B:135, C:232, C:234).*

Occasionally the prefix changes according to the first letter of the base element. The most common examples of this are the variations of **in-** when used as a negative prefix. If the first letter of the next morpheme is **l**, then we use **il-**: **illegal, illiterate**. If followed by **r**, it is **ir-**: **irrational, irresponsible**. And if it is **b**, **m** or **p**, then we usually use **im-**: **imbalance, immature, impossible**.

The most difficult aspect of prefixes is knowing which one to use, especially where there is a range with almost the same meaning, such as those used for negation. Only words from Latin use **in-** (and **il-**, **im-** and **ir-**), while both Greek and Latin words use **un-** as a prefix, but that only helps if you have some knowledge of these languages anyway.

In the table are some common prefixes with their meanings:

Prefix	Examples	Meaning/Notes
TO MAKE NOUN, VERB OR ADJECTIVE NEGATIVE OR OPPOSITE		
dis-	dishonest, dislike	
in-	incomplete, informal	also *im-*, *il-* and *ir-* *(See below)*
non-	non-smoking, non-toxic	
un-	untidy, unlucky	
TO INDICATE REVERSAL OF VERB'S ACTION		
de-	defrost, debug	
dis-	disconnect, disinfect	
un-	unwrap, undo	
TO INDICATE SOMETHING IS WRONG OR BAD		
over-	oversleep, overpopulated	too much
under-	undervalued, undercooked	not enough
sub-	substandard	not enough
mis-	misspell, misunderstand	badly

TO INDICATE SIZE OR DEGREE

hyper-	*hypermarket, hyperactive*	a lot or too much
mega-	*megastore, megabyte*	extremely, a million
super-	*supermarket, supermodel*	very big or extreme
ultra-	*ultrasound, ultra-modern*	extremely
micro-	*microwave, microchip*	very small
mini-	*miniskirt, minibus*	small

TO INDICATE OPINIONS AND ORIENTATION

anti-	*anti-nuclear, anti-clockwise*	against
contra-	*contradict, contraception*	against
pro-	*pro-government*	for, in support of

TO INDICATE POSITION AND RELATIONSHIPS

extra-	*extra-curricular*	out of or in addition to
inter-	*international, internet*	between
intra-	*intranet*	within
mid-	*midnight, mid-twenties*	in the middle, during
para-	*para-Olympics, paramedic*	beside
sub-	*submarine, subtitles*	under
tele-	*telephone, telescope*	over a long distance
trans-	*transatlantic, transplant*	across

RELATED TO TECHNOLOGY

e-	*e-book, email*	related to internet
cyber-	*cyberspace, cybercrime*	related to internet
techno-	*technophobe*	related to technology

TO INDICATE TIME AND SEQUENCE

ante-	*antenatal*	before
ex-	*ex-wife, ex-footballer*	former
neo-	*neo-fascist, neoclassical*	new
post-	*postwar, postgraduate*	after
pre-	*pre-school, preloaded*	before
re-	*recycle, rewind*	again

TO INDICATE NUMBER, FREQUENCY OR SHAPE

mono-	*monorail, monologue*	one
uni-	*universal, unisex*	one, same
bi-	*bilingual, bicycle*	two
tri-	*triangle, triplicate*	three
poly-	*polytechnic, polygon*	many
multi-	*multinational, multi-storey*	many
semi-	*semicircle, semidetached*	half

RELATED TO THE ENVIRONMENT

astro-	*astrophysics, astronaut*	related to stars and outer space
bio-	*biorhythm, biodiversity*	related to living things
eco-	*eco-friendly, ecosystem*	related to preserving the environment
hydro-	*hydro-electric*	related to water
thermo-	*thermometer, thermostat*	related to heat

As well as different prefixes with the same meaning, there are several pairs of prefixes with similar spelling and different meanings that cause confusion *(See C:234)*.

Anti- and *ante*-

Anti- means **against** or **opposed to** something. So a government that is opposed to discrimination might pass **anti-racist** laws. You can protect yourself against malaria by taking **anti-malarial** drugs. This prefix can also refer to direction, so you turn the steering wheel **anti-clockwise** to turn left in your car (note: **counter-clockwise** in US English).

Ante- means **before** and is much less common. A woman may attend an **antenatal** clinic before she has a baby. An **anteroom** is a small room where you wait before going into a large important room (in a palace for example). If the stress falls on the **ante-penultimate** syllable of a word, it is the third syllable from the end, one before the penultimate.

Dis- and *dys*-

Dis- means **not** or **the opposite of** and gives us such words as **disagree**, **dislike** and **disadvantage**. It also means **to reverse** something. If you don't pay your fuel bills, your electricity may be **disconnected**. If some cables have become entangled, you may need to **disentangle** them.

Dys- means that something is wrong or fails to work as normal. If somebody has **dyslexia**, they may have problems with reading and writing. A **dysfunctional** relationship does not work well and usually makes the people involved in it unhappy.

Hyper- and *hypo*-

Hyper- is used to describe a lot or too much of something. If a child is **hyperactive**, he or she cannot sit still. If someone is **hypersensitive**, they are more sensitive than normal and so you should be careful what you say! A **hypercritical** (/haɪpəˈkrɪtɪkəl/) person is always criticising others in an excessive way.

Hypo- is a less common and rather complex prefix, meaning **under** (a **hypodermic** needle goes under the skin), **low** (if your body temperature falls very low because you have been exposed to extreme cold for a long time you may get **hypothermia**) or **deficient** in some way (a **hypocritical** /hɪpəˈkrɪtɪkəl/ person criticises others for things that he or she also does).

Inter- and *intra*-

Inter- is used to show relationship between two or more different things. If an event is **international**, it involves people from many different countries. The **internet** allows people who are not connected in any way to communicate on-line.

Intra- shows a relationship within an organisation or group. An **intranet** is a network of computers all from the same organisation, which people from outside that organisation cannot access. An **intradepartmental** meeting would only involve staff from within that particular department. **Intra**- is much less common than **inter**-.

Hyphens

When should there be a hyphen between a prefix and base element? In most cases there is no hyphen, the prefix is attached directly to the word, but sometimes there is one. In fact the usage is rather arbitrary. A writer can check in a dictionary, but should not be surprised to see some variation there too. I checked the word **nonfiction/non-fiction** in three popular

English learners' dictionaries[23]: two gave it as **non-fiction** and the other as **nonfiction**. Similarly **anticlockwise** was given in two of the dictionaries and **anti-clockwise** in one. Here are a few guidelines, however:

- British English uses hyphens more than US English.
- The only time a hyphen is obligatory is when the prefix comes before a capital letter, **anti-Nazi**, **pro-European**, because a single capital letter cannot appear inside a word. However, even this is changing, as we now find commercial names like PowerPoint and iPhone.
- Single-letter prefixes are usually hyphenated too, such as **e-commerce**, however, **email** is nowadays usually written as one word.
- Hyphens are often used (especially in British English) if the prefix causes a double vowel or a common digraph that could be confused for a diphthong: **co-operation**, **re-align** (to avoid the reader being confused into thinking the word started with **coop** /ku:p / or **real** /rɪəl/).
- If a word including a prefix looks the same as another word, a hyphen may be included to differentiate them: **re-cover** (cover something again)/**recover** (get better after an illness).

Suffixes and inflections

Suffixes are found at the end of words and generally change the part of speech. So the verb **vary** can be changed to the adjective **various** or the noun **variety**. Occasionally suffixes also change meaning. For example, the noun **care** plus the suffix **-ful** becomes the adjective **careful**, but it can be an adjective with an opposite meaning if we add **-less** instead of **-ful**.

Inflections are also at the end of words but these are grammatical in that they help to indicate tense, person, and plurals. For example, **-ed** often indicates a past tense.

On the next page are some common suffixes and inflections. They have been divided according to the part of speech, but also according to whether they are vowel suffixes (on the left) or consonant suffixes (on the right).

How do suffixes and inflections affect spelling?

Adding suffixes is not quite as simple as prefixes, which are always added to the whole word. The rules are more complex; however, they are generally very regular. A word may carry more than one suffix: **hope** + **ful** + **ly** = **hopefully**.

Consonant suffixes and inflections

Consonant suffixes are added to the whole word or base element, hence: **absolutely** = **absolute** + **ly**. The final **e**, for example, is usually retained when adding a consonant suffix. We have already examined some changes to spelling that take place when suffixes or inflections are added to words ending C+**y**, **f** or **fe**, and **o** *(See A:56)*.

---

[23] Macmillan English Dictionary for Advanced Learners (2002), Oxford Advanced Learners' Dictionary of Current English (2000), and Cambridge Learners' Dictionary (2007).

Suffixes and inflections

Suffixes starting with a vowel		Suffixes starting with a consonant	
Suffix	**Examples**	**Suffix**	**Examples**
NOUN SUFFIXES		NOUN SUFFIXES	
-age	baggage, wastage	*-dom*	*freedom, kingdom*
-al	dismissal, fatal	*-hood*	*childhood, likelihood*
-ant	deodorant, applicant	*-ment*	*payment, amazement*
-ee	employee, trainee	*-ness*	*fitness, awareness*
-er	teacher, singer	*-ship*	*friendship, championship*
-or	actor, doctor		
-ism	communism, sexism		
-ist	optimist, artist		
-ity	obesity, continuity		
-ion, -ian[24]	education, electrician		
VERB SUFFIXES			
-ate	participate, hyphenate		
-en	strengthen, sadden		
-iate	differentiate, humiliate		
-ify	intensify, beautify		
-ise, -ize[25]	organise, synthesize		
ADJECTIVE SUFFIXES		ADJECTIVE SUFFIXES	
-able, -ible[26]	manageable, edible	*-ful*	*careful, helpful*
-al	professional, accidental	*-less*	*useless, fatherless*
-ic	basic, economic	*-ly*	*lovely, friendly*
-ish	selfish, bluish		
-ive	active, decisive		
-ous	famous, generous		
-y[27]	sunny, noisy		
ADVERB SUFFIX		ADVERB SUFFIX	
-ally[28]	critically	*-ly*	*quickly, absolutely*
INFLECTIONS		INFLECTIONS	
-ed	*planned, hoped, ended*	*-s* (plural)	*girls, notes*
-ing	*running, facing*	*-s* (3rd person)	*walks, knows*
-er	*bigger, braver*		
-est	*biggest, bravest*		

---

[24] This suffix is often shown as **-tion**, **-cian**, etc but the bases of these words are **educate** and **electric**, so we only add **-ion** or **-ian** — therefore these are the suffixes.

[25] Most of these words finish with **-ize** in US English. In British English, both forms are often possible but **-ise** is generally preferred nowadays. Some words are always spelled **-ise**, in British and US English: **advertise**, **advise**, **arise**, **circumcise**, **comprise**, **compromise**, **despise**, **devise**, **disguise**, **exercise**, **franchise**, **improvise**, **merchandise**, **revise**, **supervise**, **surprise**, and **televise**.

[26] See A:58.

[27] -y follows the patterns for vowel suffixes.

[28] Only used after adjectives ending in -ic.

Vowel suffixes and inflections

If the base element ends in CVC then the final C doubles in a one-syllable word: ***run + er*** becomes ***runner***, ***sun + y*** becomes ***sunny***. Remember some letters, such as ***w***, ***x*** and ***y***, cannot be doubled: ***sewing***, ***boxed***, ***payee***.

If a word has more than one syllable, the same CVC doubling rule applies only if the stress is on the last syllable of the base element. So ***beGINning*** has a double ***n*** because the stress is on the final syllable of ***beGIN***. But ***Opening*** has only one ***n*** because the stress is on the first syllable of ***Open***.

However, in British English, base elements of more than one syllable that end CV+***l***, double the ***l*** even if the stress is not on the final syllable: ***TRAvelled***, ***MARvellous***. This is not so in American English.

If the base element ends in ***e***, the ***e*** is usually dropped: ***wastage***, ***fatal***, ***famous***.

However, if the previous morpheme ends in ***ce*** or ***ge***, and the suffix begins with ***o*** or ***a***, the ***e*** is often retained, to preserve the soft ***c*** /s/ and ***g*** /dʒ/ sounds *(See A:50)*: ***courageous***, ***irreplaceable***.

If the word ends in ***ee***, ***oe*** or ***ye***, the final ***e*** is not dropped; ***agreeable***, ***canoeing***, ***dyeing***.

For the few words ending in ***ie***, change the ***i*** to ***y*** and drop the ***e*** before ***ing***: ***die + -ing = dying***, ***lie + -ing = lying***.

How are compound words spelled?

A compound is a word that is made of two free morphemes. Some examples:

- Nouns, ***lunchtime, skyscraper, takeover, car park***
- Verbs, ***windsurf, sleepwalk, blow-dry***
- Adjectives, ***three-legged, seasick, English-speaking***
- Adverbs, ***wholeheartedly, absent-mindedly***
- Pronouns, ***anything, everywhere, nobody***
- Numbers, ***eighty-two, three quarters***.

Compound words are made of two complete words. No changes take place. So for example in ***skyscraper***, the ***y*** does not change to ***i*** before the ***s*** of -***scraper***. In ***takeover***, the final ***e*** of ***take*** is not dropped as it would be if ***over*** was a suffix. Using two complete words sometimes gives rise to double letter patterns (across the boundaries of the two words) that are normally 'illegal' in English: ***hitchhiker*** has double ***h***, ***slowworm*** has double ***w*** and ***bookkeeping*** has double ***k***.

So as long as you know how to spell the two free morphemes the spelling of a compound word will be easy. The only problem is knowing whether it is spelled as one word, a hyphenated word or two separate words. Just as with prefixes, there are no real rules about this, which makes it difficult for the user to know how to write it. On the positive side, however, even the dictionaries do not agree about this, so it is best to see it as a relatively flexible system. For a compound adjective describing something made at home, two dictionaries give the spelling **home-made** (hyphenated) while the other offers **homemade** as one word. In the *Cambridge Grammar of English*, Carter and McCarthy admit,

> *The use of hyphens in compounds and complex words involves a number of different rules, and practice is changing, with fewer hyphens present in contemporary usage.*

(Carter & McCarthy, 2006)

In fact, there is a common pattern in the evolution of the hyphenation of a compound. Cook explains:

> *The longer a word has been in English, the more likely it is to have lost its space and its hyphen. The Oxford English Dictionary records a progression from tea bag 1898 to tea-bag 1936 to teabag 1977.*

(Cook, 2009, p. 211)

There are a few patterns we can see:

- When a compound adjective comes before a noun, a hyphen is often used to show which words are compounded, so we write about **a well-educated person** or a **close-knit community**.

- When the adjectives involve numerical compounds hyphens are also found: **a three-wheeled car**, **a 500-gigabyte hard drive**, or **a sixty-five-year-old man**.

Which takes precedence, the morphological or the phonological system?

As mentioned above, morphology is not related to sound, and in fact it over-rides phonological aspects of spelling.

The clearest examples of this are the Verb 2 and Verb 3 -**ed** inflections. Although **walked**, **owned** and **excited** all end with -**ed**, their endings, they all sound different: /t/, /d/ and /ɪd/ respectively. By all looking the same, reading is much easier than it would be if they were all phonologically spelled.

Compounds provide another good example. Look at the word **hothead**; a reader who did not know the word may see the **th** in the middle and pronounce it accordingly. But as the **t** is from the morpheme **hot** and the **h** from **head**, these two are not combined to make a /θ/ or /ð/ sound. Similarly **shepherd** does not contain a /f/ sound.

Summary of Chapter 7

- A morpheme is a unit of meaning within a word. These units can be used as building blocks which are combined to make more words.

- A free morpheme is one which can be used as a word in its own right, while a bound morpheme cannot.

- A wide knowledge of base morphemes allows us to make lexical links and gives reliable clues about the spelling of particular words.

- Prefixes, which are attached to the beginning of a whole word, modify the meaning. They don't change the form of the base element, so the main challenge is choosing the right prefix.

- Suffixes, which are added to the end of words, change the part of speech and occasionally the meaning. They sometimes necessitate minor changes to the end of the base element. There are some pretty reliable patterns to follow here, depending on whether the suffix begins with a consonant or vowel.

- Inflections are grammatical changes to the word and also appear at the end. They tell us about tense, person or plurality. They also sometimes require minor changes to base words and follow the same patterns as suffixes.

- Compound words are made from two free morphemes in their original form. The meaning is usually evident from the two elements but this has sometimes changed over time. The rules about hyphenating these are vague and often flexible.

- The morphological system clearly takes precedence over the phonological one and gives much more accurate clues to the spelling of words.

Chapter Eight:

Lexical system

What is the lexical system?

What are some useful examples?

How are these related to homophones?

What is the lexical system?

The lexical system is perhaps one of the most interesting systems, although it isn't as well-documented as the others we have examined. People know that there is a phonological element to English spelling (in fact they probably over-emphasise it), they know about prefixes and suffixes, they are at least vaguely aware that history has a part to play, and some basic graphemic patterns are taught in schools. But lexical links don't get the attention they deserve.

The lexical system is very closely related to etymology and also to morphology. What is it?

It is the lexical system which gives us similar spellings of words with related meanings. It is purely visual. We can *see* that words are related by an element they have in common, even though those elements may not *sound* the same in the different words.

For example, it is the lexical system which accounts for the silent *g* in the word *sign*. The *g* is there to show the semantic link it has to many other words. This is most clearly shown in the diagram below, in which we can see that many words include the letters *s-i-g-n*, whether the *g* is pronounced or not. What links them is the general meaning of *sign*, which comes from the Latin *signum*, meaning **mark**, **token**, **indication** or **symbol** *(See C:193)*.

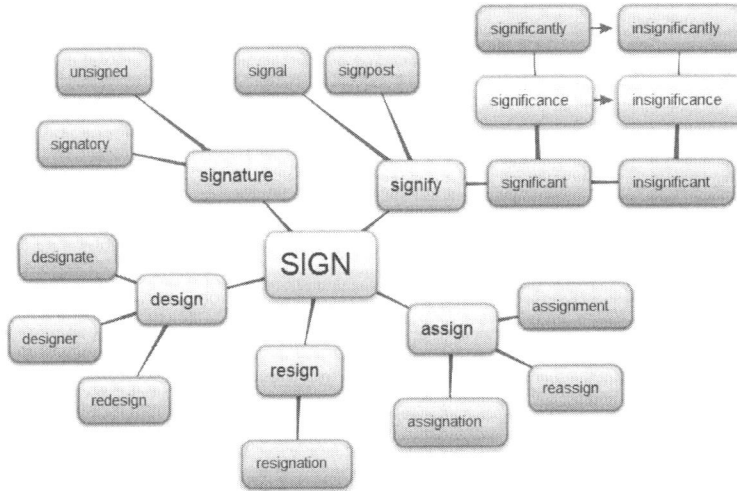

Figure 6: *A word web for* **sign**

There is a surprisingly high degree of regularity here.

> *... conventional orthography is much closer than one might guess to an optimal orthography, an orthography that represents no redundant information and that indicates directly, by direct letter-to-segment correspondence, the underlying lexical form of the spoken language.*
>
> (Chomsky, 1972, p. 12)

Noam Chomsky claims that these relationships in spelling help us to understand the meaning of words much more than the pronunciation does. Others agree:

> *... a spelling (or orthographic) system has to do more than simply record speech sounds; ultimately the written representation of a language is for the eye rather than the ear.*
>
> (Templeton & Morris, 2001, p. 2)

> *Spelling can show links between related words or morphemes which are lost in the actual spoken forms. Most claims that English spelling is deficient are based on the view that English spelling corresponds to the sounds of speech. The purpose of English spelling is instead to link to the underlying lexical representation.*
>
> (Cook, 2004, p. 78)

There are many other examples of this lexical spelling. Here are just a few:
Whole words:
- ***Know***: **knowledge, knowledgeable, acknowledge, acknowledgement**
- ***Real***: **reality, really, realism, unrealistic, realise, realisation, realtor.**

Base elements of words (from Latin and Greek):
- ***-sci-*** (related to ***knowledge*** or acquiring of it): ***science, scientific, conscious, subconscious, conscientious, omniscient*** *(See B:144, C:193)*

72

- *-rupt* (related to *break*): *rupture, interrupt, disruption, eruption, abrupt, bankrupt*[29], *corrupt*
- *-terr-* (related to the *earth*): *territory, terrain, subterranean, Mediterranean, extraterrestrial, terrace*[30], *terrier*[31]
- *-val* (related to *worth* or *strength*): *value, equivalent, interval, invalidate, evaluate, ambivalent, convalescence, prevalent*.

Prefixes and suffixes are also aspects of this lexical spelling. They give information about meaning and have consistent spelling in different words.

The examples are all related to morphemes. The difference between the morphological and lexical systems is that the former is about building up the words from parts and the lexical is about recognising visual and semantic links between words.

Some useful examples

There are some more of these groups which are very helpful for spelling, especially because they include words that are homophonous, such as *to*, *too* and *two*; *here* and *hear*; *their* and *there* *(See C:195)*.

Numbers

I was once asked by a frustrated English language learner why we say *one* with a /w/ sound when there is no *w* in the spelling and then do not pronounce the *w* in *two* when there is one. What a wonderful question! At the time I had no answer. Subsequently, however, I realised that there are reasons for the spelling, although I cannot justify the pronunciation.

The *on* string in *one* can be found in many words with a related meaning: *once, only, lonely, none* (from *not one*), *alone*, although the pronunciation of the *on* varies. Although the *w* in *two* is silent, there is a very good reason for its existence: to link it to other words from the same lexical group, namely, *twelve, twenty, twins, between, twist, twice*.

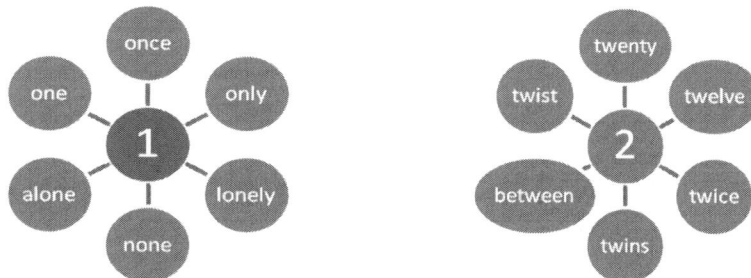

Figure 7: *Words relating to* **one** *containing the string* **on** *and words relating to* **two** *containing the string* **tw-**.

---

[29] Bankrupt: literally broken bench because the first bankers ran their business from a bench in a public space such as a market. If they became insolvent they, or maybe their creditors who were owed money, broke the bench to show they were no longer in business.
[30] Terrace — originally built on a raised mound of earth.
[31] Terrier — means earth dog, because it hunts animals that live in burrows in the ground, such as rabbits.

Place

The letter string **here** is found in three very common pronouns related to **place**: **here**, **there**, **where**, plus all the related words such as **nowhere**, **thereabouts**, etc.

Hearing

Three words related to **hearing** contain the string **ear**: they are **ear**, **hear** and **heard**.

Third-person plural function words

Third person plural function words all begin with **the**: **they**, **them**, **their**.[32]

Question words

Question words begin with **wh**-: **where**, **why**, **when**, **what**, **which**, **who** (which has a different pronunciation). The only exception is **how**, which does have the **w** and **h** but in a different order!

It is interesting to be aware of these lexical groups, some of which may not be immediately obvious, and to be on the look-out for more. As a native speaker, with the exception of **wh**-questions, I was never taught about these at school and can see no mention of them in the latest literacy curriculum used in English primary education. However, explicitly raising awareness of these can be very useful for distinguishing between homophones, remembering silent letters and writing correct letter-order in words like **two**.

---

[32] Incidentally, all the other pronouns and possessive adjectives: first person singular and plural (**I, me, my, we, us, our**), second person (**you, your**), and third person singular (**he, him, his, she, her, it, its**), come from Germanic Old English, but **they, them, their** come from Old Norse.

Summary of Chapter 8

- The lexical system is closely related to the etymological and morphological systems, but the focus is on semantic and visual links between words.

- It shows us that English spelling is often for the eye rather than the ear.

- It gives some useful, and surprising, ways to distinguish between some troublesome homophones.

Chapter Nine:

How We Spell

What's the relationship between reading and writing?

How do we spell when reading?

How do we spell when writing?

Why does seeing words in context help?

Which senses do we use when spelling?

What do good spellers do that weak spellers don't? And vice versa?

We have explored the language itself in some detail and now we should move on to look at the consumers of it. How do we approach spelling as readers and writers?

What's the relationship between reading and writing?

It is tempting to generalise about reading and writing skills — if one is weak, the other must be too. Although this is common, it is not always true. Some people read well, but have problems producing accurate spelling (Peters, 1985). Why is that?

There are important differences between reading and writing, or 'decoding' and 'encoding'. As reading is a largely passive skill, it is easier. Our comprehension of individual words is helped greatly by surrounding words that give us the context. We don't need to pay careful attention to each word or each letter, certainly when we have become more fluent readers. We can make more guesses about meaning when reading and if we get them wrong, very often nobody will know. We are rarely required to show evidence that we have understood every word in normal, everyday reading (only in a classroom!).

Here are a few experiments to illustrate:

a) Look at the sentences above between the *s. How many *e*s can you see in these sentences? Count them now and write the number in this box before you read on.

b) Think of a symbol that you are very familiar with. Here are some suggestions:

- The logo on your mobile phone
- A road sign such as 'no overtaking'
- The logo of a famous company
- A disabled sign on a toilet door

Try drawing the symbol (without looking at it):

c) Read this:

> Aoccdrnig to rscheearch at Cmabrigde uinervtisy, it deosn't mttaer waht oredr the ltteers in a wrod are, the olny iprmoetnt tihng is taht the frist and lsat ltteres are at the rghit pclae. The rset can be a tatol mses and you can sitll raed it wouthit a porbelm. Tihs is bcuseae we do not raed ervey lteter by it slef but the wrod as a wlohe.

What do these tasks show?

a) There were twenty-five *e*s in the sentences. Did you see them all? Most people don't see them all, because they read common words like **the** and common endings such as **-ed** as complete units rather than individual letters. Even words which are longer and lower frequency, like **differences**, are identified like this by competent readers. We recognise them the way that we recognise the symbol **2** to mean **two**, **%** to mean **per cent** or a particular shape tick to mean **Nike**. Not many people have to struggle to decode the word **the** letter-by-letter.

If you didn't find all the *e*s in the sentences, don't be depressed because it may well indicate that you are a better, more fluent and efficient reader than someone reading very carefully letter-by-letter (but give up your dreams of being a proof-reader!).

b) When you check (on the Internet perhaps) your drawing of the logo or sign, you will probably find that although the symbol is something you recognise immediately when you see it, and perhaps you 'read' it every day, you are unable to draw it accurately. However, if you see the symbol and it's wrong, you may have a sort of uncomfortable feeling that something isn't quite right even if you can't say what it is. A bit like having your slippers on the wrong feet! It can be the same with spelling. Unless you have consciously learned a spelling or there is a way to work it out — phonetically, morphologically, etymologically, etc. — it may be hard to remember, at least the first time you write it.

c) Many people find the text surprisingly easy to read, which illustrates how much we guess at meaning rather than decoding letter-by-letter. We guess by the context rather than the internal structure of the word. If you had just seen the word *oredr* out of context and asked to say what it was, it would have been much more difficult.

And if I now asked you to hide the text and rewrite it with the same spelling, I'm sure you would struggle because you haven't been forced to notice the spelling. For writing we need to produce every letter. We may not do this consciously when we become fluent — we write in chunks such as *st*, *ough* and *ing* — but there are always some words that we will need to spell carefully.

How do we spell when reading?

What is involved in *reading* a single word? As we've seen, common structure words are usually recognised as wholes, but if a word is less familiar we may try to answer these questions (not necessarily in this order):
- What kind of word do I expect to see? What does the context tell me about meaning and part of speech?
- What sounds do the letters make?
- Can I break the word down into chunks?
- Does the word, or part of the word, look like another similar word?
- Do I recognise any letter strings?

How do we spell when writing?

When we *write* words, the process is different.

First we usually have to choose the word. This choice is based not only on knowing what we want to say, but also the best way of saying it. Once we've decided, very often the word flows from our pen or our fingers on the keyboard.

However, we may have chosen the most appropriate word but what if we don't know how to spell it? Unless we just opt to use a less precise word that we *can* spell, we will need to go through a process of working out the spelling. Here are some ways to do this (again, not in a particular order as different people approach the task differently):

- You could try sounding out the word — if you have a good knowledge of phoneme-to-grapheme correspondence this could help you get about 50% of words right, but very often there are viable (but incorrect) alternatives, not to mention homophones.

- You could ask yourself if there are some morphemes in the word that you know how to spell — this is often useful with longer words. You need to think about how to attach these to each other too — are there any necessary spelling changes?

- Thinking about the possible origins of the word may help. If you remind yourself that academic and medical words are often derived from Greek, for example, you may consider that /k/ can be spelled **ch**.

- You might be able to relate your word to other words you do know. The sound in the other word may be clearer. For example, if you are not sure how to write **considerable** (or is it ~~**considerible**~~?), you could think about **consideration**, where the **a** has a much more identifiable sound.

- You can apply any knowledge of graphemic patterns. If you know that **ck** is never used at the beginning of a word, you are unlikely to write ~~**ckitchen**~~.

- You could use a dictionary or thesaurus. Or ask somebody.

- Of course, when using a word processor, you can try a spelling and the spell-checker will warn you if it doesn't recognise the word. It will offer you a list of words to choose from, one of which may be right. And in fact, many words can be corrected automatically, often without even the writer's knowledge. This still needs careful checking however, as homophones and other real words will not be flagged.

When we analyse a spelling that we *read*, it is usually possible to find a justification for it from one of the systems — a phonological, morphological, etymological, lexical or graphemic one. In *writing*, however, because we are starting from nothing, we can't know which system we should refer to. As David Crystal says,

> *...irregular spellings can be explained but not predicted...*

(Crystal, 1995).

Writing is certainly a more demanding activity for most people than reading, and spelling this is certainly reflected in spelling. There is a much greater cognitive load involved when writing words we are not sure of than when reading them. Although good spellers tend to spell in chunks, weaker spellers have to give attention to each and every letter.

I'll let David Crystal conclude:

> *It comes as a surprise to many to realize there is no simple correlation between reading and spelling ability. Spelling involves a set of active, conscious processes that are not required for reading. It is possible to read very selectively, as when we 'skim' a newspaper. It is not possible to spell selectively: it is a letter-by-letter act. And more things can go wrong when we try to spell. Faced with the word feep, there is really only one possible way to pronounce it, but faced with the sounds /fi:p/ there are several possible spellings (such as feep, feap, fepe and pheep). The task facing a speller is always greater than that facing a reader.*

(Crystal, 1995, p. 272)

What do good spellers do that weak spellers don't?

Not everyone approaches spelling in the same way. Research suggests that there are certain approaches that seem to typify stronger spellers and certain ones used more by weaker spellers. Of course these are generalisations and not true in every case.

Good spellers often:	Weak spellers often:
acquire spelling effortlessly from reading	do not acquire recognition of spelling patterns when reading. Too much focus on individual letters or guessing from context
can hear new words and associate them with the right letters	cannot distinguish separate sounds in a word or relate sounds to symbols *(See C:223)*
can break words into parts and write those parts	cannot hear distinct parts of words
can recognise which letters are likely to be found together, and in which order — they may see strings of letters as entities	do not see serial probability — they are more likely to see each letter separately *(See B:135, C:200, C:202, C:205, C: 226)*
can see a word in their minds and read it off	cannot remember how a word should look — they may try a phonetic spelling or make a random arbitrary guess *(See B:147, C:221, C:225, C:207, C:216, C:217)*
can see their errors, so just need to proof-read carefully	cannot see their own errors until they are pointed out *(See B:165, C:197, C:250, C:253)*
use several different strategies to improve their spelling — if one approach fails then they try something else	do not employ a variety of approaches — they may be hooked on one approach (often phonetic) or may not know any others *(See C:185)*
can see patterns and consistency in spelling — they find systems (at alphabetic, orthographic, and meaning levels) rather than chaos	do not see English spelling as anything other than chaotic and unmanageable *(See B:127, C:185. C:195)*
are interested in how words are made, their meaning, origin and spelling	are uninterested or even antagonistic towards written language *(See B:124)*
use analogy with spellings that they do know	rarely make links between words they know and those they don't *(See C:193)*

(Torbe, 1977) (Peters, 1985) (Pratley, 1988) (Scott, 2000)

Summary of Chapter 9

- When we are reading we usually don't notice spelling as we use context and other clues to make sense of words that we don't already know.

- Spelling when we are writing is a much more demanding skill which involves referring to any or all of the five systems of English spelling. If we have never seen the word before it is impossible to be sure if our spelling is right without checking another source.

- Good spellers seem to use a wider range of senses, and particularly the visual, than weaker spellers.

- Good spellers also use certain strategies (and a variety of them) that weaker spellers don't.

Chapter Ten:

Successful Learning

Do people learn differently?

How does state of mind affect ability to learn?

What role does motivation play?

Why is focus so important yet so hard?

Is thinking really necessary?

How much can the brain remember?

What's the use of recycling?

How do people learn successfully? There has been plenty of research into this. Here I will note some of the main findings that apply to learning, whatever the subject. This will serve as a useful reminder when we come to look at the best ways to improve spelling.

Do people learn differently?

We all know that there are great variations in how people learn. This may be for genetic or environmental reasons or both. There are also many similarities in how we all learn, and there are common conditions that most people need in order to learn successfully.

Each learner is, of course, unique. Each one brings a different set of experiences, assumptions, knowledge, skills and personality to the classroom. Learners, especially teenage or adult ones, don't arrive in class as a blank slate or an empty bottle to be filled with knowledge.

To make sense of new knowledge or ideas we need to be able to attach them to something that we already know. I like to imagine the brain as being covered in little hooks and when some new piece of information comes in one ear it flies around the brain looking for the most familiar hook to hang on. If it doesn't find one, it's likely to fly out of the other ear! Learning is much easier if we can hook the unknown onto something known. So people with different existing knowledge will make different connections, or maybe none.

People also have different learning styles: some are very studious, others prefer to dive into a task and just see what 'sticks', for example. There's a lot of talk of VAK: visual, auditory and kinaesthetic learning styles. Some people believe that students can be categorised into 'visual learners', 'auditory learners' and 'kinaesthetic learners'. My experience suggests that most of us are all three. People learn different things in different ways on different days. By including a visual route to learning, such as showing diagrams or photos, an auditory route, such as giving explanations, and a kinaesthetic route, doing something physical, teachers can appeal to all their learners. Some subject matter may lend itself more to one modality. Other information needs to be presented several different ways for learners to get a complete view of it *(See B:115, C:207)*.

The visual sense can be very strong. We can recognise someone we know well, even from behind in a crowded street, because we can identify their particular walk which differs from everyone else's. Have you ever found a seemingly random phrase going around in your head, and then realised that it's from a book title in your room that you weren't even aware you'd looked at? If you need to remember a foreign name that you've never heard before, don't you feel you need to see it written? On the other hand, remembering something you've seen can be very difficult if it was surrounded by lots of other visual 'noise'.

Information delivered through sound can be very memorable — think of songs and jingles. Sometimes you can't get them out of your head even if you want to. The auditory sense is also useful for very short-term memory. You look up a phone number, but your phone is in another room, what do you do? Keep repeating the number until you get to your phone (hoping nobody interrupts you on the way)? Auditory input can also be very forgettable — a lecture delivered in a monotone with no visual support is unlikely to be the most memorable way of delivering information.

Most traditional teaching for adults and teens is visual or auditory. In primary schools we may see children learning by being engaged in lots of physical activities, but does kinaesthetic teaching and learning have to cease when children go to secondary school? And do adults really learn best while sitting in a chair? I don't think so. Many people will say that 'learning by doing' is the most successful mode for them but it is by far the least common way of teaching.

So to learn well we need a mixture of visual, auditory and kinaesthetic activities — multi-sensory activities, in other words.

How does state of mind affect ability to learn?

The mind has to be ready to learn. It is difficult for it to be receptive if there are obstacles blocking that learning. These obstacles may be lack of self-esteem, stress, embarrassment, frustration, fear of being judged, or even an antagonism towards the subject.

People generally live up to expectations — or down to them! If they are told that they are not good at something, this belief often becomes lodged in the mind and they are unlikely to shine in that skill. Other people who are always praised may feel they have too much to lose if they fail at something so they work particularly hard to remain at that standard or get even better. Praising someone for something they are obviously not doing well won't make them an expert, just as the odd criticism won't make someone who is confident in their skills useless. But belief has been shown to have a strong influence on our performance *(See B:122, C:263).*

Stress and anxiety can inhibit learning. They raise the 'affective filter', as Krashen calls it. Negative emotions obstruct the brain from focussing clearly on the target. While a teacher is trying to help, the learner's brain may be busy thinking, "I've got to get this right or they'll think I'm stupid", rather than listening to the explanation which would provide the right answer. Learners are more successful when they feel relaxed and feel secure. If they recognise that asking questions is a sign of learning, not a sign of failure, they will be happier to seek help. A confident learner knows that it is 'normal' not to do something perfectly the first time. They enjoy that challenge as long as they know that the task is ultimately manageable.

What was your least favourite subject at school? Were you good at it? I'll take a guess that you weren't. If we are antagonistic towards a subject for any reason, we don't learn it well (and we usually don't like a subject that we're not good at).

What role does motivation play?

Motivation is, of course, a major factor in successful learning. If somebody doesn't want to learn there is no way they can be made to. We say, "You can lead a horse to water but you can't make it drink".

To learn something, somebody needs to know why it is useful and relevant to them and they need to believe it. The reason may just be for tomorrow's test, in which case they may subconsciously tell their brain, "Remember this until tomorrow, then you can forget it". But if they really believe that learning something will help them, they are much more likely to learn it.

So learners need to know why something is important for them *before* they are asked to devote time to it. It's so frustrating to have mentally switched off in a lesson or while reading something and *then* finding out that you really needed this information and you weren't paying attention! If somebody says to you, "We're going to look at X so you'll be able to do Y much more easily", then you know whether it's worth the effort or not.

Another aspect of motivation involves finding the content and practice engaging. There is so much competition for our attention nowadays, that if we don't find one activity engaging we soon move on to another. Boring, decontextualised, mechanical practice is just a chore. Variety, challenge and fun are much more memorable, but naturally they have to be useful too.

Why is focus so important and yet so hard?

We live in a very 'full-on' world. There is information coming at us from all directions and sometimes it's difficult to focus on something enough to really learn it. What does the following tell us about learning and recall?

I can't remember when my appointment with the dentist is so I phone the surgery to find out. The receptionist gives me the time. I'll put a reminder on my phone. Oh, what's this — a text message to phone Sue about tomorrow's class. But I need to look at the timetable before I phone her and that's on the computer. Oh great, there's a reply to Zeinab's email and this article she's attached looks really relevant to my work, perhaps I should just take a quick look at that before ...

What do you think? Will I remember what time the dentist's appointment is? Or will I have to phone back? How embarrassing!

Multi-tasking is semi-tasking! A lot of things *sort of* get done, but nothing gets done very well. And the brain doesn't get time to process and remember.

If we don't create space for learning — a situation where there are not too many other distractions vying for our attention — we don't give ourselves a fair chance to learn. This could be as simple as working somewhere quiet and turning the internet off. But sometimes it's more a case of extracting what we want to focus on from the 'noise' around it and giving that our full attention.

Is thinking really necessary?

Learning, especially where language is involved, is not a 'push' activity. Unfortunately perhaps, brains are not empty vessels to be filled by wise teachers. Learners need to 'pull' new information and skills into their brains and attach this new learning to what is already resident there. They need to understand, truly understand, and make their own connections. Our brains need to organise and make patterns. Doing this actually creates physical connections through a process of protein synthesis within the brain

There has been plenty of research which shows that when we process something more deeply in our brains, we are likely to remember it better and for longer. As Earl Stevick explains,

> *Whether new material makes it from STM [short-term memory] to LTM [long-term memory] at all, and how long it remains there, are largely affected by how much work the learner's mind does on it while it is still on the STM worktable.*

(Stevick, 1982, p. 30)

In other words, to learn we need to *think*. Deeper cognitive processing is stimulated by answering questions, doing tasks which involve organising and categorising, applying what has been learned, and evaluating how useful the learning has been.

This is fine in theory but as a teacher I know there are problems with this in practice. Many of my students seem to be rather allergic to thinking! Or at least they think they might be and don't want to take the risk! Many (not all — I should be fair) would rather be spoon-fed the ideas than make the effort to think. (I admit I'm sometimes the same too!) In fact there is often a cultural issue here as well. In some educational contexts learners are not encouraged to think, work out problems and express opinions. Their job is to learn what the teacher has told them.

How much can the brain remember?

Even the best and most motivated brains have problems dealing with large amounts of information. On average we can store between 5 and 9 pieces of information in our short-term memory. Then something has to be pushed out to make room for another bit of data. This makes each piece of information rather 'expensive' in memory terms, so we need to look for some special offers, such as Buy One Get One Free. In other words, we need to 'chunk' or group related information together, so instead of it costing, say, four memory units it only costs one. We do this with telephone numbers — remembering sets of digits rather than each individual one *(See C:200, C:202)*.

What's the use of recycling?

We know that, especially in language learning, once is not enough. We can't just tell our learners about the passive voice and then they will always use it accurately and appropriately. Language itself and the language-learning process are far too complex for that. So a great deal of recycling is needed. As well as practising a new skill at the time of learning, we need to come back to it, preferably within the next 24 hours. The reason for this is that if the information is to get to, and stay in, the long-term memory, protein synthesis must take place in the brain and it's thought that this needs to happen within 24 hours of the initial learning. Without revisiting the new information and your understanding of it, this cannot happen. (Rose, 1993)

And the recycling needs to continue, as each time we return to this learning we strengthen the connections and possibly make new ones, especially if we see the item in a different context or from a different viewpoint. So when we need to access this information we will be able to do it more easily and more quickly *(See B:156, C:187)*.

Summary of Chapter 10

- What and how quickly people learn often depends on what is already in their brains.

- Different learning styles exist but people's learning preferences may change according to the subject and other factors.

- Visual, auditory and kinaesthetic activities can all aid learning, and are probably best when combined into a multi-sensory approach.

- Low self-esteem, stress, fear of being judged and other negative emotions are all barriers to successful learning.

- Motivation to learn is fostered by relevance, need, variety, challenge and fun.

- There are so many potential distractions nowadays that learners may not easily find 'space' for learning.

- Deeper cognitive processing leads to stronger and more long-lasting learning. Thinking is important.

- The brain can't store much in the short-term memory but grouping information in chunks means more can be remembered.

- We strengthen and consolidate learning by returning to it several times and critically within 24 hours of first meeting it.

Chapter Eleven:

Common Learner Spelling Errors

What errors are common among native speakers?

What errors are common among non-native speakers?

We all make spelling mistakes sometimes. There are different reasons for them:

- Guesses — attempts at unknown spellings. These may be over-generalisations about spelling, following a 'rule' that doesn't apply or trying to base spelling too closely on sound.

- Wrongly-learned spellings. These may relate to the learner's mother tongue. For example, if *address* is spelled with one *d* in Spanish, the learner might learn it as the same in English: *adress*.

- Slips — spellings we know and can correct immediately if pointed out, but we got wrong for some reason, maybe just lack of concentration. The missing *s* on present simple third person singular verbs is a common example.

- Typos — sometimes we hit keys in the wrong order. We may type *teh* for *the*, but of course we would never handwrite it like that; the *e* finger just moves faster than the *h* finger.

There are certain words that learners across the board have problems with, or sometimes just specific parts of those words. There are some features of English spelling that are universally troublesome, such as silent letters. Then there are those difficulties that bother different types of learners, for example, native-speaker children, language learners with particular mother tongues, dyslexics, etc.

Let's look at some words that are commonly misspelled by native and non-native speakers.

What errors are common among native-speakers?

University students

Vivian Cook gives these words as being frequently misspelled by his British native-speaker university students:

accommodate	*correct*	*intermediate*	*quite/quiet*
achieve,	*correspondence*	*knew/new*	*referring*
affect/effect	*definitely*	*laid*	*relevant*
allotted	*dictionaries*	*learners*	*scenario*
appendices	*discrepancy*	*minutes*	*sense*
approved	*elaborate*	*modelled*	*sited/cited*
assess	*embarrassing*	*occasion*	*their/there*
advocates	*enthusiasm*	*occurrence*	*tires/tyres*
bare/bear	*fuelled*	*perceived*	*to/too*
beginners	*fulfil*	*positive*	*traditional*
categories	*greater/grater*	*principle/principal*	*universities*
chosen	*hindrance*	*proficiency*	*useful*
compulsory	*illicit/elicit*	*pronunciation*	*vocabulary*
confidently	*independent*	*psychology*	*well-paid*
controls	*integrated*	*questionnaires*	*where/were*

(Cook, 2004, p. 16)

He notes the main causes of spelling errors within these words seem to be related to:

- uncertainty about double consonants
- confusing vowels that are pronounced as weak forms
- choosing between homophones (and near homophones)
- making irregular spellings regular.

Some of these may just be typing errors, such as ***to/too***. Some are very surprising, for example, that native-speaker higher-education students should write ~~***dictionarys***~~ and ~~***universitys***~~, thus disregarding a very elementary spelling rule (again, they are possibly typos). And several of the mistakes are very prevalent among all native speakers, such as confusion between ***there*** and ***their***, and 'spelling demons' like ***accommodation*** and ***definitely***.

Children

Here is a list of 100 of the most common errors made by native-speaking children:

again	coming	him	people	*to
alright	course	interesting	pretty	things
always	cousin	its	received	though
an	decided	it's	running	thought
and	didn't	jumped	said	through
animals	different	know	school	together
another	dropped	let's	some	*too
around	every	like	something	tried
asked	February	little	sometimes	*two
babies	first	looked	started	until
*bear	for	many	stopped	very
beautiful	friend	money	surprise	wanted
because	friends	morning	swimming	went
before	frightened	mother	than	*were
believe	from	name	that's	when
bought	getting	named	*their	*where
came	going	now	then	with
caught	happened	off	*there	woman
children	heard	once	they	would
clothes	here	our	they're	you

(Peters, 1985)

The only words in this list which also appear in the university students' list are marked with *. Other than the word **bear** (which presumably is used in very different sense by academic students and children) the only common problems are **to/too/two**, **there/their** and **were/where**. The words in the children's list are obviously much more simple, but generally quite predictable. They indicate problems with:

- homophones
- double letters
- apostrophes
- some tricky letter strings such as **ough**
- vowel digraphs.

Children are often very creative with their spelling and Margaret Peters lists 202 different spellings of **saucer** written by 10 year-olds! (Peters, 1985, p. 19)

What kind of errors are common among ELLs?

Non-native speakers can be equally creative. Phil Brabbs (Magic Spell, 2004) reports that, in 200 test scripts at a college in the United Arab Emirates, learners produced 114 different spellings of **neighbour**[33].

Vivian Cook also gives a list of errors made by his non-native speaking university students:

accommodation	*definite*	*integrate*	*professional*
because	*develop*	*kindergarten*	*professor*
beginning	*different*	*knowledge*	*really*
business	*describe*	*life*	*study/student*
career	*government*	*necessary*	*their/there*
choice	*interest(ing)*	*particular*	*which*
			would

(Cook, L2 Spelling)

The Cambridge Learners' Corpus is a huge bank of words taken from scripts written by Cambridge ESOL examination candidates from many different countries. Analysis of these has produced this list of the ten most common misspellings. The letters in bold indicate the ones where errors were most frequently found.

a**comm**odation	definit**e**ly
advertis**e**ment	enviro**nm**ent
be**ginn**ing	gover**nm**ent
bel**ie**ve	su**cc**e**ss**ful
colle**a**gue	**wh**ich

(Cambridge University Press, 2008, p. EH12)

These shorter lists contain a few words similar to ones on the list of native-speaker student mistakes, but also several more basic words that are on the children's list, like **which**, **would** and **because** that an educated native speaker is less likely to make mistakes with.

The great challenge for these non-native students is that they not only have to cope with the irregular high-frequency words that children are struggling with and native-speaker adults have had enormous exposure to, but also have to use longer, more academic words that are difficult even for native-speaking adults.

In all of these lists we can see several errors involving:

- doubling *(See C:232, C:236, C:236, C:258)*
- silent letters *(See B:134, C:227)*
- weak vowels *(See B:131, C:220)*
- vowel digraphs *(See C:200, C:202).*

---

[33] **neighbor** in AmE.

Errors among ELLs with weak spelling

I collected samples of written work from ten adult EFL students at a private language school in the UK and analysed their spelling errors. They had all been identified by their teachers as weak spellers; in fact most had chosen to join a Reading, Writing and Spelling option (designed and advertised for students needing extra support in these skills). Of these ten in the sample, seven were Arabic speakers, two Chinese and one Spanish. They were from Pre-Intermediate, Intermediate and Upper Intermediate groups, although their writing skills were generally weaker. Some were studying academic English (IELTS preparation), others were from general English classes.

They were asked to provide some previous written work, that is, something *not* written especially for the research, as I wanted to collect as wide a sample of text types and topics as possible. I asked for work *with* spelling mistakes (rather than their best or corrected work) and that had been handwritten, so that it had not been automatically spell-checked.

Within this corpus I found 379 misspelled words, although there were more errors than this, because many words included more than one error. It was a very small sample so this may not be representative in a wider context.

Here is a list of the most frequently misspelled words in the sample:

another	*before*	*government(s)*
because	*companies/company*	*similar*
Arabic	*declined/declining*	*smoke*
beautiful	*from*	

Obviously this list somewhat reflects the particular learners in the survey, but it is interesting to see the mixture of:
- some very common words, such as *from* *(See B:140, C:188)*
- some predictably difficult ones such as **because** and **beautiful** *(See B:146, C:207)*
- some considerably less frequent ones such as *declined/ing*.

Here are the next most common words that were misspelled in the sample:

about	*happened*	*modern*	*then*
castle	*hobby (ies)*	*people*	*they*
course	*hotel (s)*	*pollution*	*think*
dangerous	*interest (ing)*	*quiet*	*twelfth*
different	*knowledge*	*sentence*	*two*
expensive	*later*	*services*	*unfortunately*
explain (ing)	*law/lawyer*	*should*	*very*
find	*magazine*	*stay (ed)*	*went*
gradually	*minutes*	*taking*	

The rest of the 379 words were each only spelled wrongly once.

Observations

From the data I collected from this small project I was able to make some observations and from those suggest some learning needs. These are not based solely on the results of this minor project however, but also on over twenty years' experience of teaching such groups.

- Learners made many more errors concerning vowels than consonants.

  - In this study, 68% of misspellings had vowel problems, while only 43% had consonant errors. If we remind ourselves that in British English we have five vowel letters for about 20 vowel sounds and 21 consonant letters for 24 consonant sounds, this is not surprising. Furthermore, English language learners often have great difficulty in distinguishing between all these sounds. However, 43% is not an insignificant number either, so we can see that consonants also present difficulties *(See B:131, C:223, C:191)*.

- Vowel digraphs posed particular problems.

  - A vowel digraph is taken to mean two adjacent letters, at least one of which is a vowel (usually both), which together form one vowel sound (including diphthongs), such as *ea* in *spread*, *aw* as in *law*. Over a third of the words with vowel problems had errors related to vowel digraphs or trigraphs *(See C:200, C:202)*.

- Weak vowel sounds were also problematic.

  - A third of the words with vowel problems were identified as having an error related to a weak sound. Again, considering there is no single way to spell /ə/, it is impossible for learners to guess the spelling of this sound in a particular word by phonological means alone *(See C:220)*.

- Spelling short vowels was more problematic than spelling long vowels.

  - There were rather more problems with spelling short vowel sounds than long ones (61% to 45%). It must be remembered that the short vowels include weak forms *(see above)*. The short vowel errors often seemed to stem from a failure to differentiate between these short vowel sounds, hence the errors such as **than** for **then**, **shot** for **shut** and ~~**vedio**~~ for **video**. Also short, and especially weak, vowels were often omitted completely, e.g. ~~**Arbi**~~ for **Arabic**, ~~**naturl**~~ for **natural**. This is especially true for some language groups. In Arabic, short vowels carry very little significance and are almost allophonic (the meaning doesn't change if a different short vowel sound is used) and in fact are usually omitted from script. (Swan & Smith, 1987, p. 143) *(See C:223)*.

- Spelling long vowels was also problematic, although less so. This may be because many are spelled with digraphs, which we have already noted to be challenging *(See C:229)*.

- Silent letters were sometimes omitted or in the wrong position.

  o Quite a high proportion of misspellings related to silent letters. They were usually either omitted or substituted. It was interesting to note that the largest sub-category here is, by a clear margin, final *e (See B:134, C:227)*.

- There were few problems with homophones but several that may have been homophonous to the non-native speaking learner.

  o There were only four confused homophones in the sample but many more words which the learner may have thought were homophones because of inaccurate pronunciation, for example *chick* for *cheek*, *then* for *than* and *casts* for *costs (See B:132, C:195)*.

- The correct letters were sometimes used but in the wrong order.

  o This suggests that learners often "half-remember", especially anything unusual or salient about the spelling. For example, a learner remembered that *guest* contained a *u* and wrote *geust*; another seems to have remembered that *assistance* had a double *s* and a single *s* but wrote them in the wrong order in *asisstance*; the *ou* (a weak form) of *dangerous* has been remembered in *dangoures*, just not the correct placement. Another interesting observation about this category of misspellings is that most of them have clearly not been spelled phonetically: *scioal* (*social*), *somke* (*smoke*), *bule* (*blue*), *preson* (*person*), *reuslt* (*result*) *(See C:198)*.

  o Some students seemed much more prone to mixing the order of letters than others and may be dyslexic (although none claimed to be so).

  o This kind of error, the transposition of letters, seems to be a mechanical one as, in my experience, learners can usually correctly respell these words instantly when they are pointed out and express surprise and frustration with themselves for having written such an error. Unfortunately they often don't see the errors until they are pointed out *(See C:253)*.

- Learners were usually able to spell prefixes and suffixes, but failed to make necessary and correct changes to the base element when adding them.

  o About a quarter of the words in this study appeared to have morphological errors, in spite of the high degree of regularity in this area. Although these were very difficult to sub-categorise, a few particular areas of difficulty appeared several times (in order of frequency):
    o changing *y* to *i* before an added morpheme *(See C:238)*
    o various problems with -*ly*
    o base word changes needed before –*ing (See C:236)*
    o various problems with the -*ed* ending
    o confusion about *f* or *v* before an added morpheme
    o spelling the -*ous* suffix.

94

- Knowing whether or not to double letters in a word was not particularly problematic for these EFL learners.

  - Only 9% of words in this study showed this problem, which was surprising. Had there been more errors by, say, Spanish students in the sample, we may have seen more occurrences of these, as Spanish often has a single consonant where it is doubled in English (Swan & Smith 1987: 78). Many of the doubling errors in this sample were in fact related to morphology (***definitally***, ***geting***) or to vowel length (***feel*** for ***fell***, ***steel*** for ***still***).

- Long words contain more errors.

  - Although only a quarter of the words in the sample were considered longer than average (more than six letters) they contained more errors per word. We must remember that short words are much more frequently used: of the 150 most frequent words in written English, only ten contain more than six letters. Learners have told me that they avoid writing long words because they are difficult *(See B:139, C:213).*

- Some misspellings were of very frequent words that learners have been exposed to many, many times.

  - Although only 14% of the misspelled words in the sample come from the 150 most frequent in writing, these words are extremely useful for learners to spell as they constitute nearly 50% of written text. This provides evidence that spelling is often not sufficiently acquired through reading *(See B:140, C:188).*

Summary of Chapter 11

The following types of errors seem the most prevalent among different types of learners.

- vowels

    - weak vowels

    - vowel digraphs

- short vowels (especially ELL weak spellers)

- homophones and words that are homophonous to learners (particularly common ones such as *there/their*, *to/too/two*, and *were/where*)

- doubling (particularly in the word *accommodation*!)

- silent letters (especially ELL weak spellers)

- longer words (especially adults)

- high frequency words (children and ELL weak spellers)

- adding affixes to base elements (especially ELL weak spellers)

- certain letter strings, such as *ough* (especially children and ELL weak spellers).

Chapter Twelve:

How is Spelling Currently Taught?

How is spelling taught in the following contexts:

UK schools — to native-speaker children?

UK Adult literacy classes?

Classes for dyslexic learners?

English language classes (EFL, ESL, ESOL etc.)?

Examining how spelling is taught in these different situations allows us to consider which methods are most useful for teaching English language learners.

How is spelling taught in UK schools?

At the time of writing, UK primary schools are teaching initial reading and spelling through a system of 'Synthetic Phonics'. This scheme, introduced in 2007, teaches children to read and write by linking phonemes (sounds) with graphemes (letters) (Department for Children, Schools and Families, 2007). Synthetic Phonics doesn't encourage children to make any guesses about words they don't know when they are reading. They should not look at pictures or use context to predict meaning before they have sounded the word out. In fact, teachers should not mix strategies for teaching reading and spelling at all. All children must learn to read and construct words by matching sounds and letters throughout the word.

This certainly raises doubts in my mind. Of course children need to know basic phoneme-to-grapheme correspondences. They need to know that the sound /b/ is written with a **b**. However, as we've seen, modern-day English is far from a phonetically-spelled language. So what happens when words are not phonetically spelled? Teachers are told to focus on the part of the word that *is* regularly spelled and then say that the rest of it isn't. I've watched a teacher teaching young children to spell the word **said by** eliciting the spelling phonetically onto the board as **sed** and so the children see it written like that. Then the teacher tells them, "But it isn't this, it's **s-a-i-d**".

The message seems to be that English is an alphabetical language with a strong phoneme-grapheme correspondence, except for a few words (which are described as 'tricky', 'funny' or 'magic'). I am sure this helps young children to learn to spell and read sentences like "The dog and the frog blog on a log" (although neither **the** or **a** are phonetically spelled) but it isn't going to be long before children see through this and realise that there are an awful lot of 'tricky' words — naughty words that don't follow the rules. They will be right of course — *if* you say that English spelling is phonetic it *is* a very defective system. If, on the other hand, you expose learners to real English and the wonderful children's stories that are full of magic and intrigue, they can start to build a love of all words — because of the messages they convey. Then we can show that, hey, look, some of these words are spelled how they sound! That's handy! And some are spelled like other words with a similar meaning. That's handy too! Some of them, we need to learn, but we'll probably see those lots of times so we'll soon get used to them. And let's play with the words — let's look at their shapes and try to remember those, let's look and see if we can find other words inside them, etc., etc.

In fact, before 2007, spelling was taught through a different approach called Analytic Phonics. One major difference is that the teacher was free (and encouraged) to use a variety of methods to teach spelling, not just grapheme-phoneme correspondence. This means different types of spelling could be approached in different ways and it probably catered for a wider variety of learning styles too. However, the results of a study in Clackmannanshire in Scotland changed that. Over seven years, schools there trialled a synthetic phonics programme with great results. This much more rigid system gave children much better reading and writing scores within a very short time. It has been argued however, that there were many other interventions at the same time and maybe after all it wasn't the Synthetic Phonics that had caused the improvement. (Rosen, 2006). Synthetic phonics has only been compulsory in England for a few years so it will be interesting to see the results in a few years' time. Incidentally, the Letters and Sounds document[34], produced by the Department for Children, Schools and Families to guide teachers in the Synthetic Phonics approach, has some excellent resources as well. (Department for Children, 2007)

I am not a primary teacher and have never taught children to read and write from scratch, but common sense tells me that there is likely to be a problem when using only one method of teaching English spelling because:

- the English spelling system is much more complex than straight sound-to-letter correspondence;
- individual learners are also complex;
- classes usually contain learners who learn differently;
- teachers have different teaching styles.

Adult Literacy

You might assume that the syllabus for UK Adult Literacy learners would bear some relation to that for primary school children described above. But it is very different, encouraging a variety of different methods for teaching spelling. Of course, there are great differences in how children and adults learn in that adults can apply more real-life experience and

---

[34] *Letters and Sounds* is available for download, at time of writing, from http://publications.teachernet.gov.uk/ . Just type 'Letters and Sounds' into the search box.

knowledge to their learning. But many of the suggestions given are in direct opposition to those given to primary teachers:

> *People do not learn spellings in the same way. Learners participating in a spelling programme need to be given opportunities to learn more about their own way of learning. Explore a wide range of multi-sensory spelling strategies. It is important that learners are aware that they can choose approaches that work for them: visual, auditory, kinaesthetic, tactile or motor.*
>
> (Learning and Skills Improvement Service, 2010)

It also advises tutors to use Look, Say, Cover, Write and Check techniques to learn spellings that are otherwise difficult. Synthetic phonics specifically warns against this.

Some other recommendations from the Teaching and Learning Spelling document:

- Use words that are relevant to the learners' home and work lives.

- Encourage an inductive approach — learners try to discover spelling patterns from words.

- Link meaning to spelling through exploring words that belong to the same family.

- (Explore) words borrowed from other languages (loan words).

- (Explore) words created through morphemes from other languages.

- Look for words within words: ***business***, ***teacher***.

- Outline words to help see the overall shape.

- Homophones ... should be learned individually in context, rather than as pairs.

Classes for dyslexic learners

Teachers of dyslexic learners often have to find new ways to help their students with spelling. There are a lot of different ideas about what dyslexia really is, but all the theories have a few beliefs in common:

- that people with dyslexia have some differences in the brain;

- that information received via the senses is processed in a different way;

- that there is a timing deficit — brain connections have formed that make it difficult for dyslexics to process information in the right sequence;

- that there are also phonological processing difficulties. Dyslexics often find it difficult to distinguish separate parts of words.

Various methods have been proposed to deal with these specific difficulties in reading and writing. Most of these fall into two main groups:

- **Structured cumulative approaches.** These include approaches such as Orton-Gillingham, Alpha to Omega and the Hickey Method. All of these are commonly used in mainstream education (sometimes in combination) to help dyslexic children and they have certain features in common. They are all based on phonics and take a very structured, sequential and cumulative approach to matching sounds and letters. This often involves multi-sensory activities and techniques.

- **Person-centred approaches.** The Learning Styles Approach, for example, is much more eclectic and individualised so it is always relevant to the learner. The student is given writing tasks and from these samples, the teacher prioritises and groups some of the spelling errors made. These are then dealt with in an appropriate way which could be visualising, Look Say Cover Write Check, mind-mapping, using plastic letters or clay P, using highlighters and coloured pens, chunking letters, or looking for lexical links. In the Davis Counselling Approach, learners are always taught one-to-one. According to Davis's theory, people with dyslexia think in pictures rather than with verbal dialogues, so they find it particularly difficult to visualise abstract function words such as ***the*** or ***although*** and this makes those spellings very tricky to memorise and causes learners to panic. (Davis R., 1997) Another person-centred approach is based on Neuro-Linguistic Programming (NLP and is described fully in the book *Seeing Spells Achieving* (Bendefy & Hickmott, 2006).

So we have one group that starts with the language, or the content, and teaches that very systematically at whatever pace the learners needs. The other set of approaches start with the individuals and work with their strengths, weaknesses, needs and interests.

ESOL

In the UK, the ESOL (English to Speakers of Other Languages[35]) Spelling and Handwriting curriculum is almost identical to the Adult Literacy one.

English Language Learners

English language teaching is generally in a vibrant state of new ideas, discussions and methodologies. New methodology books are constantly appearing on bookshelves, an ever-increasing number of conferences to attend and a plethora of blogs on all aspects of language teaching. Approaches to language teaching range from the very conservative (I tell you — you learn it — I test you) to the highly unstructured and experimental.

In practice, most of us probably teach somewhere in the middle of these extremes. Much of the language teaching around the world nowadays at least claims to follow a communicative approach. This means that learning to communicate and interact in the target language is

---

[35] See Glossary page 7.

the aim and classes use pair and group work to practise the kind of tasks learners might do outside class. Texts are often authentic and grammar is not necessarily the primary focus.

Language classes based on the communicative approach have certainly become more fun and more relevant to learners' lives. They produce learners who are used to listening and speaking, not just reading and writing.

However, there can be a problem when it comes to an area such as spelling which demands accuracy. Learners may find that they can communicate well enough (in their opinion) and not strive for more accurate spelling. Their spelling errors become fossilised. Many teachers have recognised this and know that they need to remedy the situation. But where do they turn? Where are the fun and relevant spelling activities that other areas of English language teaching offer?

They just don't seem to exist, so in desperation many teachers turn back to activities that pre-date the communicative approach. We find dictations, decontextualised word lists to learn for a test, rules (and their exceptions) that are given and then practised, gapfills, multiple choice (which spelling is correct?) and spelling bees.

Where is the communication? The interaction? The authenticity? The relevance? Usually these are absent and replaced by guilt! Have we gone back to a kind of audio-lingual approach which is about repetition, memorisation and good habit-forming? The learner repeats a correct model given by the teacher and then substitutes part of it for something else to practise the pattern — perhaps *all*, *tall*, *wall*, *ball*, etc. The focus is firmly on the language itself and the memorisation of it, not on the learner or what you can do with the language.

But maybe that is what spelling demands.

I decided to ask some English language teachers[36] for their opinions about activities and techniques for teaching spelling. They were asked to evaluate the following as 'Very useful', 'Quite useful', 'Not very useful' or 'I don't know'. They are presented here in order of perceived usefulness, with comments:

1. "**Explicitly teaching strategies for using dictionaries to check spelling**". Skilful dictionary use can provide learners with independence and reassurance. One teacher pointed out that if a learner has the wrong perception of a word, it's very difficult to look up the spelling, but bilingual dictionary or thesaurus could be used for this purpose *(See B:149, C:255)*.

2. "**Asking learners to learn spellings that have derived from classwork or material studied in class**". This is popular with learners, and also with many teachers as long as students are learning meanings as well *(See B:145, C:207)*.

3. "**Focusing explicitly on prefixes and suffixes in class**" Breaking down words into separate morphemes often helps students learn the spellings of long words, or at least be able to make informed guesses about them *(See B:135, C:240)*.

---

[36] Twenty-three teachers from private language schools in the UK, German secondary schools, a Libyan language school, and a UK teacher training institute.

4. "**Explicitly referring to spelling rules in class**" This was seen as a useful aid to students but some teachers admitted that they didn't often do it or didn't know many spelling rules. "Rules" which teachers mentioned were:
    - *y* to *i* *(See C:238)*
    - *i* before *e*
    - final *e* *(See C:229)*
    - doubling of consonants *(See C:236)*.

5. "**Explicitly teaching strategies for learning new spellings**" There certainly appears to be a need for some learner training here, but some teachers confessed that they did not really know many strategies that could be used *(See B:145, C:207, C:213, C:217)*.

6. "**Explicitly referring to sound-spelling relationships in class**" Teachers had mixed reactions to this, varying from "All spelling-sound work is useful" to "Probably too many anomalies to make it useful" and "Only if they don't read regularly".

7. "**Explicitly referring to common English letter patterns in class**" This is a strategy that is used widely in teaching L1 children spelling, but rarely mentioned in EFL *(See C:200)*.

8. "**Training learners to use spell-checkers more effectively**". This was not seen as useful by most teachers (but I disagree!) *(See B:150, C:256)*.

9. "**Asking students to learn spellings of common words not derived from classwork or material used in class.**" This was not popular and is rather an outmoded way of teaching spelling.

Summary of Chapter 12

- In UK schools, native-speaker children are currently taught to spell using a very structured and sequential programme of synthetic phonics. This is based on linking sounds to letters. During this time no other methods (such as guessing meaning and learning word shapes) should be used.

- Recommendations for teaching spelling to UK adult literacy and ESOL classes are very different from those used with children. The use of a variety of multi-sensory and cognitive methods which are relevant to the learners' lives and needs is encouraged.

- There are several approaches to teaching dyslexics to improve their spelling and these either start from the language, as in synthetic phonics, and are strictly sequential and cumulative, but move at the learner's pace or, alternatively, start with the strengths, needs and interests of the learner.

- Within English language teaching, there really is a lack of any methodology at all at present. Spelling doesn't fit very neatly into a communicative approach that values oral fluency so highly. So teachers often fall back on very traditional spelling activities. A sample of teachers said they thought it was most useful to teach dictionary skills, test students on words arising from classwork, and deal with morphological issues.

In Part B of this book we will attempt to fill the gap in English language teaching methodology by taking the best and most appropriate elements from other sectors.

Chapter Thirteen:

The English Language Teacher's Perspective

How do English language teachers feel about teaching spelling?
What are some of the challenges they face?

How do English language teachers feel about teaching spelling?

In the last chapter I described part of some research I conducted with a group of English language teachers about spelling. In the second part of the questionnaire I asked them about their attitudes to teaching spelling. The results are summarised here.

Some learners urgently need help with spelling

Many teachers were concerned about weak spellers in their classes, and felt that these learners' difficulties were an obstacle to their general English language progression. This depended on the learner's objectives, but unless their language needs exclude writing, weak spelling must be a hindrance. A common problem was that some learners developed very effective oral communication skills and listening comprehension but were unable to succeed at external examinations, because their spelling impaired their writing (even when answering listening questions).

Reading alone isn't enough

The majority agreed that these weaker spellers cannot acquire an adequate amount of English spelling through extensive reading alone — a conscious focus on spelling is also necessary. As one teacher commented "Recognising the word doesn't mean they can produce it". In my analysis of spelling errors in Chapter 11, I remarked on the number of misspellings of very common words. The learners who wrote them must see these words many, many times in their reading but do not seem to acquire the correct spelling. They need some help to notice spellings *(See C:188)*.

A phonics approach is inappropriate

All the teachers agreed that English was phonetically irregular. In addition, at least half of them had students who could not always discriminate between individual sounds within words (e.g. they can't hear that the vowel sound in 'big' is the same as the vowel sound in 'build', but different from the one in 'bag'). In my own experience I have found learners' inability to discriminate to be a major problem, especially with short vowel sounds and certain consonants, depending on the learner's mother tongue. This reinforces my suspicions that a purely phonics-based approach to teaching spelling to English language learners is not helpful.

Teachers don't know how to help

Although teachers recognised the need for more spelling tuition and knew that extensive reading was not the complete answer and nor was pure phonics, less than half the teachers felt that they were generally successful at helping these weaker spellers to improve their English spelling. Just imagine if less than half of teachers thought they were unsuccessful at helping learners improve grammar or vocabulary! Most felt they lacked an adequate range of techniques and activities to help the weaker spellers and there was a very clear message that these learners' needs are not being met in general coursebooks.

What are some of the challenges teachers face?

So we have seen some challenges already. Learners need help; reading and phonics are inadequate solutions but teachers don't really feel equipped to help in other ways. Why not?

Training? What training?

Firstly, there is a lack of training in the teaching of spelling. There is usually little focus on spelling in pre-service teacher training courses, such as CELTA (Certificate in English Language Teaching to Adults); although there is now an "English Spelling and Punctuation" point on the syllabus, which requires trainees to be able to:

- identify some English spelling patterns and some strategies to help learners develop their spelling skills;
- identify some ways in which punctuation contributes to meaning in written text;
- apply a basic understanding of English spelling and punctuation to practical teaching.

Secondly, general English language teacher development books scarcely mention spelling. Three books that are commonly used by trainee teachers make very scant mention of spelling. Jeremy Harmer's *The Practice of English Language Teaching* (Harmer, 2007) does touch on the complexity of English orthography and there are a few paragraphs about the teaching of spelling. This mainly involves phonics and a recommendation for extensive reading. Another popular methodology book, *Learning Teaching* (Scrivener, 2005), seems to have no mention of teaching spelling at all. And The CELTA Course (Thornbury & Watkins, 2007), a book specifically designed to provide "full coverage of the CELTA syllabus", hardly addresses the teaching of spelling even though there is a unit on literacy.

Materials

It is not just teacher training materials related to spelling that are lacking, there is a general short supply of spelling materials for English language teaching, particularly in printed form. Searching the major UK English language teaching booksellers comes up with:

- *Teaching English Spelling* (Shemesh & Waller, 2000), which is part of the Cambridge Handbooks for Teachers series. This presents ways to teach certain features of English spelling (especially vowel sounds) via a phonological route. It contains some very useful activities.
- *Spelling and Pronunciation for English Language Learners* (Boyer, 2003), which also takes a phonological approach, as the title suggests. It explores different spellings of 14 vowel and 3 consonant phonemes.
- *Understanding English Spelling* (Bell, 2004) focuses on the irregularities of English orthography and states the case for spelling reform, which is not of immediate use to our learners.
- EFL coursebooks have not generally given much attention to spelling (although ESOL ones have). *English Unlimited* (Tilbury, 2010), an adult general English coursebook, includes a new literacy strand called *Writing Essentials* (by Thake & Brabben) which deals with spelling. This works on strategies as well as patterns. The lower levels of *English Unlimited* also deal with sounds and spelling.

More details about materials that teachers may find useful can be found on The Spelling Blog at http://thespellingblog.blogspot.com

Research

Teachers may turn to scholarly literature, but they won't get much help from the academics: in 1980 Frith wrote:

> *Active spelling production is a field of research that has been even more neglected than passive and often unconscious use of spelling knowledge in word recognition.*
>
> (Frith, 1980, p. vii)

More recently (and relevantly to English language teaching) in 2004 Vivian Cook agreed, that L2 spelling had hardly been researched at all. Cook also complained,

> *I began to look for a system [for teaching spelling] in what was happening and discovered that there simply wasn't one in language teaching. In EFL, 'writing' usually refers to the higher level discourse skills not the everyday task of spelling.*
>
> Cook (quoted in White, 2004)

This is so true. I have spent a lot of time over the last few years researching spelling and have found very little in books or on the web that is directly aimed at English language teachers.

Lack of training and materials are not the only problems teachers face, however.

The select few

Usually, particularly in multi-lingual classes, it is only a minority of students who have serious difficulties with spelling. And these difficulties may be very divergent depending on their mother tongue. If this is the case, whole class spelling tuition may be inappropriate and unpopular. Many teachers complain that they don't have time to follow the syllabus as it is, let alone find time for extra activities.

Not a 'sexy' subject

Another problem is the assumed dullness of spelling lessons. I was surprised to read in a newspaper after a successful British TV spelling bee[37] programme:

> *A black belt in spelling is this year's coolest youth accessory.*
>
> (Glover, 2004)

However, it is not generally seen as an engaging and communicative part of the syllabus. Shemesh and Waller describe their first attempt to introduce a spelling programme into their Israeli junior and high school EFL syllabus:

> *Our students responded positively. They liked the idea of 'rules', even if their teachers called them 'spelling patterns'.... Most teachers were enthusiastic too — we were finally doing something. But, as it turned out we weren't doing it very well. The spelling generalizations were accompanied by detailed explanations, thus, some of us were confused! There were also no practice exercises for the students. No practice, no learning! Slowly, the teachers abandoned the new spelling programme, some more quickly than others — a fact that many students didn't mind, since it had become a trifle boring.*
>
> (Shemesh & Waller, 2000, p. 2)

Because spelling is usually about accuracy, it tends to be taught in a very bottom-up way which is unfashionable and risks lack of engagement *(See B:160)*.

The nature of the beast

And, of course, as we've seen, English spelling is not easily teachable. The interplay of different systems and the irregularities resulting from the history of the language do not provide us with a neat set of rules which we can impart and our students can apply. If only!

---

[37] A 'spelling bee' is a contest in which people, usually children, compete to spell English words correctly. It is thought to have originated in the USA. The BBC Hard Spell website mentioned above can be found at http://www.bbc.co.uk/hardspell/ .

Summary of Chapter 13

- Teachers are often all too aware of the spelling problems that at least some of their learners have and the consequences of these if nothing is done to help them.

- Extensive reading is not seen as a complete solution; nor is a purely phonics-based approach thought to be appropriate.

- Many teachers don't feel well-equipped enough to be able to help their learners.

- Many teachers have not been trained sufficiently in teaching spelling and there is very little research to refer to, especially for EFL teachers.

- Classes, especially multi-lingual ones, may be even more mixed ability than usual when it comes to spelling.

- Spelling is traditionally seen as a dull subject.

- It is also a difficult subject to teach as it is complex and can seem illogical.

Summary of Part A

In the first part of the book we have explored issues that face those learning to spell in English and those attempting to teach them. These issues relate to the language itself, the learners and the teachers.

The importance of spelling, even in a wired 21st century, can't be doubted. Those who cannot spell risk their reputations, the ability to express themselves accurately and potential opportunities in business and education.

If English spelling is seen in purely phonological terms, about 50% of words are 'regular'. However, if we acknowledge that there are actually five systems at work, the phonological, etymological, morphological, lexical and graphemic, we see a much higher incidence of regularity.

The history of English spelling accounts for much of the complexity that we see in the language today. It has been influenced by Germanic tribes, Vikings, Romans, French, Greeks and many others. Perhaps it is fitting that it should become the world language as it has borrowed from so many other languages. Within the last 500 years or so, English pronunciation has changed considerably but spelling has not, as printing has made it less flexible. Etymology often over-rides all other spelling systems, certainly the phonological, and an understanding of this and knowledge of some specific features bequeathed from each language can give us useful clues to modern-day spelling.

The phonological system at the core of English spelling is very complex with so many different ways to pronounce each letter and different ways to spell each sound. Some phonological spelling patterns that are traditionally taught are generally reliable, others are not.

There are also graphemic patterns: orthographical conventions which are not related to sound, which influence word features such as word length, doubling, position and word endings. This also covers common and 'illegal' letter strings.

The morphological system is relatively simple and regular. Knowledge of a wide range of base elements, prefixes, suffixes and inflections, plus how to attach them to each other, gives pretty reliable guides to spelling long words in particular.

Closely related to the etymological and morphological systems is the lexical system, which focuses on the semantic and visual links between words. It seems to be particularly effective at helping us to distinguish between some problematic homophones.

The process of spelling is much easier for most people when reading (decoding) than when writing (encoding). Good spellers seem to use a wider range of strategies for spelling and make more use of the different senses, especially the visual.

Learning seems most effective for the greatest number of people when it is multi-sensory, motivating and the information is 'chunked' and recycled.

There are errors that are common to different types of learners and the most persistent seem to be problems with vowels (writing weak and short vowels, and digraphs), homophones and near homophones, doubling, silent letters, longer words, high-frequency irregular words, affixation and certain letter strings.

In UK primary schools spelling is currently taught via a strict system of synthetic phonics, but Adult Literacy and ESOL students use an eclectic range of multi-sensory and cognitive methods, as do teachers working with dyslexic students.

Within English language teaching, the approach to spelling is usually haphazard and there are few resources to help teachers. However, many teachers recognise the need for teaching spelling to some of their learners and are frustrated at their inability to help.

In Part B of this book we will attempt to fill the gap in English language teaching methodology by taking the best and most appropriate elements from other sectors. This joining of the dots may in turn help teachers who are working in other contexts too.

PART B

Teaching Spelling Effectively

Introduction to Part B: Teaching Spelling Effectively

In Part One of the book we have clearly seen three general problems with teaching spelling to English language learners:

- English orthography is highly complex. It is certainly not based on sound alone, and pretending that it is does nobody any favours. However, neither is it chaotic, as many people think; it is a system of systems. There are many satisfying patterns to be found, but learners' eyes often need opening to these.

- Learners differ. They differ in their motivation, skills, approaches, lifestyles, mother tongues and interests. There are some commonalities in how most of us learn and these are useful guides for us as teachers. However, it seems clear that one size cannot fit all.

- Teaching spelling seems to be the Cinderella of language education. It is paid scant attention in training and literature and many teachers feel unprepared for dealing with a problem that they see daily.

So now it is time to suggest some solutions.

We start by outlining some general principles of the approach (Chapter 14), then move on to examine how to deal with psychological factors, such as lack of motivation or self-esteem, which may otherwise inhibit learning (Chapter 15). Then there is the question of *what* we should teach. This is divided into spelling patterns (Chapter 16) and strategies for spelling (Chapter 17). We then need to find ways for learners to practise their spelling (Chapter 18) both in and out of class. The teacher needs to consider the best way to correct learners' writing (Chapter 19). And finally, we confront the thorny question of testing spelling in Chapter 20.

Any approach must take account of context. In other words, what works well in the UK may not be appropriate in China. A tried and tested method in Poland may be useless in Saudi Arabia. So the suggestions given below should be adapted and applied to your context. Not everything here will be appropriate for your classes, but everything, I believe, is worth careful consideration. Teachers who want the best for their students and for their own professional development must always question. They question new ideas rather than accepting them blindly. They also question traditional ways, acknowledging that there may be better methods that may be more effective, especially in such a rapidly changing world. They use what they know about their students, try things out and adapt them as they see fit.

Chapter Fourteen:

General Principles

Why do we need a new approach?

Isn't it rather 'bottom-up' to teach spelling?

Should spelling be taught separately?

How can we help different learners with different issues?

Why do we need a new approach?

Too much that is known about how to teach spelling isn't being put into practice. I can think of no subject we teach more poorly or harbor more myths about than spelling.

(Gentry, 1987)

Has the teaching of spelling moved on noticeably since the above quote was written in 1987? Materials for teaching English language learners to write usually contain plenty of practice activities, especially for sentence-length and text-length writing. But where is the input? Where is the language focus? Where do students learn how to do it before they practise? Materials for teaching grammar will either give an explanation or lots of examples so learners can discover the patterns for themselves. Spelling materials rarely do this and that means that the 'practice' is often really just *testing* what learners already know, rather than helping them to understand how and why. So we need to look at *how* we can teach and how students can learn patterns and strategies for dealing with the complexities of English spelling.

We need an approach that is applicable to ELLs — that takes account of the fact that their mother tongues may cause interference and may lead them to very different expectations about English spelling. It must also recognise that the phonological route is often not the best, or certainly not the *only* one for them *(See A:76)*. Where we do need to work on sound-spelling relationships, we have to make sure second language learners have an accurate perception of the sounds *(See C:223)*.

The approach also needs to recognise that people have different learning styles and that humans are not all model students. We have to accept that students and teachers are at least as irregular as English spelling is said to be!

A new approach must take into account psychological factors that could obstruct learners' acquisition of spelling.

It also needs to be suitable for the twenty-first century — a time when we seem to be busier than ever before, or at least offered more distractions, when we write much more, but in new genres and registers, and when we have a multitude of different technological opportunities to help us out.

But overall, we need *an* approach to spelling for English language learners because at present one doesn't seem to exist.

Isn't it rather bottom-up to teach spelling?

Some people feel we shouldn't *teach* spelling at all as it's too 'bottom-up'. In other words, they fear that by teaching spelling we are focusing too much on details to be memorised and not involving higher level thinking processes or recognizing that conveying communicative meaning is the ultimate aim. They worry that we are not relating the language to our students' pre-existing knowledge. There are several valid responses to this.

Spelling is a micro-skill and so should not have as much time devoted to it in a language class as, say, speaking or writing more generally. However, where learners have fallen behind in this micro-skill or are finding it particularly difficult, remedial work is needed to boost this level. Otherwise, it hinders confidence and general language improvement. Of course meaning is more important, it's paramount, and that is why we have a duty to help our learners speak and write as fluently, precisely and confidently as possible. Without a firm foundation in micro-skills like spelling, this cannot happen.

Sometimes the reason why learners have fallen behind with spelling is that they have never been explicitly shown any patterns or strategies. When I have pointed some of these out, adult learners have often said, "Why hasn't anyone told me this before?" We can make the learning load much lighter by showing patterns that can be followed rather than leaving the learner to think every word has to be memorised as an instance *(See C:185)*. As Vivian Cook reminds us:

> *"Written language is at the centre of many uses of language, particularly in the computer age and its characteristics are no more likely to be assimilated unaided than are those of the spoken language."*

(Cook, 2001)

Besides, the approach described here *does* involve plenty of top-down processing, using higher order thinking skills. Learners are encouraged to think, to develop skills and strategies and to find relationships between new information and what they already know.

Reading consolidates spelling but very often we just don't notice spelling, and learners often need help with focussing in on patterns. Here, texts are first approached communicatively,

114

discussing the subject matter and reacting to the content. The target language (e.g. particular spelling patterns or words) is shown in context, so the meaning can guide the learner to the spelling.

Only then, after checking meaning, are target words singled out and tackled with more bottom-up activities. These are temporarily extracted from the text, so learners can focus on them more clearly. They are removed from the 'noise' of the surrounding words, which weak spellers often find distracting and confusing. They can later be returned to the text, and revisited in their natural habitat *(See C:238)*.

Should spelling be taught separately?

When can, and should, we teach spelling? Should it be confined to 'spelling classes' or 'writing classes'? There may be situations where you have such classes in which you can really focus on aspects of spelling and strategies for improving the skill. In most contexts, however, this is unusual and we generally need to integrate spelling work with other skills. It is usually something that is dealt with as the need arises or perhaps is related to a grammar point (e.g. adding *-ing* in continuous tenses). Maybe learners ask you for a spelling while they are writing, or maybe you notice that several of your learners have made similar errors in their work, or perhaps you are discussing spelling problems with an individual student in a tutorial. Spelling can be tackled without necessarily being a discrete area of the syllabus.

Integrating spelling also allows words to be seen in context, which is very important as the way a word is spelled is often closely related to its meaning. Not to mention, of course, that it makes the lesson more interesting and engaging. So, for example, a lesson may start with a lead-in discussion and then the reading of a text. Discussion of the content of the text follows and perhaps some vocabulary work. Only then should the focus turn to aspects of spelling. We should not lose the vital primacy of meaning just because we need to focus in on details. Spelling, like every other aspect of language, is ultimately about communication. Being able to spell easily allows for much more fluid and precise written communication as the writer doesn't lose the flow while struggling over a spelling or doesn't avoid difficult words.

How can we help different learners with different issues?

There is no one method for teaching spelling. The approach used should vary according to the structure of the word as well as the individual learner's capabilities.

(Schlagel and Schlagel, 1992)

Results indicate that using one method alone to teach children, when their individual styles are not known, can result in lower spelling age increases than an eclectic group of methods, one of which should suit every child in the class.

(Brooks, 1998)

———————————————

It is doubtful if you can teach someone to spell; but you can show someone how to learn to spell. There is no one system which can guarantee to improve a person's spelling because each of us has a unique set of learning styles, and we tend to use different spelling strategies depending on the word in question.

(Abell, 1994, p. 38)

We saw in Part A that there are those who take one approach to teaching spelling and stick to it. The UK National Curriculum, for example, starts with a synthetic phonics approach which does not allow for any visual methods.

Why? We have seen that English spelling is made up of several inherent systems: morphological, lexical, etymological, graphemic, as well as phonological *(See A:20)*. So an effective methodology needs to address these different systems by using a variety of approaches. The way we learn to spell **cat** can't be the same as the way we learn to spell **unhappiness** or **neighbour**, for example.

Each person learns different things in different ways on different days. Students have different skills and different approaches to spelling. While some will relish sitting down and learning a list of words for a test the next day, others don't need this, as they pick up spelling effortlessly from reading. Some like to sound words out, phonetically or alphabetically, while others clearly see a picture of the spelling in their heads. And although individuals often have preferred ways of learning, they can also benefit from 'style stretching' — trying out other methods that may be more effective. A new perspective may make some learning finally sink in. So why persist with one method only?

Different activities can tap into different senses — visual, auditory, kinaesthetic, logical and semantic (Abell, 1994, p. 11). Of course, these will require unequal amounts of attention, but awareness should be raised about them all and the ways in which they can interact. A learner fed on one of these alone, phonics for example, will be a very confused and frustrated learner. Those who use a mixture of strategies tend to be more successful spellers so we need to demonstrate several different strategies ourselves.

That's why I propose a multi-dimensional approach to spelling, with an eclectic range of activities. In this book I'm going to consider *multi-dimensional* learning as meaning visual, auditory, kinaesthetic and cognitive modes. All these routes could be used at some time during a whole course, a week, a lesson or even just one particular language point. In fact, I would argue for the latter whenever possible, so if some students don't 'get it' straight away, a different route might help them.

Let's take a brief look at what visual, auditory, kinaesthetic and cognitive routes to spelling are.

Visual

Visual methods of learning are highly effective for many people. We read in Part A that good spellers are generally better at visualising words than weak spellers and so this suggests that it is a skill that we should aim to develop in learners who struggle to spell. People who find it difficult to 'see' words in their heads can often be trained to do so. But visual techniques also include looking at the written words and making links that are not related to sound. Some examples of visual techniques and activities are:

- finding words within words *(See C:213 and following pages)*

- noticing the shape of a word or part of a word *(See C:216, C217)*

- identifying and visually highlighting 'hard spots' (the difficult parts) of words *(See C:207)*

- noting visual similarities with other words and exploring semantic and etymological links between them *(See C:193, C:195)*.

Auditory

We have already noted that spelling in English is partly based on sound, although there have been many other influences that have made present-day English spelling far more complex. There's no doubt that we need to address the basic sound-to-letter correspondences: learners must know that **t** makes the sound /t/ (although they should also know that **ed** can make the sound /t/ as well, as in **missed**, for example). And there are more complicated patterns concerning the position of a letter in a word and how one letter can affect the pronunciation of another. On the other hand, a list of all the ways of writing a certain vowel sound, such as 13 options for representing the sound /uː/, is unlikely to be very useful (although learners may ask for such lists).

One problem we do need to address, however, is phoneme discrimination. Where words, or parts of words, are spelled according to their sound, there is a problem if ELLs can't identify that particular sound. For example, if a Spanish speaker can't distinguish between **cap** and **cup**, or an Arabic speaker can't tell the difference in the spoken form of **park** and **bark**, then they can't use a phonological route to the spelling. So helping them to hear and say the different sounds, within words, helps them eventually with spelling *(See C:223)*.

Other auditory activities could include:

- spelling aloud *(See C:222, C:207)*

- rapping spellings and patterns *(See C:222)*

- explaining why you made the error you made *(See C:198)*

- using a 'spelling pronunciation' *(See B:145)*.

Kinaesthetic

Kinaesthetic activities can bring an extra dimension to the classroom, and these physically engaging activities help learners to link memorable actions to mental symbols. They can be especially helpful for those who have more serious problems with spelling such as dyslexic learners.

Writing itself is, of course, a kinaesthetic activity. The more often we write something (correctly), the more likely we are to remember it, as if there's a memory system in our hand muscles. We may be able to heighten this memory aid by writing in some kind of substance or on a rough surface so the tactile sensation is increased *(See C:224)*.

For some, words are too abstract to remember, especially common structure words which lack a strong conceptual meaning and often have quite irregular spelling. We can help these learners make the intangible more tangible by letting them physically construct the words with toy letters, modelling material or just blocks to represent the shape of the word *(See C:219)*. Besides making the words more concrete, the actual process of physically building letters and words is a great memory boost. While working, learners are forced to focus on the spelling and the meaning for much longer than they would if they were only writing the word. This increases the likelihood of the spelling making it to the long-term memory.

Another set of activities involves the whole body. We can:

- illustrate certain spelling patterns by using drama to create scenarios, which could be videoed[38];

- play physical games to spell words or describe word shapes *(See C:225, C:226)*.

Besides making spelling more tangible and accessible, the elements of fun and surprise create more memorable lessons. Getting learners out of their seats and moving around, and perhaps even raising their heart rate and the oxygen to their brains, can't be a bad thing.

However, these activities will not be suitable for all. Classroom management may be problematic if the only available space is small with fixed seating, or there are learners with mobility problems. The age of students, availability of materials or time may all be limiting factors, but some kinaesthetic activities should be possible with most classes.

Cognitive

Our ultimate aim is to make spelling in English an invisible process. We want learners to gain an automaticity in writing words which frees up their minds for thinking about content and style in the text as a whole. But the route to that automaticity involves learning and we know that deeper mental processing helps us learn more effectively. So how can we get learners to engage their brains fully when learning to spell?

---

[38] See some delightful examples at:
http://www1.teachertube.com/viewVideo.php?video_id=47089&title=Drop_an_E_before_adding_vowel_suffixes&v
pkey=bb7ea7081e .

In a very traditional classroom, learners are told spelling rules and are then given practice activities in which they apply the rules. An inductive, or discovery, approach involves looking at a sample of language and hypothesizing about the patterns yourself. Then the hypothesis can be tested out on other words. For example, a text includes some CVC words with short vowels such as *mat*, *pen*, *admit*, *lot* and *but*, and some CVC+*e* words, like *late*, *Pete*, *nine*, *alone* and *tube*. By listening, or using their previous knowledge, the learners hypothesise that adding an *e* makes the previous vowel long. They can then test the hypothesis out on other words they know or find.

Other cognitive activities include:

- linking unknown spellings to known ones

- ordering and organising spellings according to patterns, etymology, sound, theme, personal reactions, etc. *(See B:140)*

- using words creatively and expressively

- creating mnemonics *(See B:148, C:198)*.

Which modality to use when

Before teaching a specific point, a teacher needs to think which routes are most appropriate. For example, let's look at four possible ways to show that prefixes are added to whole words. Which do you think would be most appropriate?

- **Visual route** — After the learners have read and dealt with the meaning of a text, **some** words with prefixes are identified and learners are asked to highlight the base element and the prefix in different colours. So in the word *unnecessary*, they could see that there are two *n*s because one belongs to the prefix *un* and the other to the base element *necessary*. But in *unable*, there is only one *n*, because it belongs to the prefix and the base element starts with a different letter.

- **Auditory route** — As above but the learners are asked to say the words, making a clear break between the prefix and the base element.

- **Kinaesthetic route** — After dealing with the meaning of the text, each learner is given a card with a base element or prefix (from the text). They try to match them, by finding their partner, referring back to the text to check. When they finish, they stand together to make the word. They are guided to identify that the prefix is added to the whole word. Then they write out the words, spelling the prefix without taking the pen off the paper, then lifting the pen before writing the base element *(See C:232)*.

- **Cognitive route** — After reading the text for meaning, learners look at the given words and are asked to mark the following statement true or false:

We usually add prefixes to the beginning of whole words. We don't need to make any other changes to the word when we add the prefix. T/F

When they have found out it's true with these particular words, they are asked to think of some more prefixes that are used with the same base elements, or more words that can be used with those prefixes, to test out the hypothesis.

While variety is essential, some consistencies can be beneficial too. It helps learners if we use consistent terminology, show links between new language and that already covered, and have similar expectations of students from one day to the next.

On the other hand, what do we remember — things that are the same as usual or things that are different? When you get home from holiday, do you remember brushing your teeth every day, or do you remember the new and different things that you saw and experienced?

Summary of Chapter 14

- We need a new approach to spelling for English language learners that takes account of the fact that they are not native speakers, that they have many different learning styles, that there are psychological obstacles to be negotiated and that the 21st century presents new opportunities and challenges.

- The teaching of spelling is necessary and is appreciated by many students. By approaching texts first for meaning and by calling on learners' cognitive skills and previous knowledge, we avoid the dangers of bottom-up teaching.

- Usually spelling will be integrated into other work, but there are times when it needs single-minded focus.

- A multi-dimensional approach will help more learners with more types of spelling. This means using appropriate visual, auditory, kinaesthetic and cognitive approaches in spelling tuition and practice.

Chapter Fifteen:

Tackling Psychological Barriers

What role does state of mind play in the learning of spelling?

How can we motivate our learners to work on spelling?

How can we make spelling activities enjoyable?

How can we get the level of challenge right?

Does age matter?

How can we help our learners see that English spelling isn't chaotic?

How can we help our learners to take responsibility for improving their spelling?

State of mind plays a very important role in all learning. The pressure to master the skills that we need for everyday life is urgent and therefore 'failure' can cause increased stress. Spelling is one of those vital skills.

What role does state of mind play?

Poor spellers may lack self-esteem and confidence in spelling, and this may even affect other areas of their language learning or lives. Those who have a poor view of their abilities may resort to one or more 'face-saving' strategies, such as avoiding writing altogether (so they can't fail), blaming others for their weaknesses, denying that there's a problem, or just making out that they don't care (Littlejohn, 2008). This can translate into an apparently bad attitude in class, which can frustrate the teacher, other students and ultimately the student him or herself. Of course, the majority of learners who have spelling problems behave just as well as everybody else.

Writing is a commitment. As we write a word, we are giving our spelling attempt some kind of permanency. It is there for somebody to criticise, to notice our mistakes, to judge us. And the judging may not only be about our spelling, but also about our intelligence or reliability. No wonder some people prefer to say that they've forgotten their glasses!

Labelling a student as a weak speller can actually promote the weakness. For example, while there are many advantages in having dyslexia diagnosed, one disadvantage may be 'wearing' this label. Similarly, having extra classes to help with reading and writing can be extremely useful, but it can also carry a stigma. It can give the learner an excuse for not trying to improve and a lack of belief in the possibility that he or she can. "It's not my fault that I can't do it. I'm a bad speller and I always will be." To rise out of this and improve spelling takes a great deal of care, persistence and motivation. How can we help learners on that journey?

People learn best when they are relaxed. If they feel stressed or are experiencing strong negative emotions this can block concentration and learning. Krashen calls it the affective filter (Krashen, 1981). So it is worth investing a few minutes at the beginning of a lesson on something fun and non-threatening, or even just chatting, to relax learners. We also need to guard against merely testing when we believe we are teaching *(See B:171)*, as this can also result in more stress.

Within a lesson, aim for early success. In other words, activities at the beginning of the lesson should require only a small number of right answers; optional tasks can be longer and activities can become more challenging as the class progresses.

Encouragement helps most people, but only if it is believed to be genuine and is specifically related to your progress. Being able to see your own improvement or achievement by the end of a period of study makes you feel good about yourself and confident that you can have similar success in the future. Of course, the teacher needs to be skilful and knowledgeable about his or her learners here. Judgements must be made about what is encouraging and what is patronising. A learner who gets a lower result on an activity than his or her classmates, but has succeeded in something that was previously difficult, could have any of these different reactions to praise:

- may glow with pride;

- may not react to the praise but unconsciously add it to the bank of encouragement that increases self-esteem;

- may feel that you are patronising to praise something that falls short of what classmates can do.

Unguarded criticism or too much correction can further damage self-esteem. There is nothing to be gained from reacting negatively to a learner's errors. Of course, if something is wrong we should point out the error but this needs to be accompanied by a way to remember it in the future. The learner may continue to repeat the error many times but it is unlikely that he or she is doing it specifically to annoy us.

Knowing how much to praise and how much to correct is a difficult call, but it is a skill that good teachers become remarkably adept at (and one of the many reasons that teachers will never be completely replaced by technology!)

How can we motivate learners to work on spelling?

As we've noted, to improve your spelling, particularly if it's something you're not very good at, takes great determination and effort.

Appreciating the importance of accurate spelling

Learners who are not convinced that spelling is important are unlikely to be sufficiently inspired to improve. Their teachers need to know what kind of situations the learners may find themselves in that will require this skill, for example, exams, business, job applications, social networking, teaching, etc. And then this importance needs to be conveyed in a frank and honest way. Learners may argue that spelling is no longer important in this age of spell-checkers but although that day may come in the future, I don't believe we've arrived there yet. It certainly isn't working at the moment as one large recruiter of UK graduates reported that they reject 56% of job applications because they contain spelling errors[39]. And do your learners really want to become so deskilled that they have to rely completely on technology? It sounds unempowering and dangerous to me. So spelling is still important and learners need to believe it *(See C:250)*.

That's the bad news! The good news is that improving spelling can be interesting, fun and manageable (yes, really!).

Making spelling relevant

Target spelling words need to be presented in context and need to be seen as relevant to the learners. There really is no point in teaching the spelling of a list of words that the learners neither know nor need. Learning words related to, say, a popular sport will be more engaging for more class members than words about an obscure form of knitting (unless, of course...). By using authentic, or authentically-styled, texts, using the words for communicative purposes and showing links between work in class and life outside it, we illustrate clearly the relevance to their lives.

In an ESOL class, relevance is particularly important. Learners have a very urgent need to be able to perform certain tasks if they are living in a target language country. In this case, being able to write the name of your street is much more important than being able to write about your favourite sport. The teacher must decide or find out what will motivate his or her students and what their short-term and long-term needs are.

Creating interest in words

Anecdotal evidence indicates that learners who are interested in words, and how they are made, are likely to be better spellers than those who see words as their enemy. This may, however, be a chicken and egg situation: which came first the poor spelling or the antagonism to words?

The teacher who will see most success is the one who can create a climate of interest in words and in English spelling itself. It may sound like a tall order. But there are really

---

[39] http://business.timesonline.co.uk/tol/business/career_and_jobs/graduate_management/article1291098.ece .

interesting stories to be told about the development of English orthography and there are some very neat patterns to discover. Spelling is all about communication and humans love to communicate.

Probably the worst way to start a spelling lesson is by saying, "*I know spelling is really boring but we've got to do it*". The teacher also needs enthusiasm and interest. We need to build a sense of curiosity in our students, to create a hunger for learning before the information is served up. When learners start asking me questions, then I know we are going to succeed.

How can we make spelling activities enjoyable?

Unfortunately, spelling activities are traditionally dry and boring and consist mainly of rote learning of rules (that are then shown to be defective because they are full of exceptions) or of words from prescribed spelling lists. No wonder the only people who like spelling are the people who are good at it. It really doesn't need to be like that (and of course in many classes it isn't). A teacher who sets out to challenge that tradition and who is determined to make spelling classes (or parts of classes) even more fun and engaging than other elements of the curriculum will soon see his or her learners change their attitude and make huge strides in achievement.

What are some potential elements of 'fun'? Perhaps:
- surprise
- humour
- relaxation (but with some challenge)
- creativity
- concentration/involvement/flow
- novelty
- a sense of progression
- an engaging context
- an element of competition
- a result
- interaction
- curiosity.

To make spelling fun we need a variety of activities. What is fun and effective for one person may not be fun and effective for another, so we should try not to get too stuck on one type of activity. Obviously not every activity will or should include all of these elements of fun but if none are present, then you may be about to bore your learners into hating spelling.

Some learners may reject fun activities as a waste of time if this is not how they have been used to learning. It is important to explain the reasoning behind such activities so learners don't think it's *only* fun. They need to see the usefulness too. It may even be worth discussing the value of fun in learning.

Some kind of pay-off can be motivating too. As in computer games, some reward or satisfaction can be offered for successful completion, such as 'go to the next level'. In fact computer games are so addictive, that we can learn a lot from them in terms of motivation.

How can we get the level of challenge right?

The optimum level of challenge for learners is very difficult to judge. Too easy and learners won't learn anything or take it seriously. Too difficult and they may turn off and let negative feelings come to the fore.

Learners should not be expected to already know what you are teaching (what would be the point?) but they should be able to work it out from data given. An inductive approach — discovering patterns for themselves — is much more satisfying and memorable than just being told, even if it takes longer. It's a valuable investment of their time and yours as they are more likely to remember the information.

The words we teach or use as examples to illustrate patterns should be at the learners' general English level. So an otherwise upper intermediate student whose spelling is elementary needs to work with upper intermediate level words, as those are the ones he or she needs, though remedial work will also be needed with other words.

In a mixed ability class (in terms of spelling) some differentiated activities are useful or if that's not possible, an instruction to 'do as many as you can' or 'do the first five'.

Does age matter?

There are, of course, differences between teaching children, teens and adults and this book is primarily aimed at teachers of teenagers and adults. Many of the existing spelling materials and much of the research into spelling has concerned children. An adult or teenage L2 user has very different needs and abilities.

As Vivian Cook points out, a learner who has already become literate in one language is bound to approach a second language writing system in a different way (influenced by their particular L1) and be able to reason in a more abstract way (Cook and Bassetti, 2005). For example, a Chinese learner has largely had to remember symbols for different words, and may therefore find it relatively easy to learn spellings visually. An Arabic student, meanwhile, is used to writing phonetically, and may be searching for more sound-to-letter correspondences. We can use adults' experience and maturity to compare and contrast writing systems to encourage them to make sense of English spelling.

We can also make tasks more cognitively demanding for teens and adults than for young children. They can make more deductions about the language as well as links between what they already know and what they need to know.

If adolescent or adult learners are to use writing to express themselves fully and precisely, they will need to be able to spell a more sophisticated vocabulary than a child would, so texts and target words need to reflect their ages. Again the use of strategies is important here — learners need the tools to find the words they require. They should also be able to relate the strategies to ones they use in other areas of their lives, thus reinforcing their usefulness.

It goes without saying that topics, images, texts, design and tasks should all aim to appeal to the appropriate age-range.

How can we help our learners see that English spelling isn't chaotic?

Not surprisingly, many learners who have struggled with English spelling have a negative attitude towards it. Those who speak languages with a much more "shallow" orthography may be under the misapprehension that English is also phonologically-based, but just full of exceptions — a very 'faulty' system. I have heard students call English spelling *illogical*, *chaotic*, *impossible* and other names I can't repeat!

What I have tried to show in this book is that it is none of those — it is just *complex*. It isn't short of logic — it's just got too many different strands of logic going on at the same time! I hope by the time you've got this far through the book you'll agree.

Echoing negative opinions about English spelling won't help your students. In fact, the teacher needs to be openly positive about English spelling, focussing on what is regular and relatively easy to learn before highlighting irregularities. Starting the term with a poem about all the different pronunciations of words spelled with **ough**, for example, gives the message that spelling is a jungle that will probably defeat you. It is effectively giving learners an excuse for bad spelling, and low expectations of mastering it. Nobody should pretend that it's like Italian or Finnish in its phonetic regularity, but it is important that learners should be aware that there is certainly a sense of system there. The more we can demonstrate these systems, the more manageable mastery of English spelling becomes.

By dealing with all the layers that build up English orthography, we can demonstrate this system to learners. Therefore we should explore and refer to etymological, morphological, graphemic and lexical, as well as phonological, reasons for spelling. We can point out patterns that are reasonably consistent, before we deal with irregularities. We may not be able to justify the spelling of some very common words in phonological terms but we can make learners aware of the historical background that has led to this situation.

While teaching language generally (not necessarily a 'spelling lesson'), we can:

- point out words that have come from other languages so learners see a reason for the seeming irregularity, e.g. *chef*, *khaki*, *psychology*;

- relate unknown words to known ones with semantic links so learners can see similarities in spelling, e.g.
  - sign, signature, design, designate
  - value, evaluate, interval, validate
  - hear, ear, heard;

- show that prefixes are joined to whole words and that the adding of suffixes follows predictable patterns;

- mention if there is a graphemic reason for a silent letter, e.g. a silent final *e* on a word otherwise ending in *v*, because native English words don't end in *v*;

- correct learners' pronunciation of phonologically regular words, if this is likely to affect their spelling of them (or of course somebody else's understanding of them). For example, in Arabic writing, short vowels are not usually important and an Arabic speaker may be under the misapprehension that English is rather the same. Writing "My uncle lives in a bog house"[40], may seem like a very small error (just one little vowel), but knowing how silly it can make you sound may give a motivation boost for a lesson on vowels.

I have heard teachers 'boast' to their students that they are terrible spellers too, ha ha! They think it makes the students feel better. Does it? Or does it make the student think, "Well, if even my teacher can't spell, I don't stand a chance!"? Teachers who are not confident about their own spelling would do better to share the strategies that they use when they are not sure, whether it's looking in a dictionary, relating to other words or seeing if it looks right with alternative spellings.

How can we help our learners to take responsibility for improving their spelling?

Whose responsibility is the motivation of learners? Many people would say it is the teacher's, but is it really possible to take responsibility for another person's learning? We can do our very best to make the reasons clear, the subject engaging and the progress achievable, but the learner must take the ultimate responsibility for learning. Remember, you can lead a horse to water, tell it how refreshing the water is, tell a story about how the water got there, and play horsey games in the water ... but you can't make it drink. If learners want to improve their spelling they will have to recognise that they are the agents of change.

To help learners to take responsibility for their own learning, we can try the following:

- make it clear that we expect them to do so;
- discuss the issues of motivation and self-study with them;
- teach them spelling strategies that they can use *(See Chapters 17 and 23)*;
- provide opportunities for them to read more *(See C:190)*;
- give them some choice in what and how they learn;
- let them discover patterns rather than telling them;
- make practice activities engaging and relevant;
- show that we value the work they have done;
- help them see their own progress - rather than compare it to the performance of others *(See C:263)*;
- tell them that we can't and won't try to force them to learn.

Learner autonomy is a complex issue and we may not succeed easily in getting some learners to take responsibility, but it's certainly worth a try.

---

[40] The learner, of course, means a big house, but has suggested rather impolitely that his uncle lives in some kind of toilet block!

Summary of Chapter 15

- State of mind plays a major role in learning to spell, especially if self-esteem is low. We should consider the effect that this has on students when we correct, encourage and assess them.

- To motivate our learners to make the extra effort needed to master English spelling we need to convey why it's so important and make lessons engaging.

- A healthy dose of fun elements in spelling lessons can keep learners engaged, relaxed and receptive and make content more memorable.

- Learners need to be able to work out patterns for themselves to be able to spell words they need.

- Adults and teenagers will need, and be capable of, more sophisticated work on spelling than young learners and materials must reflect this.

- Frequent reminders about similarities and patterns within English spelling make the whole task of learning it seem much more manageable.

- We can take steps to encourage students to take responsibility for their own learning.

Chapter Sixteen:

Teaching about Spelling Patterns

Should we teach spelling rules?

How can we help with:

      vowels?

      homophones and near homophones?

      doubling?

      silent letters?

      common letter strings?

      morphemes?

      the letters *c*, *k* and *s*, and the sounds /s/ and /k/?

Should we teach spelling rules?

There certainly have been spelling rules imposed on English in the past. The spelling is not arbitrary as many people seem to think. However, sets of rules have often been laid over other sets of rules without completely over-riding them. As a result, many of the phonological and graphemic rules that are taught really are very poor ones. In Part A we debunked the so-called rule: *When two vowels go walking, the first one does the talking*. Not much better is the *i before e except after c* rule. The moral is: check their validity before teaching them or, better, task your learners with finding out if the rule is correct or not.

'Rules' are usually handed down from above, whereas it is more useful for learners to approach spelling via 'patterns' that can be discovered. From these, hypotheses can be made and tested. The very act of searching and exploring these patterns provides learners with deeper cognitive engagement with the written language, and consequently more likelihood of durable learning than if they were just presented with rules.

Interestingly, it seems that even if you do know a range of spelling rules, it might not make much difference to your spelling ability. An Australian study found that weak spellers at university knew as much about phoneme-grapheme correspondences as their classmates who could spell well. Spelling well is about much more than knowing rules. (Beason, 2006, p. 183)

In this chapter, we look at some of the most useful patterns to teach and how to do so in general terms. Specific activities that you can use or adapt are in Part C of the book.

How can we help with vowels?

We saw in Part A that vowels tend to be more problematic than consonants because:

- they are often quite similar to each other in sound *(See C:223)*;

- there are several ways to write each phoneme;

- there are several ways to pronounce each vowel letter;

- weak forms of vowels give no clue to the spelling;

- some vowel letters have rather similar shapes (no sticks or tails) *(See B:147)*;

- they are less important in some languages *(See A:93)*.

Vowel phoneme discrimination

Can your learners tell the difference between the different vowel sounds?

It is useful to compare:

- the different short vowel sounds — some of these are more difficult for some nationalities than others, for example, /æ/ and /ʌ/ are generally problematic for Spanish speakers and they may not be able to hear the difference between **ran** and **run** and so they may be unsure about the spelling, if they are using a phonological route;

- long and short vowel sounds. Probably the ones that most learners can't distinguish are /ɪ/ and /iː/.

They may need to work on phoneme discrimination for these problematic sounds. If they can't hear the differences in the sounds when they are isolated or in short words, it may be useful to show how mouth shape differs to help learners to produce them. Then they need lots of practice in distinguishing between the sounds, first in isolation, then in words, and finally in sentences.

If this doesn't work, if learners really can't hear the differences between the vowel sounds, then it may be best to stop trying this, otherwise they'll just get over-stressed about it. There are plenty of alternatives ways to learn spellings in this book.

Writing long and short vowel sounds

Being able to identify the vowel sounds is only half the challenge. Using the correct letters, especially for vowel digraphs and for weak vowels, is even more difficult for some.

Extensive reading will help many learners to match different letter strings to sounds. Simultaneous reading and listening is particularly useful because it helps learners link the spelling, the sound and the meaning.

A list of all the possible spellings of each vowel phoneme is unlikely to help learners with vowel digraphs, as it would surely overload them. It is better if they can discover some of these patterns, the most common ones, themselves. There is, however, a list of these spellings for reference on page 271.

As the phonological system rather lets us down here by offering too many possibilities, it is often better to turn to visual and kinaesthetic methods. The different vowels can be assigned different colours *(See C:220)*, or they can be highlighted in some other way to make them visually salient and therefore more memorable. A range of kinaesthetic activities would be useful.

It is also helpful to elicit links between words with similar patterns. If there is a digraph in a word that learners have particular difficulty with, they can be encouraged to link it with other words with the same pattern that they do know. So if a learner has problems spelling **double**, but knows the words **you**, **should** and **out**, we can use a sentence such as **You should go out for a double espresso**.

How can we help our learners with homophones and near homophones?

Not only does English have more than its fair share of homophones but added to these are the words that sound similar and to many learners are in fact homophonous. Some very common words are homophones or near homophones, such as:

- *there/their/they're*
- *its/it's*
- *your/you're*
- *to/too/two*.

However, the teaching of homophones (and near ones) is a risky business. Drawing attention to them can sometimes make learners confused when they weren't before. If they have learned **hear** (as something you do with your **ear**) then there is really no reason to mix it up with **here** (which is about location, as are the similarly-spelled words **there** and **where**) *(See C:195)*. But if you make a big thing of the fact that **here** and **hear** have the same sound and are often confused, this can actually plant a seed of doubt about which is which. It's much better to link words by meaning and spelling, rather than by sound. Unfortunately, spelling books and the web are full of activities about the spelling of homophones. Use them at your own (or your learners') risk![41]

Here are some more ways for learners to remember the spellings of the words above without comparing them with their homophones:

- **_there_** is spelled like **_here_** and **_where_** which are semantically related words about location;

- **_your_** and **_their_** are possessive adjectives. They both add an **r** to the personal pronoun **_you_** and **_they_** (respectively), but the **y** in **_they_** changes to an **i** in **_their_**;

- **_its_** is one word and it happens to end in **s**, just like **_his_** — another possessive adjective;

- **_they're_** is a contraction of **_they are_**, **_you're_** is a contraction for **_you are_**, and **_it's_** is a contraction for **_it is_** or **_it has_** — the apostrophe tells us there's a missing letter;

- **_to_** is a preposition and has two letters like many other prepositions (**_in_**, **_at_**, **_on_**, **_by_**, etc.);

- **_too_** — remember there's another **o** too, or there are too many **o**s;

- **_two_** is related to **_twin_**, **_twelve_**, **_twenty_**, **_between_**, etc.

So teaching each word in its own right or with lexically related words seems to be much more useful than comparing a word with its homophone.

How can we help with doubling?

In many languages a double letter is pronounced differently from a single letter. In English that usually only happens with vowels (**_meet/met_**). With consonants doubling doesn't usually change the sounds at all (**_rabbit/habit_**), though it may make a difference to the preceding vowel (**_rabbit/rabid_**). Double or single letters in English are as likely to be related to etymology, morphology or graphemic patterns as sound. So we can deal with many double letters by showing how:

- prefixes and suffixes are usually added to the whole word:
  person + **_al_** + **_ly_** = **_personally_**
  mis + **_spell_** = **_misspell_** *(See C:232)*;

- CVC words usually double the final C before a vowel suffix:
  running/skipping (CVC words)
  walking/hiking/sleeping (not CVC words) *(See C:236)*;

- some letters are never doubled in native words:

> *rowing*, *payee*;

- some spellings come from the original language:
  *le**tt**er* from French *le**tt**re*;

- a double *e* or *o* *may* make a longer sound than a single one:
  teen/ten, ***shot/shoot***;

- a double consonant *may* make a preceding vowel short:
  able/apple; diner/dinner

How can we help with silent letters?

This is perhaps one of the most frustrating elements of English spelling for many learners, especially if they don't have any in their own language.

There isn't just one way to teach words with silent letters — we really need to consider *why* there is a silent letter in the word first. This will determine the routes we can use to teach it.

You would think that, by definition, silent letters could not be learned phonologically. But in fact sometimes a letter is silent (in that it is not pronounced itself) but it affects the pronunciation of other letters in the word. The most common example of this is the final silent *e* — "the magic *e*" — such as in ***rate***, ***eve***, ***fine***, ***alone***, and ***use***. But also consider the *r*[42] and *l* in words like ***sort*** and ***walk*** — they also affect the pronunciation of the preceding vowel. We need to make learners aware of these.

Many silent letters have historical roots. So words like ***ballet*** have the silent *t* because they come from French. They can be learned with other words of similar spelling and etymology, such as ***buffet***. They can also be grouped with many other words that have a similar ending but that came into the English language earlier and so had their pronunciations anglicised (***budget/secret/cabinet***). We just have to make sure ELLs are aware of the pronunciation differences.

Some words have silent letters purely for graphemic reasons. The silent *e* at the end of ***give*** doesn't make the *i* long, it's only there because English words never end with *v*. The extra *o* in ***too*** exists to distinguish it from the preposition ***to***. By teaching learners some of these graphemic patterns, we reduce the number of words that have to be learned visually as individual 'instances' of words that are seemingly irregular.

Many silent letters are the result of changes in the pronunciation of words. There was a time when the *w* was pronounced in ***write***, the *gh* in ***right***, the *k* in ***knife***, and the *t* in ***listen***, etc. The pronunciation changed but the spelling had already been prescribed in early dictionaries. So the legacy is words which have silent letters that just have to be learned.

How can we help learners with these? We can give them the background knowledge to help make sense of these anomalies and make them more memorable. We can also help them

---

[42] In non-rhotic accents, see Glossary page 7.

look for common patterns that they can consider using when trying possible spellings. We can certainly use visual and kinaesthetic methods to help them remember these words.

How can we help with morphemes?

For word-building *(See B:139),* learners need some knowledge of morphemes and how they attach to each other, for example:

- that prefixes are added to whole words;

- when to drop the final *e* before a suffix;

- when to double a consonant before adding a suffix;

- when to make changes such as *y* to *i*;

- various plural patterns;

- some conventions for adding vowel suffixes and consonant suffixes;

- that compound words can break normal graphemic rules, such as the double *h* in **hitchhiker**.

Also they do need to know the spelling of some of the common prefixes and suffixes and the differences between some of the confusing ones *(See C:234).* Here are some tricky prefixes:

- *anti-* and *ante-*
- *pre-*, *per-* and *pro-*
- *dis-* and *dys-*
- *inter-* and *intra-*

and suffixes:

- *-er*, *-or* and *-ar*
- *-ist* and *-est*
- *-ion* and *-ian*.

How can we help with common letter strings?

There are certain letter strings that occur so often in English that learners need to be able to write them automatically as 'chunks' of spelling, rather than letter-by-letter. They are too numerous to list here but they do fall into certain categories:

- blends — two or three consonants commonly found together at the beginning or end of words, such as *st-*, *br-*, *spr-* *-nt*, *-sk*;

- digraphs — two letters used together to make one phoneme, like *ch*, *th*, *ng*, *oa*, *ie*, *er*, *oy*;

- affixes — prefixes, suffixes and inflections: *auto-*, *-ful*, *-ed*;

- strings related to etymology but not sound:
  - Old English — *-ough*, *-igh*, *-aught*, *-ould*
  - French — *eau*, *-ette*.

These need to be brought to their attention, and practised extensively. Known words can be used to help with unknown words with similar letter strings: ***sigh*** is spelled like ***light***. A variety of visual and kinaesthetic means can also be used. It is very important that learners do write and type these words often to establish the muscle memory that will enable them to produce each string as one item rather than two, three or four separate letters.

Teachers may also like to do some work on 'illegal' letter strings if these are cropping up a lot in students' writing. There are some combinations we just don't find at all in English words, such as *jj*, some are only found across morpheme boundaries, like *lr* (***already***) or only found in certain positions in a word, such as *ck*, which can't be used at the beginning of a word. However, most classes won't have time for this and hopefully extensive reading will make these spellings 'look funny' for most learners.

How can we help with the letters c, k and s, and the sounds /s/ and /k/?

Although this area is rather confusing, there are some strong patterns that are useful to teach. If you heard the word *concise*, for example, and tried to spell it phonetically, you might consider any of these (although some letter strings are illegal in English): *concise*, ~~*consise*~~, ~~*concice*~~, ~~*koncise*~~, ~~*quoncise*~~, ~~*choncise*~~, or ~~*ckoncise*~~ and many more combinations of errors surrounding these sounds and letters. With so many ways to spell the /k/ sound, two main ways to spell the /s/ sound (that can be interchanged in different varieties of English), two main pronunciations for the letters *c* and *s*, there's little wonder mistakes occur.

There are some reasonably predictable patterns in the usage, however. Some of these are graphemic and depend on the following letter, or on the position in the word. Others are etymological, with the *ch* spelling /k/ in words from Greek and *que* found in French-origin words.

Looking at and referring to some of these systems allows learners to make considered choices when they are faced with uncertainty over such words.

People often think there are equivalent patterns for the letters *g* and *j* and the sounds /g/ and /dʒ/, but they are actually far less reliable guides than the ones above.

Summary of Chapter 16

- 'Rules' should be approached with caution, whereas getting learners to find patterns in example words avoids presenting the language as defective.

- We often need to help ELLs with vowels, particularly phoneme discrimination and assigning the right symbols to the sounds. Visual methods, perhaps with colour, and making links with other words may be the most effective approaches.

- To avoid confusion, it is better not to teach homophones together, but teach each word in its own context so learners can see links with words with similar meanings.

- Referring to etymological, graphemic and morphological patterns helps learners with double letters.

- Silent letters appear for different reasons and the way of dealing with each one depends on why it is there.

- Learners need to know how to break words up into morphemes, how to spell each morpheme and how to attach them to each other. With this knowledge, many longer words become easier to deal with.

- Common letter strings need to be firstly noticed by learners and then practised extensively to gain automaticity in writing these chunks.

- The letters *c*, *k* and *s* and the sounds /s/ and /k/ present many spelling options but there are some fairly predictable patterns that are worth exploring.

Chapter Seventeen:

Teaching Spelling Strategies

Why should we focus on strategies?

How can we help learners see useful patterns in spelling?

How can learners cope with spelling long words?

What about the most frequent words?

How can we encourage learners to record spellings?

What strategies can be used to learn new spellings?

How can dictionaries and spell-checkers be used most effectively?

How can editing be improved?

What common strategies may not be helpful?

Why should we focus on strategies?

Existing spelling materials seem to focus primarily on discrete features (such as when to change *y* to *i*). While this kind of input has its place, we need a far greater emphasis on *strategies* for improving spelling. For example, if we can train learners to look more closely at words, to relate their spelling to other known words, to see patterns or other words within them, to break them down morphemically, use reference tools, etc., we can help them to be more autonomous in the quest to improve their spelling.

However, it would be dangerous to think of teenage or adult students as blank slates when it comes to strategies. We will want to find out what strategies they already use to tackle spelling and get them to assess how well these work for them. Sharing and discussing these strategies among classmates can also be very useful *(See C:185)*. Those who use only one strategy may take some persuading to try others, whether their way is working well for them or not.

How can we help learners see useful patterns in spelling?

Noticing spelling patterns gives clues about serial probability — which letters are likely to come next. When learners are stuck on how to spell a particular word, they can consider different possibilities and make more informed choices based on their knowledge of typical patterns.

Learners who want to improve their spelling do need to read. They are unlikely to get very proficient otherwise. So we may need to suggest reading sources that will appeal to them *(See C:190*. However, reading alone is not enough for many people as they don't really notice the spelling of words. They recognise most words by the context and the rough shape. However, explicitly focussing on certain spelling patterns *in class* increases the possibility of learners noticing these *out of class*. You could give occasional activities in class which prompt the reader to search for particular patterns either in a text they are all reading or one that they have chosen *(See C:249)*.

We can also encourage students to record certain common spelling patterns in a spelling log book *(See B:140)* and add new words they find to a page for a particular pattern.

How can learners cope with spelling long words?

Because long words can look so daunting to spell, we need to make sure learners can break them down into more manageable parts. They could be broken down into syllables or into morphemes. The latter is more useful for spelling most long words as it relates to meaning and gives more clues to the spelling. If we break *educational* down into morphemes we have:

educat(e) + ion + al

That is the base element *educate* (we drop the final *e* before a vowel suffix) + the common noun suffix *-ion* + the common *-al* suffix that turns a noun into an adjective. It's all very logical and we don't have to worry about whether the word ends with *-tion* or *-sion* or *-cian*, as the *t* from *educate* tells us. Also we don't need to remember that this word ends with *-al*, rather than *-le* or *-el*, as long as we know about the common *-al* suffix that changes a noun into an adjective.

But if learners try to tackle the spelling by dividing *educational* phonologically into syllables, it would be:

ed + u + ca + tion + al

Here all reference to the meaning has gone and the spelling clues are now missing too. So it leaves questions like:

- How many **d**s?

- How do you spell the /ju:/ vowel sound? Or is it /dʒu:/? (Does it sound like **you** or **Jew**?)

- We know there are several ways to spell the sound /k/ — which is it?

- -**shun**, -**tion** or -**sion** or -**cian**?

- -**al**, -**el** or -**le**?

The first way, by morphemes, not only presents fewer elements to remember but also gives clues to the spelling. It goes without saying that learners will need to have worked on common morphemes and how they are attached to each other *(See Chapter 7)*. Breaking up by syllable may provide a useful check *after* the word has been written by the morphological method — to check each part has been included.

Finding words within words is another strategy that helps memory of long spellings *(See C:213)*. The most useful is when we can find words with related meaning that help us to spell. So a commonly misspelled word, *definite*, is difficult because the second two vowels are weak forms. As these can't be spelled phonetically, learners need to know how to relate them to other words in the family, where the weak form has its full value. The spelling of **definite** can be remembered because it contains the related word **finite**, which has a much clearer sound-to-spelling relationship. However, this only works if the learner can pronounce that word correctly.

But even just remembering that there's **a rat** in **separate** will help learners remember that the weak vowel is an **a**. The longer and more carefully somebody looks at a word, the more likely they are to remember the spelling, so finding words within words is a useful memory strategy *(See C:213)*.

What about the most frequent words?

As already noted, many of the most common words are phonologically irregular in spelling, basically because they have been hanging around in English for so long. But these words are vitally important — remember, being able to spell the most common 150 words correctly means being able to spell about 85% of text accurately. Merely knowing this is a great motivator for learners. So we definitely need to ensure that learners can cope with these. Reading will help but more explicit work will be needed by some.

Many of these high frequency words need to be learned visually as 'instances' (words with less predictable spelling that just need to be mentally stored). There is the added problem for dyslexic learners that structure words, which many of these most frequent words are, seem to be more difficult for them to learn as there is no tangible meaning attached to them. There is no visual picture to fix the word **although** or **because** to; they are too abstract. By teaching such words in context we can provide a mental picture for learners to visualise when they are trying to spell the word *(See C:216)*.

Many of the techniques and activities explored throughout this book can be usefully applied to learning these common words, such as:

- working on word shape *(See C:216)*

- drawing an interpretation of the word or a context for it *(See C:216)*

- modelling words *(See C:224)*

- overwriting 'hard spots' – i.e. the difficult parts *(See B:146)*

- colouring vowels *(See C:220)*

- mnemonics *(See B:148, C:198)*.

How can we encourage learners to record spellings?

How should learners record spellings? Some learners keep vocabulary notebooks in which they write new words. In my experience, these tend to be written chronologically as they are encountered in class. The only way to access a word is to remember when it was entered in the book and then try to find other words that were met at the same time. Lots of cognitive processing, but not related to the spelling! These vocabulary books are better than nothing, but I do tend to agree with whoever first nicknamed them 'vocabulary graveyards' — they are where words may rest in peace, never to be disturbed again! To keep this new learning alive, kicking and useful, the words need to be accessible, organised and frequently recycled.

Personal spelling log

One alternative for recording spelling is a personal spelling log. This can be a book, but a small loose-leaf file affords more flexibility. It is best to make this in two parts.

Part 1 — A-Z Record
The first part is an alphabetical list of words that the student wants to learn. There should be at least one page for most letters of the alphabet, depending on how common the letter is. The learner writes new words on these pages (with a definition, picture or translation) and then is able to find them again when needed.

If the learner thinks it may be difficult to remember the first letter of a word, he or she could write a note on another page. Let's say the word is ***psychologist***; as well as being recorded on the ***P*** page, it could also be written in brackets at the bottom of the ***S*** page.

When students write the words, they should be encouraged to highlight the parts of the spelling that they find difficult, preferably by overwriting these letters with a different colour pen.

The purpose of the first part is a reference — a place where learners can easily look up a word that they have forgotten how to spell. It can also be used to populate the second part.

Part 2 — Spelling Organiser

The second part of the spelling log is organised in another way. Learners should make pages for different types of spelling, for example:

- various spelling patterns, such as *-igh*, *wh-*, *VC +e*

- words containing different silent letters

- particular etymological patterns, such as the Greek *ch* for /k/

- prefixes and suffixes, such as words ending with *-ible* and *-able* (in separate columns)

- irregular plurals, or those that follow particular patterns

- words related to a particular topic

- words within one family, such as all the words related to *form* (*formula*, *information*, etc.).

These pages can be made as they are needed. The words from the first part, the alphabetical list, can be transferred onto these pages. Possibly some words will fit on several pages and there is certainly no reason why they shouldn't be repeated. The words may be written in lists but learners should be encouraged to consider other visual layouts too, such as mind maps, annotated pictures, flow charts, etc.

The very act of reorganising the words, and thinking about how they should be presented, helps learning as this involves higher order thinking skills and consolidates the memory of the spelling. This part of the log also acts as a different kind of reference. The learner can see a range of related words and start to appreciate patterns. By grouping the words it helps them to make predictions about other spellings based on recurring patterns. The sense of system is reinforced. It also makes it easier to revise patterns rather than a list of unconnected words.

Digital spelling log

While a loose-leaf folder makes it easier to organise and add pages, such folders do tend to be rather large and students may find one cumbersome to carry around. Computers offer some great alternatives. The most appropriate tool that I've found is Microsoft OneNote. This program is included in Microsoft Office packages, but many people who have it don't know they have. It can also be bought as a standalone program and there are web and phone apps for it too.

Here is a MS OneNote 'Notebook' designed as a Spelling Log:

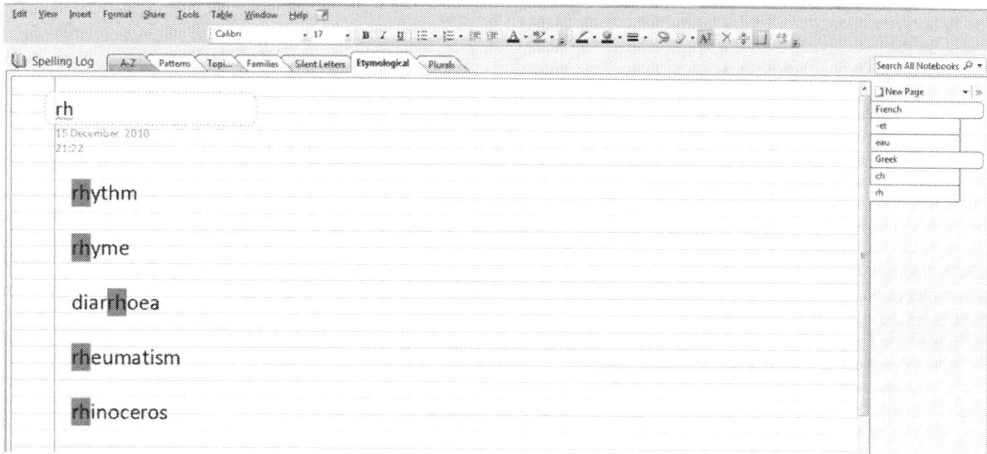

Figure 8: *Microsoft OneNote used as a Spelling Log*

You will see that different Tabs have been created to make sections of the notebook:

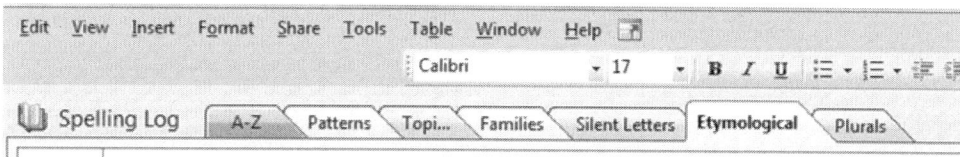

Figure 9: *Microsoft OneNote tabs for different sections*

Within those Tabs you can create different Pages, and even Sub-pages, all of which are easily searchable:

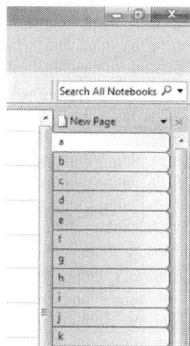

Figure 10: *Different pages can be made for the alphabetical list of new words*

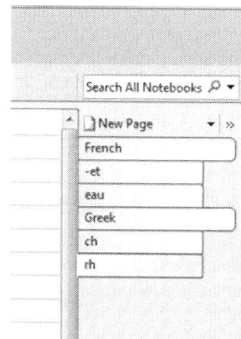

Figure 11: *Pages and Sub-pages can be made for different etymological patterns*

On the Pages themselves you can:

- type

- paste text, images and videos from the web or elsewhere on your computer

- draw mind maps and flow charts.

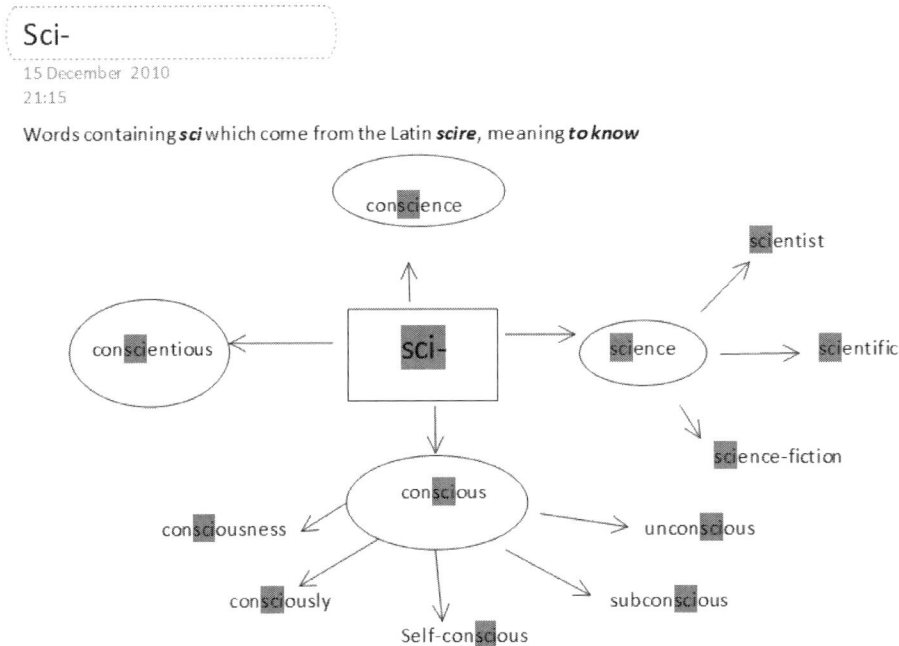

Sci-

15 December 2010
21:15

Words containing *sci* which come from the Latin *scire*, meaning *to know*

Figure 12: *An example of a mind map for showing lexical/etymological relationships between words*

If learners don't have MS OneNote, there are several free alternatives on the web, such as Evernote. They all have different features.

What strategies can be used to learn new spellings?

A learner may well be able to work out a spelling or look it up, they may assiduously record words in a spelling log, but what about the next time he or she needs the same spelling. Will it come automatically to mind? Will it flow from the pen or fingers without hesitation?

Because not all words can be learned the same way, a learner needs to know some patterns or precedents for sound-to-letter correspondences, morphological patterns and so on, but also must learn some words as 'instances'.

As we've seen, there's learning and there's acquiring. Many people acquire spellings as they read. They see words several times and the spelling gets absorbed by the brain. However, as we've seen this isn't always the case.

A considerable amount of extra effort is required to consciously learn spellings. Teachers often ask their students to learn spellings, but sometimes learners just don't know *how* to do it. They may have one strategy that they always use but it may not be very efficient or not effective at getting the word into the long-term memory. This can result in 'Friday spellers' — those who can remember the spelling just until Friday's test and then forget it as it's no longer perceived as needed.

Here are some learning strategies that can be introduced.

Look Say Cover Write Check

One of the most frequently used methods is Look Say Cover Write and Check. The learner looks very carefully at the word, which is written in the first column of a table, and says it aloud at the same time. Some teachers ask learners to just say the word and others suggest they spell out the word letter-by-letter. Then the word is covered and the learner tries to write it. The original word is uncovered and checked. This is then repeated at spaced intervals.

There is a template for an improved version of this in Part C *(See C:207)*. The same basic sequence is followed but there is more emphasis on the Looking part. Students are guided to say the word *and* the letters, count the number of letters, identify hard spots, look for common patterns, use the meaning to help remember, relate it to known words and to visualise the word shape. The learner then covers the word, writes it from memory and checks it. By spending this extra time on each word and looking at it from different angles, the memory of it is likely to be stronger and more long-lasting.

Let's have a look at some of those stages in more detail as they are useful strategies in themselves.

Saying the word

Should the learner say the word, or the spelling? Why not both?

As a learner looks at a word, he or she can say it aloud and take time to explicitly notice how similar or different the sound is from the spelling. It may also sound like another related word. If these words have come from classwork, hopefully the teacher will have already worked on pronunciation.

Saying the letters out loud can also be very useful for some learners who find it easier to memorise aurally. Some words seem to have a natural rhythm which lends itself to this, like **Mississippi** — **M-I**-double **S-I**-double **S-I**-double **P-I**.

Some proficient speakers say they often spell difficult words by saying them with their 'spelling pronunciation', so for **comfortable** they will say 'com-for-table' when they need to spell it. Although this is a useful strategy if you are proficient in the language, it is rather a dangerous one for ELLs as we don't want to encourage them to use and learn such unnatural pronunciation.

Identifying 'hard spots'

When learners look at a word they can usually see some letters that are easy. Most words are at least partly phonetic. So as they say the word aloud they can start by acknowledging these. The rest, the bits that aren't obvious, are the 'hard spots' — these are where they need to direct their energies. It can be helpful to 'overwrite' these, that is, trace over the top of those letters in a thicker, brighter or contrasting coloured pen. This makes the 'hard spots' more salient and helps to imprint these letters on the visual memory.

Also by isolating what is difficult in the word they realise that less needs to be learned; it may be two or three letters rather than seven or eight.

Searching for common patterns

If learners have knowledge of some common spelling patterns in English they can look at the word and see if there are any they recognise. These then become one chunk rather than, say, three letters *(See C:188 C:200)*.

What's inside the word?

Sometimes another word can be found inside a longer word. When these are closely related in meaning, learners can hook unknown information onto what is already known, and so help memory retention. The word **clean** can be found in c**lean**liness, and **govern** is hidden in **govern**ment, for example. This gives a useful clue to the spelling of the longer word which is phonologically irregular. This can also be applied to parts of words. The word **their** can be related to **they** and **them** (to remember that the **e** is before the **i**).

Sometimes that meaning relationship can be stretched somewhat to help with memorisation: there's a **lie** in be**lie**ve. Or words can be found within longer words that are not related to meaning at all, but still help memorisation of the spelling *(See C:213)*. In the word **materialistic**, for example, we can find **mat**, **material**, **mate**, **ate**, **is**. Setting learners the task of seeking these out not only encourages them to spend longer looking at the word, but can also help them to remember the difficult parts. In **materialistic**, the first vowel is usually pronounced as a schwa /ə/, so gives no clue to the spelling, but words like **mat** and **mate** will. And even the *lack* of words can help: the fact that **real** is not in the word helps remind us that the spelling is not ~~**materealistic**~~.

Incidentally, it is important that the letters appear in the long word in the right order — just finding letters that make up words but are in the wrong order doesn't help with spelling the source word. So the word **real** *is* in **materialistic**, but only in that the long word happens to have the letters **r-e-a-l** somewhere in it: **matERiAListic**. This gives us no useful clues to spelling it, however.

146

Word shape

One way that we seem to remember at least whether a word 'looks right' or 'looks funny' is by the word shape — its length and where any 'sticks' and 'tails' are, in other words, where the letters rise above others (*b d f h k l t*) or fall below the line (*g j p q y*). The easiest way to focus attention on this is to have the learner write the word clearly and neatly in lower case letters and then draw around its outline *(See C:217)*. For some learners this image imprints itself on the memory and helps them recognise if the word is wrongly spelled when met again later. It also involves them looking closely at the word and interacting with it as they draw the outline. This may help memorisation.

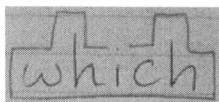

This strategy can also be used to memorise parts of words, such as the -*ly* on adverbs or the string *ough*

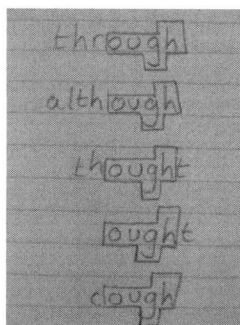

In Part C you will find several activities for exploiting word shapes.

Colour

Colour also helps visualisation. We can make the parts we need to remember, the 'hard spots', stand out in a different colour so this imprints on the memory *(See C:220)*.

Holding the word in the mind's eye

Once learners have managed to 'see' a word, we also need to help them hold that word in their memory, or at least access it again at will. That is why many of the activities in this book involve visualising a word and then spending a bit of time doing something with it, rather than just writing it and moving on. The longer you can hold the spelling in your brain, the more likely you are to transfer it your long-term memory. It may be that learners can visualise words but don't trust what they see. Plenty of practice at these sorts of activities should build up their confidence in their intuition.

Mnemonics

Mnemonics, little tricks for remembering spelling (or anything else), are useful for words that just refuse to stick in the brain any other way *(See C:198)*.

They should be used with caution however, as they don't really teach you to spell a word; they teach you a way to be able to produce it accurately. They are a crutch and people usually find they have to stop and access the mnemonic whenever they need to spell the word and this doesn't help at all with automaticity. A personal illustration: I could never spell the word **rhythm** until I learned the mnemonic *Rhythm Helps Your Two Hips Move*. Excellent — now I can always spell the word with 100% accuracy. But ... I don't think I'll ever be able to spell it automatically, because I *think* I can't spell it without the mnemonic. I've tried to do it without but the mnemonic always pops into my head and insists that I check the spelling. It's like trying not to think of an elephant once someone has told you not to think of an elephant!

But when nothing else works, they can be relied upon. There are different types of mnemonics:

- a word for each letter;
  - *rhythm* — Rhythm Helps Your Two Hips Move
  - *because* — Big Elephants Can't Always Understand Small Elephants

- a clue for the hard spots only (the parts the learner has trouble with):
  - *ne<u>cess</u>ary* — It's necessary to have one *c*oat and two *s*ocks
  - *ac<u>comm</u>odation* — The best accommodation has two double beds (two double letters)
  - *emba<u>rr</u>assed* — When you're embarrassed you have two *r*ed cheeks (two *r*s)

- a clue for more common patterns:
  - when it sounds like *E*, *i* before *e*, except after *c*.

Mnemonics are most memorable, and therefore effective, if they are:
- **P**ersonalised — it might be best if learners make up their own;

- **A**musing — if it's funny it's more memorable;

- **M**eaningful — meaningless mnemonics take more effort to remember than the spelling;

- **P**ictorial — if the mnemonic creates a visual picture in the learner's mind that will help;

- **E**asy to remember — not too complicated;

- **R**ude — yes, sorry, but it seems the ruder the better!

If you find it hard to memorise that list, just remember "PAMPER yourself with mnemonics'!

How can dictionaries and computer spell-checkers be used most effectively?

The reply to a 'How do you spell...?' question is often, 'Look it up in a dictionary' (especially if the person being asked doesn't know!). But is that an effective strategy?

Using a bilingual dictionary

Of course, using a bilingual dictionary is one of the easiest ways for an ELL to check the spelling of a word. Assuming the dictionary contains the word and is accurate, it's quick and effective. The downside is that it transports the learner back into their first language. It also demands no cognitive processing, so the word looked up may be just as easily forgotten. It's important, therefore, to encourage learners to record and learn the spellings they look up.

Using a monolingual dictionary or thesaurus

Monolingual dictionaries do require more thought (and therefore more time). The learner really needs to know at least the first three letters to be able to find the word. Knowledge of the spelling of prefixes helps with this. Also knowing which letters commonly do and don't appear at the beginning of words.

More user-friendly, perhaps, is the thesaurus, although this is not usually thought of as a spelling tool. If, for example, a learner wanted to know how to spell **wonderful** and had looked up **wunderfull** in a dictionary to no avail, he or she could look up **good** or **fantastic** in a thesaurus and would soon find the word **wonderful**. So words with synonyms (or near synonyms) which have easier spelling can be accessed via this overlooked resource. If learners are not familiar with the layout of a thesaurus, this needs to be explored in class *(See C:255)*.

Using electronic dictionaries

Electronic dictionaries come in several forms:

- Published dictionary software for computers. Many of the learners' printed dictionaries come with a CD-ROM.

- Dictionaries within other educational software. Nowadays, there is often a CD-ROM or DVD-ROM for students packaged with coursebooks. These usually include a dictionary feature — just for the words included in the course.

- Online dictionaries. These may be free or paid-for by subscription.

- Portable electronic dictionaries. Many students have these pocket-sized devices that have dictionary software within them. The software may be bilingual or monolingual or 'bilingualised', meaning that the main information and the definition is in English but there is also a translation into the learner's language.

All these dictionaries have many advantages over a paper one, including portability. But one of their main benefits is the flexibility and 'searchability' they offer, especially if you don't know the spelling of the word. If you get it a little bit wrong, very often the program will suggest alternatives. If I type **wunderful** into the Cambridge Dictionary Online[43], I am offered the following:

wonderful
wonderfully
wunderkind
undercuts
undersold
underfoot
undersell
undercut
wunderkinds
underfunded

Note that **wonderful** is offered before **wunderkind**, which starts with the same six letters.

Wildcard

Another little known but incredibly valuable feature of some electronic dictionaries, particularly the portable ones, is the 'wildcard'. If you type a * or ? in place of any letters within a word that you don't know, the program will offer you suggestions. In some dictionaries, * stands for one or more letters and ? represents a single letter. So if you know how many letters are missing but not what they are, just type ? for each unknown letter. Whereas if you have no idea about the ending, type * after the letters you do know.[44]

Training

So what can teachers do to help learners use these tools more effectively? Firstly, make sure that they are aware of any features mentioned above that will help them with spelling and perhaps advise them on the best dictionary to buy. If necessary, we may have to teach them alphabetical order and how to use it (especially for second and subsequent letters). We can also make learners aware of abbreviations in a dictionary that give extra information about spelling, when adding suffixes for example, or if there's a difference between American English and British English.

Whether to help them use paper or electronic dictionaries largely depends which your students are likely to use. Training in the use of both would be ideal.

Computer spell-checkers

People ask, "Why bother teaching spelling nowadays? We all use spell-checkers". This not only assumes that all writing is done electronically (which most of it is for some people but not all), but also that people know how to use them well (which some don't).

In my corpus of 372 handwritten spelling errors from adult EFL learners with spelling problems *(See A:92)*, I found 16% of the errors wouldn't have been flagged by the spell-checker at all because they were homophones or other real words. 15% were shown as

---

[43] See http://dictionary.cambridge.org/.
[44] I have written an article about the use of portable electronic dictionaries at http://www.elgweb.net/ped-article.html .

errors but the intended word (as indicated by context) was not offered. So in over 30% of cases the spell-checker wouldn't have helped.

Another problem is that very often learners are offered several alternatives to choose from and the one at the top of the list may not be the one they need. Many of the errors offered up to five alternatives. Of the 261 errors that were picked up by the spell-checker and where the right word was offered, 21% required the user to choose a word other than the first one shown, i.e. the second, third, fourth or fifth word. So thinking still needs to take place. Some learners have admitted to me that they always take the first option shown. Blind faith!

The good news, perhaps, is that in 51% of the total sample, the intended word was the one offered first. But even then usually there were still other options that the writer needed to discount.

Maybe the easiest is when there is only one spelling offered. For example, a student who wrote ~~culdn't~~ would have only been offered **couldn't**. There were 62 cases where only one word was offered (16% of the total sample). But of these 62, 11% didn't offer the correct word, so a writer can't even have complete confidence in this. An example to illustrate: a learner who wrote ~~*funately*~~ meaning ***fortunately*** would only have been offered one alternative, ***finitely***, which would have made nonsense of his sentence if he'd accepted it.

One limitation of spell-checkers is that they can't distinguish between homophones. So in ***I can't ~~bare~~ marmalade***, the word **bare** would not show up as an error because it is a real word. In fact, even a word that is completely different, but still a real word, such as **pair** in ***I can't ~~pair~~ marmalade*** won't be flagged.

So although spell-checkers are undoubtedly useful, if learners are too far from the original spelling or if they confuse two words, the spell-checker may not be helpful. Some learners need training in the effective use of them and encouragement to use other strategies too. Like much learner training, there is a danger of patronising learners — many will already know how to use a spell-checker well. But the following training could be useful:

- looking at the words underlined by the spell-checker and trying to guess what it should be before right-clicking on it;

- choosing the right word from the list offered *(See C:256)*;

- recording the word so it is less likely to be misspelled in the future;

- realising the limitations of spell-checkers and the need for supplementary editing tactics.

Learning the spellings that have been checked

Before all this technological help was available, teachers sometimes had problems persuading learners to look up words they didn't know in a dictionary — it was time-consuming, you needed to know the first few letters and be able to work well with alphabetical order. Now some teachers complain about the opposite problem — learners are too reliant on electronic dictionaries and spell-checkers. They may be producing the right spelling (*may* be) but are they really learning? The process of looking up a word or clicking on a word with red wavy underlining is so quick that there may be minimal cognitive processing going on and without a deliberate effort the spelling is unlikely to make it to the long-term memory.

The deliberate effort needed by learners could take several forms:

- The words found in an electronic dictionary can be saved either into a notes page within the software (if available) or into a word processing document. The learner later reviews these. In some of the electronic dictionaries there is a facility to play games with words you have chosen.

- Learners look carefully at the word, then cover it and try to write it. Then they check.

- The word is carefully copied onto a Look Say Cover Write Check chart, for learning later.

- It is added to an appropriate page in a spelling log book to learn later.

- Learners try to think *why* the word is spelled in that way, considering other words with similar meaning, spelling and/or sound. They apply any etymological knowledge they have that will aid memory. The dictionary may even help with this.

- Related words from the same family are noted down if they are given — this not only helps them learn several words instead of one but also gives them an opportunity to notice spelling similarities which may then stick.

How can editing be improved?

Errors can prevent people understanding what we really want to say, but the fear of making errors can also prevent us saying clearly what we want to say. Maybe a writer will use a different word because the one he or she really wants to use has a difficult spelling. So we can encourage learners to write the content first without worrying about spelling — the most important thing is the communication, getting down the ideas that they want to convey in the language that they think best. They can underline words which they are not sure they have spelled correctly. When they have finished writing they work on editing: fluency first, then accuracy *(See C:252)*.

We all make mistakes when we write or type. Some people go back and correct their errors, some don't bother and some try but don't correct them all because they don't see the errors or don't know how to correct them. It has been argued,

> *There is little point in telling poor spellers to check their work for spelling mistakes; they will fail to spot the mistakes for the same reason as they made them in the first place.*

(Mitton 1996: 72).

Fair point, but on the other hand, if they are guided to look for their recurrent errors and to identify spellings that they are not sure of, there is certainly value in this.

So there are three types of help we can give:

- Make the importance of careful editing clear. We can show how unedited work can cost much-wanted jobs, make people look foolish, affect the way others think about the learners, prevent them from passing an exam or gaining a good grade in written assignments even when the content is good *(See C:250)*.

- Help learners seek out their own errors in a piece of writing:
  - by checking for red wavy lines in word processing documents;
  - by looking for common 'spelling demons' (such as tricky homophones) and their own personal ones. Armed with a list of these, learners can type the misspellings into the Find function of the word processing program;[45]
  - by reading the text aloud (privately), as this makes the reader slow down and the different mode of delivery may make the misspelling more noticeable.

- Help learners to correct their own errors by referring to their own knowledge or notes, using reference sources, or even asking.

What common strategies may *not* be helpful?

Sounding out

What about the practice of 'sounding out' words? Both in reading and spelling it may help with some words. If I want to spell the word *laptop*, I could probably do it by saying the six individual sounds to myself. But what a mess I'd get into if I used the same method to spell *conscientious* — maybe something like 'con-ski-entio-us'. Often there are *parts* of words that can be sounded out, but learners should be aware that it is not a very reliable technique for constructing spelling. We have to remember that letters really don't represent sounds, except in combination.

Another danger with 'sounding out' is that learners may put a schwa on the end of a consonant phoneme and say, for example, /kə/ instead of /k/, /tə/ instead of /t/. They may sound out the word *cute* as kuh-u-tuh-e, /kə-ʌ-tə-e/ instead of /kjuːt/. Or if they want to spell /kjuːt/, sounding it out may well encourage a spelling something like ~~kyoot~~.

The problem with spelling by sound is that there is no way of knowing if it's right. If a word has been learned visually then the writer can often recognise if it looks right or not.

Choose the correct spelling

It's great when learners go online and get involved in spelling games. Some are very useful. But some aren't. I mean this sort of thing:

---

[45] In MS Word this is accessed via CTRL + F.

Which is the correct spelling?
  a) crissificate
  b) chrissificate
  c) crisifficate
  d) chrisificate

If learners ever had any idea how to spell this word (which I've made up, by the way), they would surely find themselves thinking "...or is it that one?" Thus the seed of doubt is sown and it grows. So where there was never any problem, now there is. And if they didn't know the word before, they'd just be guessing anyway, which is rather pointless. We need to help learners trust their intuition more when spelling. If they have been exposed to wrong spellings several times (and it is often the same words that crop up in these exercises) they may be visualising the wrong spelling.

Reading aloud

Asking weak readers to read aloud in front of a class can be cruel — especially to the reader, but usually quite painful for the listeners too! For many, it's far too stressful an experience for them to gain any benefit from it in terms of reading. Some teachers argue that it helps the learners with their pronunciation, but there are much better ways to work on pronunciation than reading aloud.

Reading aloud can be beneficial for spelling, however, if learners have had a chance to read and study the text previously, so they have been able to think about how the spelling relates to the sound. Dialogues are better than prose for this type of reading as they are more interactive and students read shorter sentences.

Spelling may also be helped by the teacher reading aloud to the students as they read silently in their books. However, many people, native speakers or not, do not read well aloud, so the teacher might need to practise the reading first.

Summary of Chapter 17

- We may need to focus on strategies to allow our students to improve their spelling beyond the classroom.

- To get learners to notice patterns in their own reading we need to first flag some of these in class to make them more salient.

- Breaking words down into morphemes and looking for words within words are useful strategies for coping with long words.

- As many of the most frequent words are phonologically irregular and conceptually somewhat intangible, they may need to be learned visually as instances.

- Learners need to record and organise new spellings, ideally in a Spelling Log, either paper or digital.

- Different words can be best learned in different ways, so students need a range of multi-dimensional learning strategies. A Look Say Cover Write and Check system can include all of these.

- Dictionaries and spell-checkers can lead to accurate work and spelling improvement, but some learners will need training in order to be able to use them to their best advantage.

- Editing is a vital part of the writing process and we need to make this clear to learners if necessary and then help them to find their errors and correct them using suitable tools and methods.

- Some strategies that should be used with caution are sounding out, seeing misspelled words and reading aloud.

Chapter Eighteen:

Practising Spelling

What kind of restricted practice activities are useful?

How can we make freer practice most effective?

How can we help students learn spelling from reading?

How can we help learners to improve spelling out of class?

> *It is only when we have achieved ... spelling that is automatic, predictable, and infallible that we are really free to write with confidence, with no backward glances to see if a word 'looks right', and with no offering of a less precise synonym or phrase because the right one is too difficult to spell.*
>
> (Peters, 1985, p. 5)

We know that practice and review are vital if spellings are to be transferred from the short-term to the long-term memory. This practice needs to involve repetitive mechanical tasks (handwriting or typing) to build up the 'muscle memory' and lead to automaticity — the would-be speller's ultimate aim. In addition, these tasks need to be complemented by others which demand deeper cognitive processing. All these activity types should ideally approach spelling from various angles, to appeal to different learners, to provide access to the spelling via different sensory routes and to stimulate engagement through variety and, whenever appropriate, real communication.

We can divide these activity types into 'restricted' and 'freer' practice.

What kind of restricted practice activities are useful?

We say 'practice makes perfect' but it may be more precise to say 'practice makes permanent'. 'Restricted', or 'controlled', practice is about establishing links within the brain and consolidating them through repetition, thus transferring new knowledge into the long-term memory. It also focuses on accuracy (with an eventual aim of improving fluency). Restricted practice might deal with letters of the alphabet, letter strings, individual words, words in sentences or whole texts depending on the aim of the activity.

Letters

Those who are just starting out on their spelling adventure, who are meeting the Roman alphabet for the first time, or who need to go back to basics might have to work on practising the shape of individual letters, writing from left to right or keeping the writing on the line. They may need help to see that handwritten letters don't always take the same form as printed ones. Other learners may need to consolidate knowledge of sound-symbol relationships, at first for individual letters and then taking into account their position in the word. Or alphabetical order may need to be practised, to allow the student to use reference books, like dictionaries or telephone directories.

Letter strings

If learners practise letter strings until, say, **ing** or **eau** become like one symbol, rather than three separate ones, they will lighten their own memory load when spelling words including those strings. Plenty of practice of these strings within words can lead to automaticity.

Words

While it definitely helps to meet words within a context, the target language can also get rather lost in a forest of words. Sometimes specific lexical items need to be isolated from their context in order to work on them and group them with others that have related spelling. It's rather like capturing a live wild animal (humanely!), taking it off to the lab to examine it and tag it. Then it is safely returned to its natural environment and we can use the knowledge gained to deal with it more effectively.

Sentences

Teachers often find that learners can spell a word learned for a spelling test in isolation, but are unable to spell it when it is in a sentence. There are many other language challenges competing for their attention in a whole sentence, so we need to give plenty of practice of using the same words in different sentences too. By doing this we are reinforcing the spelling of other words in the sentences as well.

Texts

Restricted practice can also work with longer texts such as dictation. Dictation is a traditional (some would say *old fashioned*) activity, which has been much maligned, but can actually be very useful if used thoughtfully. It is often assumed that a dictation involves the teacher reading a text and the learner listening and trying to write what the teacher says. This can be a nightmare for someone who can't spell well. They listen, they write what they hear and then they are told that they got it wrong! Much more effective is the so-called 'humane dictation', in which the teacher leads in to the topic of the text to get the learners interested in it and then reads the text aloud and checks their comprehension and reactions to it. The teacher then allows them to see and read the text while it is read aloud again and asks them to identify any words that they think will be difficult to spell. The learners spend some time learning these words, using strategies such as Look Say Cover Write Check. When they are ready, they put away the text and any notes and do the dictation in the normal way, with the teacher reading it aloud. They check their own or each other's texts, with special focus on the words they learned *(See C:207)*. It doesn't have to be the teacher who reads; it could be one or several other students. There are many excellent ideas for variations on dictations in the book, *Dictation: New Methods, New Possibilities* (Davis, 1988).

Making restricted practice effective and engaging

Looking at the above paragraphs, one thing strikes me. Spelling practice could be so boring! Could be … but needn't be. While encouraging the necessary repetition of such isolated surface details of writing, we need to find ways to sugar the pill. So all our creative powers are needed to come up with activities and games that are fun and relevant as well as providing the repetitive practice needed.

We need plenty of variety and surprise in the activities we use. Multi-sensory activities should provide this and appeal to a wide range of learners. Variety also means that learners can try out more strategies and decide which ones suit them and which don't.

Activities are often best when kept short and snappy. But ideally, they should be used frequently, either as part of a class dealing with spelling or perhaps as warmers at the beginning of lessons, energisers for a flagging class, or to fill in a few minutes at the end of a class. Recycling content from the previous day's lesson is particularly valuable, as so much of what is learned is forgotten within 24 hours unless reviewed.

Using technology

There are plenty of opportunities nowadays for digital practice and this is very valuable. The interactive and visual nature of many of these activities adds extra motivation and interest. They also often have a built-in addictive element. Computer games (as well as social networking) can keep people from their beds, homework, business and families for much longer than is healthy. But if we can harness that addictiveness and channel it into learning to do something useful like spelling, then at least the bleary-eyed student can know he or she has achieved something.

Another great advantage of digital media is that they often demand such a high level of accuracy. Getting an email address or URL *nearly* right is only as good as getting it completely wrong! In a game, players soon learn that they have to be 100% accurate too. So the computer or mobile phone or Playstation is a very strict taskmaster. Would a teacher get away with saying to her students "If you don't get it 100% right, you'll get zero"? And yet this ruthless intolerance is seen positively, as a challenge, in computer gaming. The beauty of it is, though, that technology is completely non-judgemental and infinitely patient. It never says "But we studied this last week, you should know it" or "For goodness sake, don't you know that?" There is a sense of privacy and freedom for risk-taking allowed by digital media.

As so much writing is typed nowadays rather than written, of course our students need to practise typing as well as handwriting. We have discussed the need for handwriting practice to develop 'muscle memory' of letter strings and common words. The same is true for typing. Whether a person touch types or not, the fingers will soon start to move towards the keys with less conscious attention to the individual letters, especially in common letter strings like -***ing*** or -***tion***.

How can we make freer practice most effective?

Perhaps one of the greatest challenges in restricted practice of spelling is making it not only useful, but also motivating and engaging. Freer practice is another matter. It lends itself much more easily to communicative and engaging activities.

Any spelling programme must include free practice activities as well as restricted ones, to give learners the opportunity to use words in a meaningful context. It is after all the whole point of learning to spell, to be able to write well and express exactly what you want to say without distracting or confusing the reader with misspellings. As learners write to express themselves, they relate meaning to spelling which helps them to see semantic links in spelling patterns.

By setting freer writing tasks, we give learners the chance to use both spellings that they have recently learned and others that they may need in order to express themselves. This can lead to what has been called " *'a teachable moment' for spelling — a moment when getting the right spelling is important, salient and learnable*" (Scott, 2000, p. 78).

Weak spellers are often reluctant to write, especially if they know their writing will come back from the teacher covered in red (or green or whatever colour) pen. They may feel that they are unable to express their thoughts in writing because of the limited number of words they can spell confidently. Other students seem happy to write freely and at length, eager to express themselves, with no regard at all for correct spelling, but regrettably the reluctance often appears at the editing stage. In other words, they have provided plenty of potential 'teachable moments', but failed to capitalise on them. Both types of learners should be encouraged to write 'little and often' with a keen eye for editing. We need to help them build a writing habit, so they can consolidate their knowledge of the most common words and recently-learned patterns. Short tasks show them that expressing themselves in writing can be manageable, whereas a long task may feel too daunting. Also, if they attempt to write at length, the editing stage often seems to get rushed or omitted. By encouraging learners to get their ideas down on paper first and edit later, we help them produce more meaningful and more accurate work *(See C:252)*.

Word processing tools

Editing is often easier on word-processed documents than handwritten ones as the second draft doesn't need to be completely rewritten. There are also several tools within a word processing program to help us with accurate spelling. Here I will describe some from Microsoft Word, but there are no doubt equivalents in most other word processing packages.

Autocorrect

With this turned on, the program will automatically correct common spelling or typographical errors, such as **teh** and **adn**. If you have spelling errors that you often make, you can add these to the Autocorrect program. This, of course, produces a more pleasing finished product and if that is the aim, it is useful to have it turned on. However, it does not help users to *improve* spelling as they don't have to think at all. In fact, they probably don't even know that their spelling has been corrected. Turning Autocorrect off is probably best for most spelling activities when word processing. Learners may take some persuading of this though and it is useful to have a short classroom discussion about why it's a good idea.

The Spell-Checker

The spell-checker is a much more useful tool when it comes to learning because it does require some thought and input from the user. The red wavy line under a word tells us simply that the word is not in the Microsoft dictionary. It doesn't necessarily mean it is wrong, but it probably is. When the user right-clicks the word, he or she is usually offered several options and must make a decision about which one to use. Some learners need training to use this tool well *(See C:256)*.

Audience and authenticity

One of the great advantages of our 'wired' 21st century world, with its social networking, blogs, review sites and so on, is that it offers real-life audiences for our learners' writing. This makes the reasons for writing so much more natural. Writing for an authentic audience can also motivate learners to write to a higher standard than they would for a purely academic exercise. They may have more emotional investment and be keen to express themselves precisely. Here's a story from my own teaching about a time when I realised how motivating writing for an audience can be.

It was the late 1990's and blogs and social media were yet to take off in a big way. I did a project with a small group of learners in a UK private language school who took an afternoon option, 'Improve your Reading and Writing'. They were all weak in these subjects, especially spelling. One of them, Ali, didn't like writing and he certainly didn't like editing his work! Our project was about worldwide festivals and at the end of the week each learner was to write about a festival in his or her country.

Ali approached the task of writing about Eid with his usual cheerfulness but lack of enthusiasm for the written word, especially where accuracy was concerned. However, when I told them their work would be put on a website, something miraculous happened! Ali suddenly became the most demanding learner in the class: "Teacher, is this right?", Teacher, how do you spell...", "Teacher, can you check my work again?". Friday afternoon, end of the lesson and we'd got all the pieces of writing attractively presented and uploaded to the website. Ali grabbed his phone, and started shouting excitedly into it. The other Arabic speakers were laughing and they translated for me: "Dad, Dad, I'm on the Internet. I wrote something. It's in English. Quick, get Mum and have a look!"

I remember being almost tearfully pleased but also angry with myself for all the seemingly pointless writing I'd set my learners before, writing that was for my critical eyes only. Of course, not every student writing task is suitable for public consumption, but it does show how much more motivating writing can be if it is for an audience of more than one, or fulfils a real task. The internet has given us unlimited opportunities for this kind of activity.

Authentic tasks could include:

- writing a genuine letter/email to request information

- writing to a keypal or penfriend[46]

- posting to an online forum, either one specifically linked to the learning programme or a public one

- posting a comment to a blog

- writing a review

- contributing to a wiki on a subject they know about

- writing their own or a class blog

- participating in social networking (Facebook, for example) in English

- writing a class magazine or advice for other students in the institution.

While tasks aimed at authentic audiences are very motivating, they may be beyond some students, but we still need them to write. Besides the usual writing activities (descriptions, compositions, etc., etc.) that teachers often set for learners, a particularly useful medium for some students seems to be the diary. These may be for their own eyes only, or to be given to the teacher as a form of communication or to be given to the teacher for correction. It is probably best to make these optional — some people just don't 'do' diaries. If the learner is writing every day, 'I got up. I had my breakfast. I came to school. I came home. I did my homework', it becomes a pointless chore for student and teacher. Others, however, will open their hearts and be keen to express themselves fully.

Each teacher will need to experiment with different writing tasks for different classes to see what works. By 'works' I mean that learners do the tasks, they write meaningful texts, they use the type and level of language required, they provide and benefit from 'teachable moments' and they learn from editing their work. If the teacher can help to foster a love of writing that would be a tremendous bonus.

How can we help students learn spelling from reading?

Reading is also a type of spelling practice. As people read, they practise decoding words and hopefully get faster and faster at recognising spellings as whole words and need to do less letter-by-letter decoding. For some learners this will translate into more accurate and efficient encoding (writing), while others need a bit of extra help to transfer the skill.

By *reading* here I am talking primarily about silent reading. While asking learners to read aloud in class is probably not a good idea, especially for weak readers *(See B:154)*, listening to the teacher or a recording while they read can be very valuable. If they read and

---

[46] Keypals available at http://www.eslcafe.com/forums/student/viewforum.php?f=13 .

simultaneously hear an accurate rendition in which intonation helps with understanding, learners can follow the text more easily while, at the same time, seeing how the written words translate into spoken ones and vice versa.

Encouraging learners to read

Our first challenge, however, may be getting our learners to read at all. If words felt like your enemy, you might not want to swim around in a sea of them. So how can we encourage reluctant readers?

If we can find topics that truly interest them, they are much more likely to read, especially if there is something that they really want to find out. They may even cope with much more advanced level texts if they are highly motivated. My first literacy student, many years ago, was an English man in his 50s who was a pigeon fancier (a person who keeps and races pigeons). He was supposed to read out loud to me from a graded reader at his diagnosed level — it was a slow and painful process which resulted in him having no idea about what he had read. Towards the end of each lesson, we rebelled and read from an ungraded book he brought along about his passion, pigeons. It was a completely different experience — he was reading it for meaning and was determined to understand, although the language was far more difficult. He asked me questions about the written language and enjoyed answering mine about pigeon fancying.

So books, magazines, websites, or even songs about subjects of interest can be used. In a mixed class interests will vary, but by letting learners choose some of their reading and ensuring that texts are widely engaging, we can keep motivation high.

Authentic texts may be too difficult for low level readers, but there are now plenty of excellent graded readers available for English language learners. Many of these graded readers are based on popular films and learners often feel more motivated to read these if they have seen and liked the film, as they know they will be able to follow the story *(See C:190)*.

Helping learners to notice spelling in reading

As already noted, reading doesn't necessarily lead to good spelling and some people need help to notice spelling in their reading. The first reading of any text should be for meaning, but then it can be revisited to see what helpful spelling patterns are hidden within. If this is not done, Timmis warns, "*there exists a danger that they will 'see through the text' and therefore fail to achieve intake.*" (Timmis & Islam, 2003)

Work already done in class on spelling patterns should help promote noticing, but if not, after studying a text the teacher can prompt: "Can you find any words that follow the pattern we were looking at yesterday?" Alternatively, the teacher can highlight particular words and ask if students know other words with similar spelling, or why they think a word may be spelled in that way. An instruction could be more open: "Choose five words that you would like to learn how to spell."

This work in class on noticing makes certain features of spelling more salient and learners may be more likely to notice similar ones unprompted in their future reading *(See C:191)*.

How can we help learners to improve spelling out of class?

Most classes don't have the luxury of devoting a lot of lesson time to improving spelling, so learners need to work on it outside class too. This is where motivation (or lack of it) really shows. Here are some out-of-class activities that would be very useful:

- Revision of classwork. Review needs to take place within 24 hours to establish new information in the long-term memory, so some short practice activities on words or patterns already learned are very valuable. For example, learners could regroup words learned according to spelling features.

- Extensive writing. We can set writing tasks or point learners in the direction of freer writing opportunities. Frequent short tasks are better for weak spellers, as these are more manageable. Stress that writing is a two-stage process: firstly, they should try to write fluently — to get their ideas down on paper before worrying about the spelling. Then the second stage is to edit their writing, for spelling as well as other writing features.

- Reading. Even just reading for enjoyment, or perhaps *especially* reading for enjoyment, is very useful. The teacher can recommend or provide graded readers on subjects that interest learners. Reading tasks are also helpful, ones in which students first read for meaning and then look for more examples of patterns, letter strings etc.

- Dictionary work. Learners can be tasked to find spellings of words about a specific subject, using bilingual dictionaries if necessary. They can look out for similarities in spellings of related words. They can also use good dictionaries or online sources (e.g. etymonline.org) to find the etymological origins of selected words.

- Learning irregular words with Look, Say, Cover, Write and Check. As we've seen, some words just have to be learned as 'instances'. As long as learners have been taught useful ways of doing this, for example using the chart on page C:207, they should soon be able to do this independently.

- Word games. There are word games that they can play on a computer or with friends and family. Some of these are not only fun, but frighteningly addictive.

- Out and about tasks. Give a photo assignment in which students are asked to take photos of letters of the alphabet seen in the environment. They can be from street signs, billboards, building names, shop signs or even just shapes that resemble letters. These can be used for various activities in the classroom or online.

Summary of Chapter 18

- Learners may need restricted practice with letters, letter strings, words, sentences and/or texts, but we have to ensure these are engaging and varied. Technology provides some enjoyable and challenging activities.

- Freer practice activities are needed to provide 'teachable moments' and practise 'write first, edit later' skills.

- Word processing tools can help produce accurate work but may not always help with improving spelling in the long run. The internet allows us to more easily find an audience for learners' writing.

- If necessary, teachers should encourage reading and prompt learners to notice spelling patterns within texts after they have read them for meaning.

- There are many activities that can be done out of class to reinforce learning, from revising work done in class, learning words and practising strategies to doing longer creative tasks.

Chapter Nineteen:

Correcting Spelling

How can teachers correct spelling most effectively?

How can teachers correct spelling most effectively?

Most teachers would prefer to do less marking and have more time for their family and life. Maybe, in fact, that is what we should be doing. Before we correct spelling errors in our learners' work we should ask ourselves *why* we are doing it. There really is no point in correcting an error unless the learner can learn from it. Teachers should ask themselves whether each error is a learning opportunity, or just something that is wrong. In many situations it is only the learning opportunities that are worth correcting. If we correct the spelling of a word that we have already corrected several times before, this shows us that the correction technique is not working for this word for this student and we need to try something different. It is not a learning opportunity, in other words. However, if a student has tried to spell something but made a mistake because there was an unknown pattern in the word, then we have a good reason to correct it — in other words we are helping the student, not just nagging!

Some options

Imagine you set some writing and when you collect it in, you find some students' work full of spelling mistakes. What should you do? Here are some options. What do you think about each of them?

1. Do not mark the individual errors but tell the students they must work harder to improve their spelling.

2. Write the correct letters above incorrect ones in misspelled words.

3. Ignore the spelling errors and comment on the content only.

4.   Do not mark the errors in the texts, but at the bottom of each page write a list of the most important words (in your opinion) for the student to learn.

5.   Refuse to mark the work. Give it back to the students and tell them to proofread it and correct the spelling before handing it in again.

6.   Attach a few practice activities for each learner that deal with some of the spelling errors he or she has made.

7.   Write the correct spelling above all or some of the misspelled words.

8.   Underline misspellings and ask students to correct them.

9.   Give everyone's work back unmarked and guide them all to check their work carefully in class.

10. Use individual tutorials to guide students to the correct spelling.

11. Note down the most common and important spelling errors across the class and work on these in subsequent lessons.

Evaluating the options

So which would you choose? Almost too many options? That is because there are so many different contexts and learners. Most of them have some validity. Let us look first at the ones that probably do not.

1. Do not mark the individual errors but tell the student to work harder to improve spelling.
There is no point in saying this unless you can do something to help the learner improve. Otherwise you are likely to either find the learner 'forgets' to do future assignments or takes no risks and uses only simple words he or she already knows. Saying this will probably knock the student's confidence without giving any real help.

2. Write the correct letters above incorrect ones in misspelled words.
 It is more beneficial for the learner to see the whole correct word. You can highlight or overwrite the letters in the correct spelling which replace the incorrect ones in the misspelling.

3. Ignore the spelling errors and comment on the content only.
With certain very reluctant writers, they can be encouraged to write a little daily, perhaps in the form of a diary. This just gets them putting pen to paper and it may be inappropriate to correct their errors in spelling or grammar. Here we just want to show them that writing is a means of communication and so a valuable skill in its own right.

However, in most situations, we would be accused of abdicating our responsibility as teachers if we never helped our learners to improve their spelling. I have known native-speaker trainee teachers who have completed university education not knowing (as opposed to just making a slip) when they should use an apostrophe in ***it's*** and when they should not (***its***) or who spell ***a lot*** as one word (~~***alot***~~). They have claimed that nobody has ever corrected them or explained. Have their teachers, whatever the subject, not felt it was their job to correct spelling (seeing it as somebody else's job), were they embarrassed to correct such elementary mistakes from native speakers or were they unsure of the rules themselves?

4. Do not mark the errors in the text, but write a list at the bottom of the page of the most important words (in your opinion) for the student to learn.
This is a useful approach as long as you have taught your learners how to learn spellings. And you need to consider if you are going to test these. With motivated and mature students this should not be necessary — they should recognise that you have just pointed them in the right direction. However, when it comes to learning many of us are not as mature and independent as we should be! Especially if we are used to the teacher checking everything we are asked to do. So if you ask a learner to learn some spellings, he or she may expect you to check these — to give a test on them. If you think this is the case, work out beforehand if you will have time to do this.

5. Refuse to mark the work. Give it back to the students and tell them to proofread it and correct the spelling before handing it in again.
This very much depends on the context and the learner. It is a response that very occasionally may be appropriate if you have received some work from a student who usually spells well, but has made many errors in this piece of work because he or she has not given it enough attention. But you need to be sure the errors are not due to the learner risk-taking in terms of language. We certainly would not want to be dismissive about this. If you do give the work back to be proof-read, you could suggest that the student 'forgot' to proofread it!

6. Attach a few practice activities for the learners that deal with some of the spelling errors they have made.
It is very useful for the teacher to have a bank of such activities ready to use in this situation. However, the 'practice' activities must include some kind of input ensuring that the learner knows the pattern or has the strategy. Otherwise it is just a test of something that you already know the learner doesn't know! And don't forget you'll need to mark it or give the key.

7. Write the correct spelling above all or some of the misspelled words.
This is perhaps the most common kind of feedback. But is it really feedback? A learner who is a bit lacking in motivation, or just busy, may look at the returned assignment, take a mental note of how many spelling errors were marked and 'file' the paper, never looking at it again. More motivated students may learn from these corrections however. So this is another case where we need to know our students well. If in doubt, give a short task along with the corrections.

The other important point here is the "all or some". The answer partly depends on how many errors there are in the piece of work and what its purpose is. If it is full of errors, it probably means the task was too difficult for the learner and there is little point in discouraging him or her by marking every error. However, if this is a first draft, especially if it is for a real task, such as a letter that will be sent to a company, then it may be necessary to correct everything. The student can then copy your corrections, but would it not be better if thinking was required as well?

Just marking a selection of errors is often more appropriate and more encouraging. Limiting yourself to perhaps five or six spelling corrections in one piece of writing is probably more effective than marking many. It is more manageable for learners and it forces you, the teacher, to really consider carefully which ones you should choose. This may depend on factors such as whether:

- the misspelling makes it unclear or confusing for the reader;

- it involves a spelling pattern recently studied;

- this is a word the learner is likely to need again soon;

- you have corrected this error several times before (if so, it is not worth correcting it again — some other measure is needed).

If you decide to just correct a few spelling errors, learners should be aware of this, especially if they are going to redraft it. Otherwise they may think everything else was correct and copy all the other errors (thus reinforcing them).

8. Underline misspellings and ask students to correct them.
Here we see the learners doing more work and the teacher 'spoonfeeding' less. If you think your learners are able to correct their own spelling, this is an effective method as it involves some deeper mental processing and therefore more likelihood of remembering. However, without strategies or resources, learners may not be able to correct the words themselves. Underlining the letters that are wrong may help, but sometimes this becomes very complicated if, for example there are missing or transposed letters. A more effective way is to write the word as the student has written it but with gaps for the letters that are wrong or missing. So for example, if a learner writes *wich*, you write *w _ ich* above it. Or for *bueatyfull*, you write *b _ _ _ t _ ful*. This means that students should not get wrong what they have previously got right. And it also allows them to search for a spelling in an electronic dictionary.

9. Give everyone's work back unmarked and guide them all to check their work carefully in class.
For example, you could ask "Do we change a base word before we add a prefix?" (no) "OK, so check all your words that have prefixes — have you added them to the whole word?"

This is a very useful strategy. Even before you collect work from a group, ask them to check their own writing (or each other's if you think it is appropriate). Guide them with prompts to correct the most common types of spelling errors. At a low level this could involve giving out a list of the 100 most common words for them to check against. Or maybe you have encouraged them to keep a list of their most common errors that they can consult. Or it could be more direct questions, "Have you got any nouns or verbs that end in *y*, if you've added *s* what changes do you need to make?". It is very valuable for learners to take this responsibility for 'surface' editing themselves as it fosters independence. It also frees the teacher up to focus on more productive correction.

10. Use individual tutorials to guide students to the correct spelling.

This is possibly the ideal situation, but a luxury that many teachers do not have. If individual tutorials happen, they often need to focus on other matters too. Teaching a student one-to-one is perfect as you can spend as little or as much time as you see fit on each item that is difficult for him or her.

11. Note down the most common and important spelling errors across the class and work on these in subsequent lessons.

This is also an excellent strategy if a significant proportion of the class have spelling difficulties. The spelling 'syllabus' is then determined by these needs.

Summary of Chapter 19

- There are many different ways to correct spelling. Which to use depends on the context and the particular aim and task.

- Any corrections should be ones that students can learn from.

- Correction techniques which make the learner think and perform some other task seem to be the most effective.

Chapter Twenty:

Testing Spelling

Why do teachers give spelling tests?

What are the dangers of spelling tests?

What's the difference between testing and teaching?

How should we test spelling?

What do we need to consider for different types of tests:

      diagnostic tests?

      progress tests?

      on-going assessment tasks?

The words **spelling** and **test** form a strong collocation. What do the words 'spelling test' mean to you? They strike fear into some people, boredom in others and smugness in those who are confident spellers. But probably the most widespread opinion is that they are a necessary evil.

Why do teachers give spelling tests?

The impetus to test can come from various sources.

Often the teachers themselves decide to give regular tests. Some give spelling tests just because that's what teachers do, others have more considered reasons. They may test to:

- find out what students need to know before teaching them (diagnostic test)

- find out whether students have learned something that has been taught (words, patterns, strategies) or learned a prescribed list of words (progress tests)

- motivate them to study at home
- find out the general level of learners' spelling at the end of a course (achievement tests)

- provide data for a report

- provide or prepare for a fun activity (such as a spelling bee).

Sometimes it is the institution or department which insists on testing. They want to ensure consistency and measurable standards throughout the organisation. Or they just believe it is the right thing to do.

When teaching adults in particular, the request for tests may come from the students themselves, especially if they are from a culture where tests are the norm. Some say they *need* tests to make them study, some like to measure their progress and some who spell well just enjoy doing better than the others in the group! I have known students ask for daily spelling tests and I have known others who always seem to be off sick on the day of the test.

Pressure to test may also come from parents, sponsors, politicians and members of the public who feel it is a necessary measure of progress. This is one of many headlines on the subject that I've read recently:

Outrage at banning spelling tests

This one is from The Washington Post and the article goes on to complain that teachers have stopped giving spelling tests because they feel they are getting a lot of 'Friday spellers', those who do well on the end-of-week test but can't apply the knowledge to their writing. The commentator dismisses this reason as political correctness and goes on to assume that spelling will no longer be taught as it will not be tested. (Rochester, 2010) This confusion between teaching and testing is a widespread one. There are hundreds of similar articles.

What are the dangers of spelling tests?

Learn > Test > Forget

These so-called 'Friday spellers' are a genuine problem though. Many people can 'learn' the spelling of about 10 words just long enough for a test the next day, but not for the longer term. When the test is over, they clear out their minds for the next lot of words to be learned.

I recently received an email from a very worried mother whose son was diagnosed as having a very poor working memory although he was bright. Every night of the week the boy and his mother would work on words for his spelling test on Friday. This dominated their evenings and the boy hated it. His reward was usually getting 5/5 on the Friday spelling test. Fantastic! Result! But then a few days later he'd forgotten them all. What a waste of time and energy! He could have been reading and enjoying words rather than stressing over them for a test.

Furthermore, if the words given are random, or seem to be, then learners may be unable to make links to help long-term memorisation. Often children are given words to learn which derive from word lists that comprise the most frequent words. The Dolch Spelling List which was prepared in 1936 from the most common words in children's literature in still in use today, as is Schonell's Essential Spelling List (1932).

It is also relatively easy to write these words individually when there are no other cognitive demands, but much more challenging to spell the words correctly in freer writing. Here is a typical comment from an anonymous teacher on a forum:

> *I'm really frustrated with spelling. Even my highest readers cannot spell when they write. They have good knowledge of phonics, they get 100 % on their spelling tests, but they don't seem to make the connection between the words they memorize and the words they use during writing.*

Elsewhere, a primary teacher writes on his blog:

> *This year, for the first time ever, I did not give weekly spelling tests to my students. After giving the students one spelling assessment at the beginning of the year, I taught brief spelling minilessons throughout the year based on the words I saw the students frequently misspelling in their writing. … Just recently, I gave the students an end-of-year spelling assessment. When I compared their growth to that of past classes, **I found that the students made the same amount of growth as they had in previous years**, when I had done similar minilessons but had also employed the weekly tests. So I managed to get rid of the weekly spelling tests (and the dreaded spelling homework!), saved some class time in the process (which we used to do more actual reading and writing), and got the same exact results as before. Can someone remind me again why spelling tests exist?*

(Pullen, 2008)

Testing one set of words and then moving onto another set without reviewing previous sets is very unlikely to be effective. Once is just not enough in language teaching.

Learn > Forget > Test

We have been looking at the inability to carry over correctly learned spelling into written work, but also what about those who don't even do well on the tests, let alone subsequent writing? Poor spellers can become very demotivated if they really struggle with spelling and feel they 'fail' every week. They may have put in just as much work or possibly considerably more, and yet fail to get a good result. Fear of failure can lead to stress and the learner may perform less successfully anyway. They might have been given too many words to learn or the words may be too difficult for the stage they are at. If, for example, learners don't know the meanings of the words or they seem irrelevant they won't be able to make links to help them learn. We can send learners away with a set of words to learn but they may not know how to learn them, or they may have just one strategy that is not appropriate for all words.

Other dangers of testing

It is not always clear exactly *what* is being tested. Is it purely spelling, or is listening or grammar also involved? For example, a dictation used as a test is not just a spelling test unless students have already made themselves very familiar with the text; it is also a listening, vocabulary and grammar test. That doesn't necessarily make it a bad test, but it makes it a bad spelling test.

And finally, tests could actually make people's spelling worse! There have long been discussions about whether seeing wrong spellings, for example in editing or multiple choice activities, is dangerous. It was avoided for many years as it was thought that these misspellings might stick in learners' memories. Although some research has since suggested that isn't the case, and these types of activities have become very common, I have worries about this as I know it's bad for *me* to see these deliberate errors. There are words that I never had a problem with before I started researching spelling and trying out different activities. For example, I always wrote the word **separately** automatically without thinking about whether the second vowel was ***a*** or ***e***. Seeing so many activities in which I had to choose between **separately** and ~~**seperately**~~ planted a seed of doubt in my mind and now I have to use a mnemonic to remember the correct spelling! The visual sense is so strong in many people that seeing two alternatives may make them both look right. (That, incidentally, is why I ~~strikethrough~~ deliberate misspellings in this book — to disrupt the visual spelling pattern. I hope it works!)

What's the difference between testing and teaching?

Another worry is inadvertent testing. Looking through spelling books and websites, the majority of the activities seem to be testing, although they claim they are teaching or providing practice.

Teaching happens when learners can find out the right answer even if they did not know it before. Testing relies on their memory. There is room for both, of course, but we should be aware that 'failing' or doing badly in a test that you have not had a chance to study for is not good for your self-esteem, especially when others in the class are glorying in their success!

So for each learning objective we should first allow students to learn by discovering. They should be able to use the material, their minds and strategies they have learned to find answers. Teaching will probably also include some telling and demonstrating. Testing can come *after* this to check that learning has taken place.

Some teachers may prefer a test, teach, test approach to ascertain the needs of the learners before teaching. If this is the case, the purpose of the first test should be made clear to the learners and the teacher should be careful not to praise those who have done well, as by implication it suggests that the others have failed in a sense.

How should we test spelling?

Before setting any spelling test, teachers should ask themselves:

- Why am I doing this?

- What do I want to find out?

- Will the test give me that information?

- Is the test manageable and relevant for all the learners?

- Do my learners have the skills to prepare for the test?

- Are any other skills necessary to be able to succeed at the test?

- What's the best way to test this particular target language or skill?

- How can I make sure they remember the target language or skill after the test?

What do we need to consider for different types of tests?

To be sure about why we are testing and what we want to find out, we can consider three types of assessment: diagnostic tests, progress tests and on-going assessment. The notes below will give suggestions about how they can best be carried out.

Diagnostic Testing

Diagnostic testing at the beginning of a course is, in fact, very important because it informs teachers about needs. A diagnostic test doesn't have to just be a test of which words students know and which they don't. We can also test strategies and abilities to cope with the different systems of English spelling. In the table on the next page are some areas we may want to test and, for each, one possible way to do this. There is also a diagnostic test in Part C *(See C:259)*.

Of course you could also just set learners some writing and see what their spelling difficulties are. Two problems with this: one is that they may just avoid using words that are difficult to spell and the other is that it doesn't give you very precise information about why they have made an error.

Another useful tactic is to interview learners about how they learn words and see if they can think of any alternative ways. This is not always feasible with a large class, however.

To test whether learners can:	How?
write their own personal details accurately, as needed on a form, (particularly important for ESOL/ESL learners)	The learner fills in a form with certain information like nationality, job title, address (if in an English-speaking country). The teacher checks this (if necessary by asking the learners to bring in documentation).
spell common words that have unpredictable spelling	A gapped dictation. The student reads a short simple text in which some common words are deleted. The teacher reads the full text slowly, repeating as necessary, while the learner fills in the words.
discriminate between different sounds	The teacher gives some pictures of keywords that the student knows which contain the sounds to be tested (e.g. all short vowels). Then other words containing the same sounds are given orally, without meaning, and the student matches them to keywords that contain the same sound.
match sounds to letters	Some words which are phonetically regular are dictated to the student. They are not in sentences and no meaning is given. The student is told that they are regular.
use some common letter strings	One example word for each of several common letter strings is given. The learner is asked to give more words containing the same string.
make guesses about a spelling based on the spelling of other similar words	The learner sees 15 words in no particular order, three from each of five word families. Below these are five new words, one from each family, with some letters gapped. The learner finds similar words from the list and completes the words by making guesses about the spelling. The new words can be in sentences to help with meaning.
apply morphemic knowledge to build up words	Some word sums are given, e.g. *run* + *ing* = *running*, *un* + *necessary* = *unnecessary*. The learner 'solves' some more word sums, by referring to the completed ones.
apply etymological knowledge to make guesses about spelling	Learners are given some etymological information, such as 'Some technical or academic words from Greek which are about science have the letters *ch* to make the /k/ sound. They never have the letter *k*.' Then they fill in *ch* or *k* in some words below, by deciding if they are likely to fall into this category of technical or academic Greek words.
apply graphemic knowledge	Learners are shown some words that contain strong graphemic patterns, such as *q* followed by *u*, or words ending in *ve* preceded by short vowel sound. Then they complete sentences about these patterns: *The letter q is always followed by … . English words never end in … .*
use a dictionary or spell-checker	Learners are asked to write a short text on an appropriate subject or they are given a short dictation. They write on every second line and underline any spellings they are not sure about. They are given a dictionary and/or a spell-checker and asked to use this to check their spelling. They write any corrections clearly above the original spelling.

Progress Testing

If you feel the need to test your learners on words learned (or someone else feels you should), I would suggest the following:

- Be sure of your aim and how you will use the results.

- Make sure the words are related in some way (topic, spelling pattern, lexically, morphologically, etc.).

- Introduce the words within texts or use words that have arisen from classwork.

- Include words from previous tests. Warn learners that you will do this but do not tell them in advance which 'old' words will be tested.

- Consider letting learners choose the words they are tested on from the ones given (they each choose, say, three words and these are all added together for the test). You get to choose some too.

- Test strategies as well as knowledge.

- Teach learners strategies for learning words and let them share and evaluate the ones they use.

- During the test, give words in sentences. Learners write the whole sentence. Alternatively, with a stronger group, say the word and they have to write the word in a sentence they make themselves. To make it more challenging, give them a topic for the sentence during the test so they can't just learn a complete sentence by heart.

- Avoid tests which deliberately present learners with wrong spellings.

- Differentiate between learners of different abilities. Learners who struggle are not expected to get 100%, but they are expected to do at least as well as they did on the previous test, aiming for some improvement. If possible, differentiate the test itself, so that it's easier for weaker learners and more challenging for stronger ones. Words could have some given letters for weaker students.

- Encourage learners to keep progress charts of their spelling scores *(See C:263)*.

On-going Assessment

Spelling can also be assessed within writing, using a set of rubrics. Set writing tasks that arise from other classwork, learners' interests, or target language. If you are worried that learners will stick to easy words, give more challenging topics or specify some words that must be used.

Explain to learners that they should write their first draft focussing on the content — their aim is just to express what they really want to say. If they don't know a spelling they should guess the word and highlight it. When they have finished, they read what they have written and highlight any other words that they are not sure about. They then use the strategies taught and discussed to help them find the correct spelling of these words and write them above the highlighted word.

They rewrite the text as a second draft, including the corrected spellings. They hand in both drafts.

Explain to them that they are not assessed on the original spelling in the first draft, but on how well they corrected it and the accuracy of the final draft. This encourages them to stretch themselves. Show them and explain the rubric on page 265 that you will use. Of course there are plenty of other writing criteria to use, these are just concerned with spelling.

Summary of Chapter 20

- A teacher who decides to give spelling tests should be clear about the aim of them.

- Some downsides of testing spelling are that many students forget the words they have learned when the test is over (or even before the test!); they can write the words in isolation but not within sentences; proficiency in other skills may affect the test result and seeing misspelled words in multiple-choice tests may damage the learner's visual memory of those words.

- Teachers should make sure that they are not merely testing when they mean to be teaching or providing practice.

- Diagnostic tests tell us what learners need to study and these can test strategies as well as patterns.

- Progress tests check that students have learned what has been taught in class. There are many options and variations on the traditional spelling test and they should certainly include words from previous learning.

- On-going assessment can usefully evaluate learners' editing skills as these involve many other strategies and encourage students to try out words they are unsure of.

Summary of Part B

The second part of the book suggests a fresh approach to solving the problems we encountered in Part A. There are several recurring principles in this approach.

Learners should be encouraged to think hard about spelling when they are studying it to help the information to work its way into the long-term memory.

The ultimate aim is accurate automaticity.

An eclectic, multi-dimensional approach is needed to provide appropriate routes to learning for different learners and for different features of spelling. This should include visual, auditory, kinaesthetic and cognitive activities. Visual methods are particularly useful for irregularly spelled words. The phonological route is often the least reliable for English language learners.

A positive attitude to English spelling should be fostered so learners see it as manageable.

The self-esteem of weak spellers needs to be nurtured to get them into the right frame of mind for learning. Correction needs to be sensitive and useful rather than nagging.

Spelling activities have traditionally been rather dull and we need to find ways to make them more engaging for a wide range of learners.

We should take care not to confuse learners where there was previously no confusion. We can avoid teaching homophones together and asking students to look at misspellings.

Learners need a good range of spelling strategies as well as a knowledge of spelling patterns. Strategies are needed for discovering, researching, recording, learning, practising and editing.

Learning some patterns and systems lightens the load as students have fewer words to learn visually.

Technology offers some useful, engaging and demanding opportunities as well as some challenges for the would-be speller. Some training may be needed to help learners make the most of these tools.

We should encourage learners to write first (as fluently and communicatively as they can) and then spend time editing their work carefully. Some guidance may be needed.

Reading helps most people recognise whether words they spell are correct or not, but for some learners spelling is not sufficiently acquired through reading and they need some help seeing patterns within reading texts.

Spelling tests are very common but not always effective. Teachers should be very sure of the purpose of any test they give and should evaluate its usefulness. A clear distinction should be made between teaching and testing.

PART C
Activities and Resources

PART C
Activities and Resources

Introduction and notes

This part of the book offers a toolkit of possibilities for implementing the approach outlined in Part B. There are six chapters:

- Chapter 21 contains some activities that are useful for general spelling improvement, rather than for specific patterns or strategies.

- Some of the games and puzzles in Chapter 22 are for classwork and others can be used for homework.

- Many of the strategies for learning spellings that have been discussed in Part B are included in Chapter 23.

- Likewise, activities to discover and practise many of the patterns that have been shown to cause problems for learners are described in Chapter 24.

- Chapter 25 gives specific means to encourage learners to edit their work and use reference tools well.

- The chapter on testing and assessment (26) gives a sample diagnostic test, progress charts for regular tests and rubrics for spelling assessment from writing.

Together the chapters form bank of tools, techniques and activities for teachers to use as they are or adapt to their teaching context.

The aim of each activity or technique is given before the description. Every activity is an illustration of the approach suggested in this book; it has a clear purpose — nothing is included just because that's how it's always been done. That is not to say the baby has been thrown out with the bathwater — here you will find adaptations of old favourites, such as dictations and spelling tests, alongside newer multi-sensory activities. These are cross-referenced with ideas from the rest of the book, so teachers can see the thinking behind each activity.

Approximate level is indicated for each activity by four circles, representing language levels Elementary, Pre-Intermediate, Intermediate, and Upper Intermediate. The levels for which each activity may be suitable are shaded. So, ⬤⬤⬤⬤ suggests an activity is appropriate for Pre-intermediate to Upper Intermediate learners, but not Elementary.

Timings are not given as there are so many variations and you are much more likely to be able to accurately assess how long an activity will take with your learners than I can. Many of the activities can be used as warmers or fillers. Others can be set for homework.

Where appropriate there are photocopiable worksheets. Some of these are available for download in colour or a different size. There are also audio recordings for many of the activities available for download. These can all be found on The Spelling Blog at **http://thespellingblog.blogspot.com**

Teachers will probably want to adapt the activities for their own context. Notes about variations are given where appropriate. Some activities may spark an idea, but the text may not be suitable for your learners — feel free to adapt it. Photocopiable material may be used freely in class. If you adapt it, please acknowledge this book with wording such as *"Adapted from an idea by Johanna Stirling, Teaching Spelling to English Language Learners, page x."* Thank you.

Chapter Twenty-One

General Spelling Improvement

21.1 Spelling Discussion ○○○○○

Aim: To share ideas about the importance of accurate spelling and ways to improve. *(See A:Chapters 1-8)*

Materials needed: Worksheet (optional)

Activity: Learners discuss the questions on the worksheet in pairs or groups and then with the whole class.

Variations: Just use some of the questions if you prefer. With a higher level group use more challenging words in question 4.

Key and notes:
1. Try to bring out the points that accurate spelling is needed for exams, job applications, 'public' writing, email addresses and URLs, computer games, and anywhere where you want to impress! If learners say spelling is not important because of spell-checkers, point out that spell-checkers can't catch homophones and don't always offer the word that you want.
2. Learners will have different ideas. Reassure them that you can help them with these problems over the course.
3. Assure them that English is not totally irregular and is in fact largely regular, but it is complex and English spelling does not always relate to sound.
4. You could do the first one as an example or prompt learners if they don't know what to say about the words.
   - *milk* is spelled as it sounds. A short vowel is often followed by two consonants.
   - *chef* is a French word and so we write it with a *ch* although it is pronounced /ʃ/.
   - *queen* contains a *u* because *q* is always followed by a *u* in native English words.
   - *unnaturally* has a double *n* because we add the whole prefix to the whole word. We usually drop a silent final *e* before a vowel suffix (*-al*) but we usually add consonant suffixes, like *-ly* to the whole word, hence the double *l*.
   - *sign* contains a silent *g* to show that *sign* is in the same word family as *signature* and *signal* as well as other words with silent *g* such as *assignment* and *design*.
5. Encourage sharing of ideas.

Worksheet 21.1: *Spelling Discussion*

1. Why is accurate spelling important? Make a list of reasons.

2. What is difficult about English spelling?

3. Do you think English spelling is totally irregular?

4. Try to explain the reasons for the spelling of these words:

   - *milk*

   - *chef*

   - *queen*

   - *unnaturally*

   - *sign*

5. How do you learn new spellings? Which way(s) do you find most effective? Find out how other people learn.

21.2 Spelling Box ⬭⬭⬭⬭

Aim: To recycle spelling studied in class *(See A:86).*

Materials needed: A box (the lid of a photocopier paper box works well) and some paper or card cut into small rectangles.

Activity: Whenever you teach a new word in class, write it clearly on a piece of card and put it in the box. This acts as a record of words studied and there are plenty of activities you can do with the cards to recycle learning:

A. Deal out the words among the learners. They test their partners on the spelling of the words.

B. Deal out the words among the learners. They walk around the class asking other people to spell the words. If the other student gets it right, he or she takes the card and moves on. Students keep working with different people. There are no winners or losers and the length of time is up to you.

C. Give each group of two or three learners a few words (3 or 4). They memorise the words and spelling before you take the words away again. They work together to write a little story or dialogue including their words. They read out their story and just say "bleep" when they get to the words they used from the box. The other students guess the word and spell it.

D. Give each pair up to five words. They work together to write gapped sentences — the words from the box are just represented by one dash for each letter. They give their sentences to another pair to solve.

E. Play hangman. One learner comes to the front of the class and picks a word from the box. He or she draws a dash on the board for each letter of the word. The others guess the letters. If they are right the letter is added to the word. If not, one section of the hangman is drawn. If the final bar is added the class lose. Use a different image if you prefer.

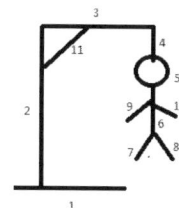

F. When you have a lot of words in the box, divide them out between pairs of students. They arrange the words into groups on the table in front of them. Give them some prompts (e.g. all the words with double letters, all the words that you think come from French). Collect and redistribute the words. Learners repeat the activity, but they decide the groupings themselves. Then learners walk around the class trying to identify each others' grouping criteria.

21.3 Did You Notice?   ⬭⬭⬭⬭

Aim: To encourage learners to notice common spelling patterns in texts *(See B:139)*.

Materials and preparation needed: One worksheet per student, folded along horizontal line, so only Part A is visible. You will need to find the answers to as many of the questions as possible before the lesson as they may vary in different parts of the world. Also before students come into the classroom, change something about the room (e.g. move a poster).

Activity:
1. When learners come into the classroom, ask them what has changed in the room.

2. Tell them you are going to give them a quiz to see how observant they are. Give out the folded worksheet. Learners do the quiz in Part A alone or in pairs. Conduct feedback.

3. Check that learners know what vowels, consonants, 'sticks' and 'tails' are. They open the worksheet and have to find the answers in Part B by referring to the questions in the Part A text. Learners work alone. Make it a race if you like, or set a time limit.

Variations: Make it non-competitive if you think weak spellers will get too stressed.
If you have not introduced them to the concepts of 'sticks' and 'tails' in word shapes, remove the last two questions.
If time, have pairs of learners write observation questions for each other. They can follow the same procedure as the worksheet — general questions and then spelling questions. They must find the answers themselves before passing the quiz to another group.

Key: Part B
1. Words with double letters: ***usually*, *traffic*, *see*, *green*, *yellow*, *door***.
2. Words beginning with two consonants: ***what*, *the*, *there*, *traffic*, *which*, *green*, *shape*, *stop*, *front*, *this***.
3. Three letter CVC words: ***how*, *did*, *sun*, *set*, *red*, *can***
4. Longest word: ***paperclips***
5. Number of *e*s: 26
6.

igh	ant	ly	wh	th	sh
lights	*observant*	*usually*	*which* *what*	*the* *there* *this*	*shape*

7. Most sticks: ***traffic*, *lights*, *building***
8. Most tails: ***paperclips***

188

Worksheet: 21.3   *Did You Notice?*

A . *Can you answer the questions?*

How observant are you?

What time did the sun set yesterday?
How many sides are there usually on a pencil?
On traffic lights which colours do you see after green? Red or yellow?
What shape is a Stop sign?
Can you describe the front door of this building?
How many bends do paperclips have?

--fold--

B. *Look at the text in the box above (the title and the questions). Can you find...*

1.   ... 6 different words with double letters?_____   _____   _____

        _____   _____   _____

2.   ... 10 different words that begin with 2 consonants? _____   _____

        _____   _____   _____   _____

        _____   _____   _____   _____

3.   ... 6 three-letter words made of a consonant, vowel and consonant (in that order)?

        _____   _____   _____   _____   _____   _____

4.   ... the longest word? _____

5.   ... the number of 'e's in the text? _____

6.   ... different words which contain these common letter strings:

igh	ant	ly	wh	th	sh

7.   ... the 3 words with the most 'sticks'? _____   _____   _____

8.   ... the word with the most 'tails'? _____

21.4 Cliffhanger Reading

Aim: To encourage learners to read out of class. *(See B:161)*

Materials needed: Graded readers or authentic texts at the learners' level.

Activity: Read a short passage aloud to the learners from the graded reader or text. Choose an exciting bit, but stop just before they find out what happens. Tell them where they can get hold of the book if they want to continue reading it.

Variations: The text could be a joke (stop before the punchline), a news story (stop before the end, when they are hooked), a sports commentary, or anything your learners are likely to be interested in. You could photocopy the part you read so they can follow along with your reading.

21.5 World Cup Vowels   ⬭⬭⬭⬭

Aim: To encourage learners to notice vowels in words. *(See B:139, B:131)*

Materials needed: One Worksheet A and B for each student. There are coloured versions of these available for download at The Spelling Blog: http://thespellingblog.blogspot.com

Activity:

1. Write these football scores on the board. Learners discuss whether they think they are likely scores.

Brazil 2 — 5 South Africa

Argentina 4 — 3 Greece

USA 0 — 4 Algeria

   Overwrite the vowels in the country names in a different colour. Ask why the games might have been given those scores. (Because that is the number of vowels in each country name.) Think of two other matches that could be played in a World Cup. What are the 'scores' (from the number of vowels in the country names)?

2. Give out the worksheet. Learners look at Part A only. They write in the 'scores' in Part A. Give a time limit — they do as many as they can. Check the 'scores'.

3. Learners choose the countries that they want to be able to spell. They learn these. They pay particular attention to the vowels.

4. Learners put away Part A and any notes they have made with the spelling on. Give out Part B. They find the countries they learned and fill in the vowels. Check answers.

Key: A.

South Africa	5	4	Uruguay
Mexico	3	2	France
Argentina	4	4	Nigeria
South Korea	5	3	Greece
England	2	4	Algeria
USA	2	4	Slovenia
Germany	2	5	Australia
Serbia	3	2	Ghana
Netherlands	3	2	Denmark
Japan	2	4	Cameroon
Italy	2	4	Paraguay
New Zealand	4	4	Slovakia
Brazil	2	4	North Korea
Ivory Coast	4	3	Portugal
Spain	2	3	Switzerland
Honduras	3	2	Chile

Worksheet 21.5   *World Cup Vowels*

Part A: *What are the scores? Count the vowels.*

Country	Score	Country	Score
South Africa	_	Uruguay	_
Mexico	_	France	_
Argentina	_	Nigeria	_
South Korea	_	Greece	_
England	_	Algeria	_
USA	_	Slovenia	_
Germany	_	Australia	_
Serbia	_	Ghana	_
Netherlands	_	Denmark	_
Japan	_	Cameroon	_
Italy	_	Paraguay	_
New Zealand	_	Slovakia	_
Brazil	_	North Korea	_
Ivory Coast	_	Portugal	_
Spain	_	Switzerland	_
Honduras	_	Chile	_

Part B: *Fill in the vowels.*

S_ _th fr_c_	N_rth K_r_ _	N_w Z_ _l_nd	S_ _th K_r_
M_x_c_	N_g_r_ _	lg_r_ _	_ _str_l_ _
_r_g_ _y	G_rm_ny	S_ _	S_rb_ _
Fr_nc_	Gr_ _c_	Sl_v_n_ _	Gh_n_
N_th_rl_nds	_t_ly	Br_z_l	Sp_ _n
D_nm_rk	P_r_g_ _y	_rg_nt_n_	Sw_ _tz_rl_nd
J_p_n	_ngl_nd	_v_ry C_ _st	H_ nd_r_s
C_m_r_ _n	Sl_v_k_ _	P_rt_g_l	Ch_l_

192

21.6   Mapping Word Families   ○○○◉

Aim: To help learners to see helpful links between words. *(See A:72)*

Materials needed: One worksheet per student. Audio recording of the text available for free download from The Spelling Blog: http://thespellingblog.blogspot.com (optional).

Activity:

1. Write "It's a fake!" on the board. Tell learners they are going to read a short text with this title. What do they think it will be about? Write some ideas they give on the board.

2. Give out the text. Learners read alone and see which are right. Check answers. Discuss any forgeries or fakes that they know about.

3. Learners find all the words containing the letters *s-i-g-n*. They decide what meaning they have in common.

4. Read the text aloud to the class and learners put the eight words into two groups according to whether the *g* is pronounced or not.

5. Give them the chart which groups the words by meaning, not sound. They fill in the gaps with the words from the text.

6. Give other roots. They try to make their own charts. Example roots: *sci, form, rupt, dict*. These could be displayed on the wall and added to as more words are discovered.

Key: The eight words in the text are: *sign designer*, *signature*, *signify*, *insignificant*, *signal*, *resign*, *significantly*. The full chart is on page 72.

Worksheet 21.6: *Mapping Word Families*

It's a fake!

Can you spot a fake from the genuine article? Forgers are at work on everything from the money in your wallet to the goods you buy in the stores. The sign in the shop window may be a well-known brand but beware - that designer watch could be a copy, the signature on a painting may be a forgery, and the change you get in return for your purchase might signify a loss if you are given a counterfeit note.

How to tell the difference between a quality item and a cheap copy
Look for an imperfect finish, poor workmanship or some apparently insignificant fault which might signal that you are holding an imitation. So check before you buy or you may have to resign yourself to being another victim of a significantly increasing crime around the world.

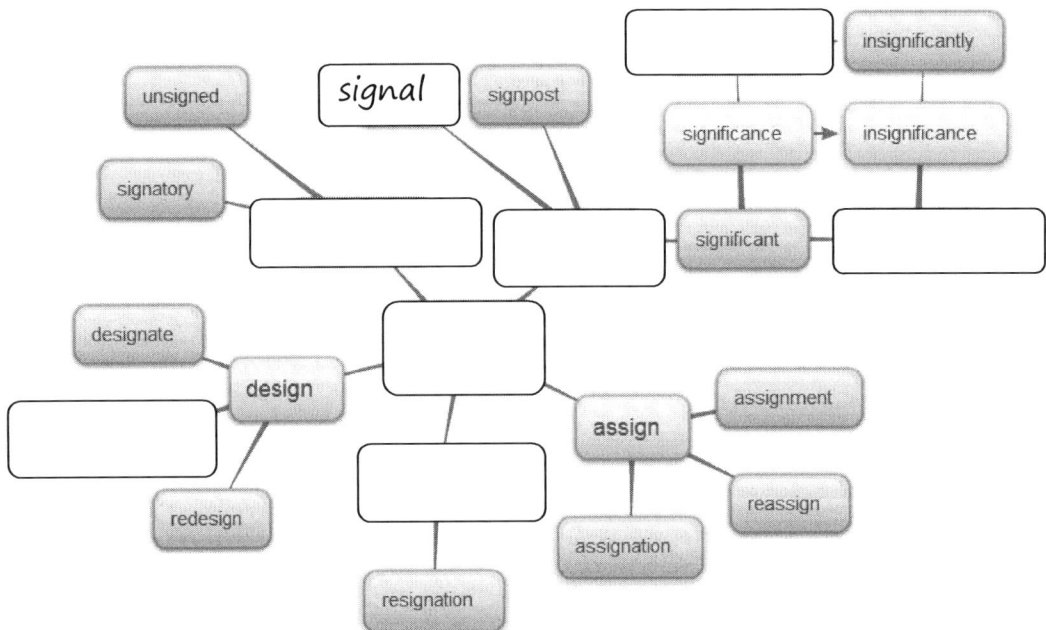

---

signal

unsigned

signpost

signatory

insignificantly

significance → insignificance

significant

designate

design

assign

assignment

redesign

assignation

reassign

resignation

PHOTOCOPIABLE ©Johanna Stirling 2011. Teaching Spelling to English Language Learners

21.7 Lexical Links

Aim: To help learners recognise semantic links between similarly spelled words. *(See A:71)*

Materials needed: One worksheet per student.

Activity:

1. Give a worksheet to each learner. In pairs, they divide the 18 words in the Wordle into four groups according to similar spelling and meaning (not sound). They write the words in the diagrams.

2. In the middle of each diagram, learners write a word, symbol or picture of what links the words in meaning.

3. Check answers.

Key:
One, *once*, *lonely*, *only*, *none*, *alone* — all related to ONE;
Two, *twenty*, *twice*, *twelve*, *twin*, *between* — all related to TWO;
Heard, *hear*, *ear* — all related to SOUND;
Where, *there*, *here* — all related to PLACE.

Worksheet 21.7:　　*Lexical Links*

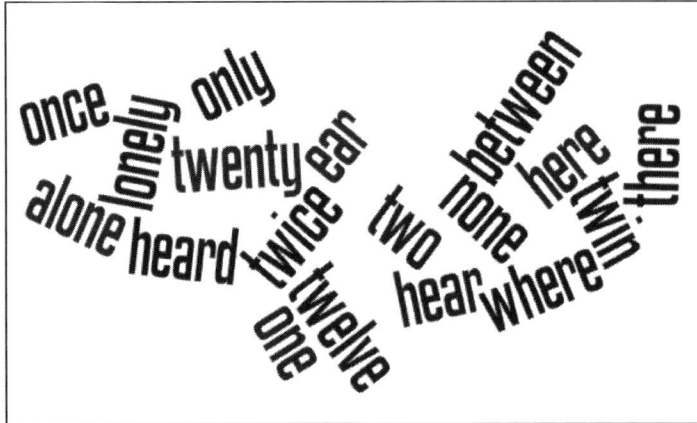

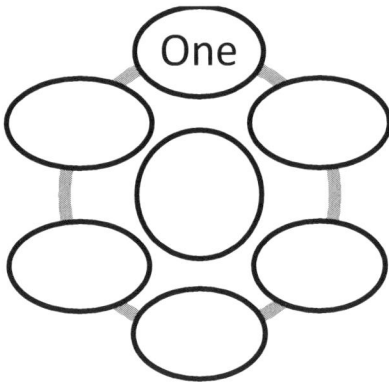

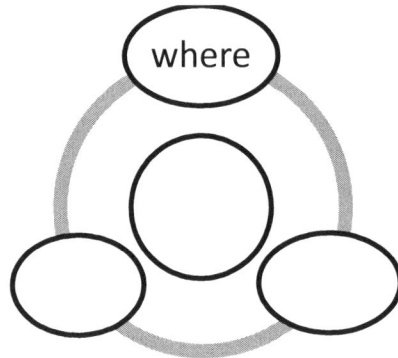

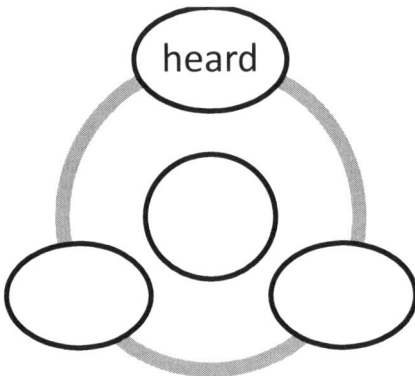

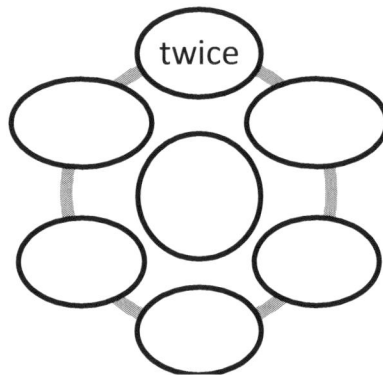

once only lonely twenty alone heard twice ear between none here twin there two hear where one twelve

One

where

heard

twice

21.8 Learn From Your Mistakes ⬭⬭⬭⬭

Aim: To help learners remember corrections. *(See B:165)*

Activity:
1. Ask learners what kind of spelling mistakes they think people who speak their language often make when writing English.

2. Draw a table like the one below on the board. Choose a common mistake made by your learners. Write it in a sentence in the first column and elicit the correction. Draw a line through the error and write the correction in the next column. Overwrite the letter that was wrong with a different colour pen. Then ask if anyone can think of a good way to remember the correct spelling. If they do, write it in the last column (you need to have an answer ready, in case they don't think of one!). Remind them they can think of the sound, other similar words, a mnemonic, etc. Here's an example:

I wrote this	I should have written this	A way to remember
I live in a ~~beautifull~~ village in the mountains	beautiful	When you hear 'full' on the end of an adjective, just write one 'l' (because it's not the full word 'full', just a suffix): like careful, awful, wonderful, hopeful

3. Learners make similar tables in their notebooks. They work alone. They look back over their recent marked writing and find some (maximum five) spelling errors.

4. Learners write one sentence containing a spelling error from their work under 'I wrote this'. They lightly cross out the error by putting a single line through it. They write the corrected word under 'I should have written this'. If they do not know how to correct it, they use a dictionary, friend or the teacher to find out. They decide which letters they got wrong or missed out and overwrite these in the second column with a different colour pen. Then they try to find a way to remember each correct spelling. If they can't think of one, they leave it blank and, when they have finished, ask other learners in the class for ideas.

5. Encourage learners to do this every time they receive any written work that has been marked.

21.9 Why I Got It Wrong ⃝⃝⃝⃝⃝

Aim: To encourage learners to learn from their errors. *(See B:165)*

Activity: When you give back some written work with spelling errors marked, learners tell a partner why they think they made their spelling mistakes. Explain that doing this will help them to remember the correct spelling in the future. Put some example language prompts on the board, such as:

- "I forgot the __ because it's silent"
- "I always get confused between ___ and ___."
- "I never know if it's _____ or _____."
- "It sounds like ____."
- "It was a guess."
- "My dictionary/friend/dad/teacher told me to spell it like that."
- "I suppose I wasn't concentrating."

Variations: If you think learners won't be comfortable talking about their errors with their classmates, ask them to write each error (with a ~~line~~ through it), the correct spelling and the reason. They hand these in to you. They may be very useful as they will give you insight into your learners' difficulties.

Acknowledgement: This idea is based on one by Adrian Underhill (Underhill, 1994)

21.10 Mnemonics ⃝⃝⃝⃝⃝

Aim: To help learners accurately produce troublesome words. *(See B:148)*

Activity:
1. Give an example of a mnemonic, not necessarily for spelling. For example, British people remember the colours of the rainbow with the mnemonic Richard Of York Gained Battle In Vain (Red Orange Yellow Green Blue Indigo Violet). Ask if anyone has any spelling mnemonics.

2. Give the following mnemonics and ask learners what spelling they think they are designed to help you remember:
   Big elephants can't always understand small elephants (***because***)
   R____ helps your two hips move (***rhythm***)
   When you are em_____d you have two **r**ed cheeks (*embarrassed — double **r***)
   The best ac_____on has two double beds (*accommodation — double **c**, double **m***)
   It's ne____ry to have one coat and two socks (*necessary — one **c**, double **s***)

3. Now learners find some words (from their notes or previous work) that they have difficulty spelling. They try to make some mnemonics to remember them.

Variations: Making the mnemonics could be set for homework.

Chapter Twenty-Two:

Games and Puzzles

22.1 Last Letter, First Letter

○○○○

Aim: To practise final letters of words, particularly silent ones. *(See B:134)*

Materials needed: A ball or other throwable object (optional).

Activity: Learners sit in a circle (or in circular groups). The teacher says a word and throws the ball to a learner. The person who catches it says a word that begins with the last letter of the previous word and throws the ball to someone else. And so on. So if one person says *table*, the next could say *elephant*, then next, *teacher*, etc. Words mustn't be repeated.

Variations: If you want to make this more competitive, each learner starts with three points, and loses a point if he or she gets one wrong.

22.2 Don't Finish the Word

○○○○

Aim: To encourage visualisation of spelling. *(See B:147)*

Activity: Learners sit in a circle (or in circular groups). Say one letter of the alphabet. The next student in the circle says another letter that together with the first makes the beginning of a word. The next learner adds another letter and so on. The aim is to spell a word, but not be the person who finishes it. Each learner starts with three points. If learners finish words, they lose one of their points. Then the next person starts a new word. If at any time someone doubts that the learner who says a letter has a real (correctly spelled) word in mind, they can challenge that person. If the challenged student can't give an appropriate word, they lose a point and a new word is started. If they can give a word, the challenger loses a point. If somebody can't continue a word, they also lose a point.

Notes: This is a good warmer or filler. Watch out for anyone starting a new word with *a* or *i*. They immediately lose a point as they are complete words. Don't warn them of this beforehand — it spoils the fun!

22.3 Pass the Pattern

Aim: To encourage learners to visualise common spelling patterns. *(See B:135)*

Materials needed: One worksheet, cut into 12 cards, for each group of 6-12 learners. A spinning top or some other type of random timer.

Activity:
1. All learners make a circle. Each learner starts with three points. Place a pile of cards face down in the middle of the circle.

2. One person takes a card and shows the others or says what it is. The learner then says a word containing that letter string. The teacher sets the top spinning.

3. The card is passed to the next person on the left who says another word containing that string. The card continues around the circle with each person saying a different word containing the string. If a learner repeats a word or says one that doesn't contain the string, they can try again. Learners lose one of their three points if:
   • they pass (don't say a word)
   • they are holding the card when the top stops spinning.

4. Whenever a point is lost a new card is taken by the person who lost the point. The game continues for as long as you like or until all the cards have been used.

Variations and notes: This game is best played either by reasonably confident learners or as revision. Very weak spellers may find it too stressful.
In a large class divide into groups of 6 - 12. Give one pack to each group.
Make your own cards to practise particular patterns.

Worksheet 22.3:   *Pass the Pattern*

ee	ea
es	le
tion	ck
ing	al
st	igh
ch	ou

22.4 Three in a Row Vowels

Aim: To give practice with vowel patterns. *(See B:135, B:131)*

Materials needed: For each group of four learners: One game board — enlarged to A3 if possible; two different coloured sets of cards, also enlarged to A3 and cut; pencils.

Activity:
1. Learners work in groups of four (or up to six if necessary). Each group has two teams. Give each group two different coloured sets of vowel pattern cards — one for each of their teams. Also give them one game board. The cards are shuffled and placed in a pile, face down, in front of each team.

2. One team turns up the first card. They make a word containing that vowel or pattern that matches one of the categories on the game board. They write the word in pencil under the pattern and place the card on the game board on top of the relevant category.

3. The next team turns up one of their cards and does the same. The game continues until one team gets three cards in a row, horizontally, vertically or diagonally. So as well as trying to make a row of three, learners need to stop the opposing team from winning a row.

4. To play again, learners need to rub out the words they have written on the cards.

Variations: Boards and cards can be laminated for reuse. Then learners write their words with a non-permanent pen and these can be washed off after the game.
You can download coloured cards from The Spelling Blog: http://thespellingblog.blogspot.com
You may want to set a time limit for the creation of each word.
At the end of the game, everyone writes personalised sentences for the words they used to help them remember the spellings within a sentence.
For an easier version of this game, each team spreads out all their cards in front of them and they can choose the pattern they use to make a relevant word.
You could use this idea to make your own game with different spelling patterns or different topics.

Game Board 22.4: Three in a Row Vowels

Something hot	A verb	Related to sport	Something pretty	Related to water	Something high or tall
An animal	A part of the body	Something indoors	Related to food	An adjective	Related to houses
Related to work	A vegetable product	Related to free time	Something cold	Related to families	A noun
A country	Something that moves	In the office	Related to money	An action	Related to technology
A mineral product	Related to weather	An animal product	Something dangerous	Related to clothes	Something outdoors
Related to travel	In the classroom	A feeling	Related to friends	In the kitchen	Related to people

Cards 22.4: *Three in a Row Vowels*

a	or	ea	ure	ir	ar
io	our	a_e	o	ue	eau
ow	e	ur	ia	air	oo
ay	ou	oa	ee	i	u_e
ei	o_e	ie	ear	ui	ai
i_e	au	u	oe	er	oi

PHOTOCOPIABLE ©Johanna Stirling 2011. Teaching Spelling to English Language Learners

22.5 Code Word Nouri

Aim: To develop skills for predicting letter patterns. *(See B:130)*

Materials needed: One worksheet per student.

Activity: Give each student a worksheet. Explain that each different letter has a number. For example, 7 represents the letter *i*, so they write 'i' above all the 7s. Do the same for the other numbers given in the table. If it's the first time learners have done this type of activity, guide them through it using the questions on the worksheet.

Key: My name is Nouri. I want to be a pilot. The course will be in English so now I am studying at a language school.

a	b	c	d	e	f	g	h	i	j	k	l	m
16	19	2	14	8	-	17	4	7	-	-	12	9
n	o	p	q	r	s	t	u	v	w	x	y	z
10	18	6	-	13	5	1	3	-	11	-	15	-

Worksheet 22.5: *Code Word Nouri*

9	15		10	16	9	8		7	5		10	18	3	13	7	.

| 7 | | 11 | 16 | 10 | 1 | | 1 | 18 | | 19 | 8 | | 16 | | 6 | 7 | 12 | 18 | 1 | . |

| 1 | 4 | 8 | | 2 | 18 | 3 | 13 | 5 | 8 | | 11 | 7 | 12 | 12 | | 19 | 8 | | 7 | 10 |

| 8 | 10 | 17 | 12 | 7 | 5 | 4 | | 5 | 18 | | 10 | 18 | 11 | | 7 | | 16 | 9 |

| 5 | 1 | 3 | 14 | 15 | 7 | 10 | 17 | | 16 | 1 | | 16 |

| 12 | 16 | 10 | 17 | 3 | 16 | 17 | 8 | | 5 | 2 | 4 | 18 | 18 | 12 | . |

Try to complete the text.

• Each different letter has a number. For example, *i* is the number 7. Write *i* above all the 7s. Do the same for the other numbers given in the table.

a	b	c	d	e	f	g	h	i	j	k	l	m
				-			7	-	-			
n	**o**	**p**	**q**	**r**	**s**	**t**	**u**	**v**	**w**	**x**	**y**	**z**
10	18		-	13			3	-		-		-

• Which two words in English have only one letter? Can you find them in the text?

• What are the five vowel letters? Which one haven't you got? This letter is often at the end of words (and usually silent).

• Can you guess the 2nd word? It's quite a common word.

• Now can you guess the first and third words?

• Continue like this. Hints:
        Think about the meaning of the text. Look at the picture.
        Think about some two letter words you know.
        Think about some letters that you often find together in a word.

Chapter Twenty-Three:

Strategies for Learning Spellings

23.1 Look Say Cover Write Check ◯◯◯◯

Aim: To introduce a multi-dimensional strategy for learning individual spellings. *(See B:145)*

Materials needed: For each student: a copy of the Look Say Cover Write Check (LSCWC) chart and Covering Card. Laminate the Covering Cards if possible. About six words that you have recently taught to your learners or that you have noticed they find difficult to spell.

Activity:
1. Write the six words on the board. Give out a LSCWC chart to each learner. They copy the words into the first column. Spot check that these are correctly copied if necessary.

2. Say the first word and learners repeat it. Then they say the letters out loud.

3. They count the number of letters and write this number in the next column (marked 'No.' — English abbreviation for 'number'). Explain that this helps them to check if they have they have the right number of letters when they learn the word.

4. Learners look at the word and decide which parts might be difficult to spell. Prompt them to look for silent letters, double letters, two vowels together, weak forms, etc. Show them how to overwrite these with a different colour pen *(See B:146)*. Demonstrate on the board.

5. Learners think about how they will be able to remember the spelling. They write notes in the How to Remember column. Ask:
    *   Is the spelling similar to another word you know? If so, is the meaning related?
    *   Is there another word inside it (consecutive letters)? Is that related to the meaning?
    *   Can you guess anything about the origin of the word?
    *   Are there any common letter strings, like **ing** or **igh**?
    *   Does it sound like its spelling?
    *   If none of the above, can they make a mnemonic to remember?

(continued)

6. Show on the board how to draw around the outline of the word (See B:147). Learners write the word neatly on the grid in the middle row of the Word Shape column. Tall letters (b, d, f, h, k, l, t) reach into the top row. The ones that drop below the line (g, j, p, q, y) reach into the bottom row. Then they draw around the outline of the word. Learners close their eyes and try to see the word in their heads.

7. Give out the Cover Cards (which include reminders to the learners about how to use the chart). Learners use them to cover what they have written and try to write the correct spelling in the first Write column. They check carefully that their spelling is right, counting the letters and saying them aloud.

8. They repeat the process with the next word, working alone now.

9. When they have finished learning the second word they test themselves on the first and second word.

10. When they have learned all the words, they try to fill in the final column, without looking back at the words or their notes.

11. Give learners extra copies of the LSCWC chart (or ask them to make their own) and suggest they use it when they need to learn other words.

Variations: There is a larger version of the chart available at The Spelling Blog http://thespellingblog.blogspot.com.

Look Say Cover Write Check template

LOOK / SAY				COVER	WRITE	CHECK	WRITE	CHECK	REVISE later	CHECK
Copy & Say the word	No	What's difficult?	How to remember	Word shape						

23.1: *Look Say Cover Write Check Cover Card*

LOOK SAY COVER WRITE CHECK **COVER CARD**				
Copy & Say the word	N o	What's difficult?	How to remember	Word shape
Copy the word very carefully. **Say** the word. **Say** the letters of the word. **Count** the number of letters. Write this in the next column. Check it's the same as in the word you copied.		**Write** which parts of the word might be difficult to remember. Think about letters that are: — silent — doubled — two vowels etc.	Some ideas to help you remember the spelling: — similar to another word? — another word inside it? — origin? — common letter string? — sound? — mnemonic? — your own ideas	**Write** the word carefully in the middle row. Tall letters (b, d, f, h, k, l, t) reach into the top row. The ones that drop below the line (g, j, p, q, y) reach into the bottom row. **Draw** around the outline of the word. **Look away** from the paper. Try to 'see' the word in your head.

THEN

Cover your work with this card.

Try to '**see**' the word in your head again and **write** it in the next column.

Lift the card. **Check** your spelling. If it's right, **tick** (✓) the next column.

If it's wrong, cross it out, look carefully at the correct spelling again, then cover and write in the next column.

If it's right, tick (✓) the next column.

Try again later.

23.2 Humane Dictations

Aim: To give practice in learning new spellings. *(See B:157)*

Materials needed: One worksheet (of one text only) per student.

Activity:
1. Lead in to the topic of the text — get the learners interested in it.

2. Set a couple of general questions about the text and then read it aloud to the learners. Check they understand by answering the questions.

3. Now give the text to the learners. Read it aloud again. They follow by reading silently.

4. Tell learners you are going to dictate this to them in a few minutes. First they underline any words they think they will have trouble spelling. Allow them time to learn these words, using Look Say Cover Write and Check or any other methods.

5. Learners cover the text and put away any papers with the spellings on. Give the dictation in the normal way. (Read a small meaningful chunk out loud, now say it twice silently to yourself while students write, then aloud again, then twice to yourself again — this seems to make the pace about right for most people, but allow more time if necessary).

6. Now check the dictations or get learners to check each other's against the original text (people who can't spell well often find it difficult to see their own errors). Any words which have been misspelled should be listed (correctly) and learned before the next lesson.

There are three different example texts given on the worksheets:

*   Text 1 contains many words with silent letters.
*   Text 2 contains various plural patterns and irregular plurals.
*   Text 3 contains several words with silent final *e*.

You could use any text, perhaps from the coursebook.

Variations:
Step 2: Cut the text into separate sentences. Learners work in pairs to put them into the correct order.
Step 5: Pairs deal the sentences out evenly between themselves. They dictate sentences to each other.

Worksheet 23.2: *Humane Dictations*

Text 1
The Debt
A banker lent a poor woman some money and told her to give him a receipt with her address on it. A few weeks later the banker wanted the money back but he couldn't find the receipt or the woman. The banker didn't know how to call in the debt. As he was walking through the market worrying about his business, he saw an old woman sitting on the ground next to a sign she had written: "Any two questions answered for twenty silver coins". He thought she looked honest and she might know where to find the woman and the receipt. "Excuse me," he said. The old woman listened carefully. "Can I ask you two questions?" "Yes," she answered. "That was one. What's the other one?"

Text 2
Heavy Metal Heroes
Two boys have been declared heroes after saving a group of women's lives with heavy metal music. The ten-year-old boys were walking home from school when they heard some cries from inside a park. They ran until they saw three ladies sitting on the branches of a tree crying. The boys saw something move at the bottom of the tree and at first thought they were foxes, so they threw their scarves at them. But then they saw that they were wolves and they didn't know what to do. Then the oldest boy had an idea. He got out his phone, turned up the volume and played the song 'Go, Go, Go' by his favourite band, the Big Metal Heavies. The wolves looked at the boy and then ran off in fright.

Text 3
Use it or lose it!
Is it a waste of time doing puzzles and playing games? New computer games are being produced for people who are worried that their memory will fade with age. Many people hope that these exercises will help them to keep their brains fit. Research shows that we have to use our brains if we want them to stay in good condition. Scientists suggest that besides playing brain games, we should write and read aloud for at least five minutes every day.

23.3 Words Within Words 1   ⟨○○○○⟩

Aim: To help remember spellings by noticing short words within longer words. *(See B:146)*

Materials needed: One worksheet A and B for each learner.

Activity:
1. Ask learners why it's useful to see words inside other words (helps you to remember the spelling).
2. Give out Worksheet A. Learners try to find a short word (with the meaning given) within the long word. They highlight the letters. It's helpful if you can show this using a projector or interactive whiteboard, or even just writing it on the board. Check the answers to A.
3. Learners look at the long words carefully as they will have to spell them in the next activity.
4. Learners put away Worksheet A so they can't see it. Give out worksheet B. Learners do the crossword. This uses the same words as Worksheet A and gives clues to the meaning as well as prompts about the short word.

Key: Worksheet A: 1. cat 2. died 3. lie 4. iron 5. should 6. end 7. ear 8. call 9. one 10. the 11. count 12. all 13. hi 14. use.
Worksheet B: **Across** 4. education 6. money 7. country 8. shoulder 10. while 13. usually 14. environment. **Down** 1. friend 2. their 3. believe 5. automatically 9. because 11. studied 12. learn.

--------------------------------✄----------------------------------

Worksheet 23.3 A: Words Within Words 1

Highlight an animal in **'education'**

Highlight a past tense verb (at the end of life) in **'studied'**

Highlight something that's not true in **'believe'**

Highlight a type of metal in **'environment'**

Highlight a modal verb in **'shoulder'**

Highlight the final part in **'friend'**

Highlight a part of the body in **'learn'**

Highlight something you do on the phone in **'automatically'**

Highlight a number in **'money'**

Highlight an article in **'their'**

Highlight 1,2,3,4,5... in **'country'**

Highlight everything in **'usually'**

Highlight hello in **'while'**

Highlight a three-letter verb in **'because'**

Worksheet 23.3 B: *Words Within Words 1*

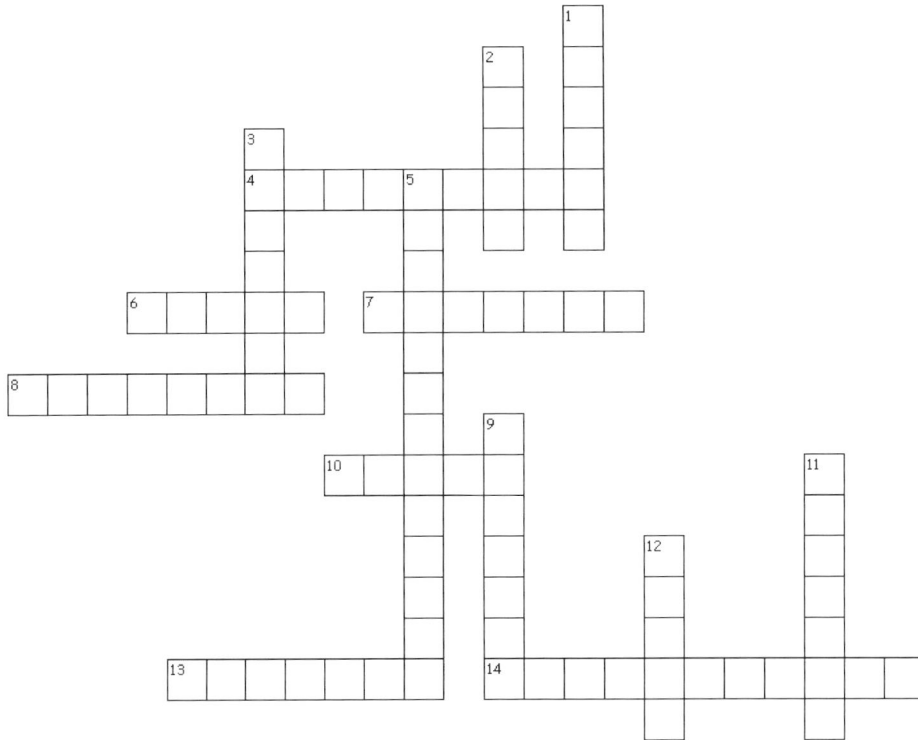

Across

4. You need a good _____ to get a good job. (contains an animal)

6. Can you lend me some _____ — I've left my wallet at home. (contains a number)

7. The food in my _____ is the best! (contains 1,2,3,4,5 ...)

8. I hurt my _____ in the gym. (contains a modal verb)

10. Wait here _____ I pay the bill. (contains hello)

13. I _____ walk to work, but I got the bus today. (contains everything)

14. Pollution damages the _____. (contains a type of metal)

Down

1. I talk to my best _____ about everything. (contains the final part)

2. That's _____ room, not ours. (contains an article)

3. I don't _____ you — it can't be true! (Contains something that's not true)

5. The door opens _____ when you walk towards it. (contains something you do on the phone)

9. I was late _____ the traffic was bad. (contains a three-letter verb)

11. I _____ hard for the test and passed. (contains a past tense verb — at the end of life)

12. I need to _____ to drive. (contains part of the body)

23.4 Words Within Words 2   ⭘⭘⭘⬤

Aim: To help learners to remember spellings by noticing short words within longer words. *(See B:146)*

Activity:
1. Write *another* on the board. Ask learners to say quickly how many words they think are contained inside this word. Tell them there are eight (see Key). They try to find them.

2. Write these words on the board: *something*, *whatever*, *father*, *teaching* on the board. Learners work alone or in pairs to find as many words inside each of them as possible.

Variation: You could also use any long words that you have recently taught if they have other words inside them.

Key:
Another: a, an, no, not, other, the, he, her;
Something: so, some, me, met, I, thin, in, thing;
Whatever: what, hat, hate, a, ate, eve, ever;
Father: fat, a, at, the, he, her;
Teaching: teach, tea, each, aching, chin, in.

23.5 Words Within Words 3   ⭘⭘⭘⬤

Aim: To help learners to remember spellings by noticing short words within longer words. *(See B:146)*

Activity: Write these words on the board: *alarm*, *diagnose*, *friendship*, *merchandise*, *obeyed*, *potatoes*, *searching*, *slippers*. Tell learners that each word contains the name of a part of the body. One word contains two parts of the body. Learners try to find the shorter words.

Variations: Write these words instead and ask them to find living things (including animals, birds and insects): *sunbathing*, *then*, *coward*, *paper*, *separate*, *fantastic*, *bowling*, *communication*. All these contain only one relevant word.

Key: al**arm**, diag**nose**, friend**ship**, merc**hand**ise, ob**eye**d, pota**toes**, sear/c**hin**g, sli**pp**ers.
sunba**thing**, **then**, **cow**ard, pa**per**, separate (it is useful to point out *a rat* in this one), fant**a**stic, b**owl**ing, commun**ica**tion.

23.6 Picture It ⬤⬤⬤⬤

Aim: To help learners to visualise the spelling of abstract common words. *(See B:140, B:147)*

Activity: Before the lesson, think of some common abstract structure words that your learners have problems with, such as: ***about, again, although, another, because, different, from, necessary, really, similar, their, then, very, which, would***.

1. Write one of the words, for example, ***although***. Each learner or pair thinks of a sentence that clearly illustrates the meaning, such as ***We played football although it was raining***. Learners share sentences.

2. Now they try to visualise a picture of one of the sentences (it doesn't have to be the one they thought of if another seems better). They draw a picture of the scene, including the word. Reassure them that they don't have to be good at drawing to do this. In fact the funnier it looks, probably the more memorable.

3. They repeat for other words.

23.7 Sticks and Tails ⬤⬤⬤⬤

Aim: To introduce learners to the concept of letter shapes to help them to visualise the shape of words. *(See B:147)*

Activity:
1. Write the word ***bag*** on the board. Show that it contains three different letter shapes:
   b has a 'stick' — it is a tall letter.
   g has a 'tail' — it drops below the line
   a is an 'in-line' letter — it has no 'stick' or 'tail'.

2. Learners categorise the rest of the letters of the alphabet into those with 'sticks', 'tails' and 'in-line' letters. (Note: **f** is a bit problematic as people write it in different ways, some with a 'stick', some with both a stick and tail, and when handwriting some write it just with a tail. In most typed fonts it has a stick.)

3. Learners have 3 minutes to write as many three-letter words as they can containing one of each of the three letter shapes, such as ***dog*** and ***got***. They need to know what the word means.

Key: Letters with sticks: *b d f h k l t*
Letters with tails: *g j p q y*
In-line letters: *a c e i m n o r s u v w x z*

23.8 Word Shapes — Outlining ⬭⬭⬭⬭

Aim: To help learners to visualise the shape of words. *(See B:147)*

Activity:
1. Choose some words to work on. They could be ones your learners are having difficulty with or a set of words containing the same letter string.

2. Write one of the words clearly on the board and show how to draw around the outline of the word, like this:

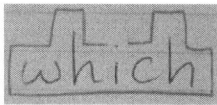

3. Write other words on the board. Learners write them out carefully and draw the outlines. Discuss whether they feel this helps them to visually remember words. If they do, encourage them to do the same with other words they want to learn.

23.9   Word Shape Matching ⬭⬭⬭⬭

Aim: To help learners to visualise the shape of words. To help learners distinguish visually between words containing *p* and *b* (useful for many Arabic speakers). *(See B:147)*

Materials needed: One worksheet per student.

Activity: Ensure learners are familiar with the concept of word shapes (see activities on previous pages).
1.   Give them the worksheet and ask them to match the words with their shapes. They write the words in the boxes.
2.   Learners match the meanings with the shapes. They fill in the gaps with the word paying particular attention to the *p*s and *b*s.

Variations: This could be given for homework.
You can make your own word shape worksheets for practising different words and patterns at http://tools.atozteacherstuff.com/word-shapes/wordshapes.html

Key: A. a. palace b. before c. lamp d. probably e. perhaps f. baker g. possible h. apart i. pages j. bargain k. about l. lamb.
B. 1. perhaps 2. lamp 3. about 4. baker 5. probably 6. before 7. lamb 8. palace 9. apart 10. pages 11. possible 12. bargain.

Worksheet 23.9: *Word shape matching*

A: Match the words with the shapes.

| perhaps | lamp | about | baker | probably | possible |
| lamb | palace | apart | pages | before | bargain |

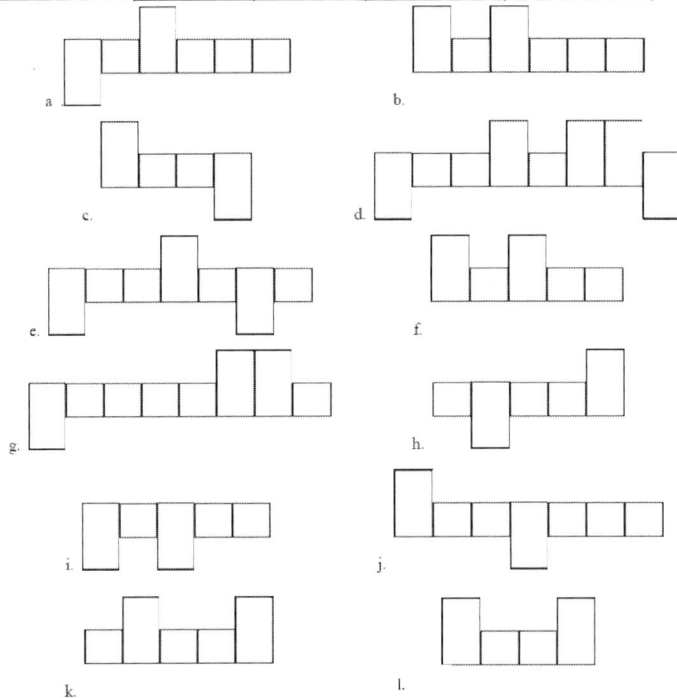

a.

b.

c.

d.

e.

f.

g.

h.

i.

j.

k.

l.

B. Match the shapes with the meanings

1. _____ means 'maybe'.

2. A _____ gives you light (for reading).

3. "There were _____ 50 people at the party. I'm not sure exactly how many."

4. "I'd like to be a _____, because I love making bread."

5. If you are 90% sure something will happen, you think it will _____ happen.

6. You have to do a course _____ you take the exam.

7. A baby sheep is called a _____.

8. A king or queen lives in a _____.

9. _____ means 'separate'.

10. The pieces of paper in a book are called _____.

11. "I don't think it's _____ to stop children watching TV."

12. "I'm going to buy it. It's a _____! It 's much more expensive in other shops."

23.10 Word Shape Dictation

Aim: To help learners to visualise the shape of words. *(See B:147)*

Materials: Cuisenaire Rods or paper shapes. To make paper shapes, cut one sheet of white paper or card into 1cm x 1cm squares. Cut another piece of coloured paper or card into 1cm x 2cm rectangles. Each student or pair needs about 7 of each shape. Some larger squares and rectangles with something to stick them to the board with.

Activity:
1. Find a word that you have focused on recently (that includes at least one letter with a stick, one with a tail and one in-line letter) and write it on the board. Use the larger squares and rectangles to stick over the letters, showing where the stick and tails are.

2. Do this with a few more words, perhaps inviting learners to come to the board to build the word shape.

3. Give out the rods or paper shapes. Learners make some words to become familiar with the technique.

4. 'Dictate' some words. Learners don't write them but they just build the shapes with the rods or cards. Learners check their shapes with a partner. Show correct shapes on the board

5. Learners dictate words to each other to build.

Here are some examples built with rods:

 which   bicycle

23.11 Coloured Vowels

Aim: To help learners visualise which vowels to use in words they find difficult. *(See B:147)*

Materials needed: One worksheet per student. Coloured pens or pencils: blue, red, green, grey (could be normal pencil), yellow. Alternatively colour version of worksheet can be downloaded from The Spelling Blog http://thespellingblog.blogspot.com

Activity:
1. On the board write the five vowel letters and the names of the colours: **blue**, **bright red**, **green**, **grey**, **yellow**. Ask learners to match the letters to the colours. If necessary, suggest that they match them by rhyme: **a** is gr<u>ey</u>, **e** is gr<u>een</u>, **i** is br<u>igh</u>t red, **o** is yell<u>ow</u> and **u** is bl<u>ue</u>.

2. Give out the black and white worksheet and coloured pens and ask learners to colour them, or give the downloaded colour version. Explain that colouring the vowels helps visual memory.

3. Ask learners to colour the vowels in the following words or to write words that they have problems with and to overwrite the vowels in the appropriate colours.

Notes: Learners can keep the coloured vowels somewhere handy, so they can refer to them. On The Spelling Blog http://thespellingblog.blogspot.com there is a colour version, and several other configurations of the vowels — including a classroom poster and bookmarks.

--✂--

Worksheet 23.11: *Coloured Vowels*

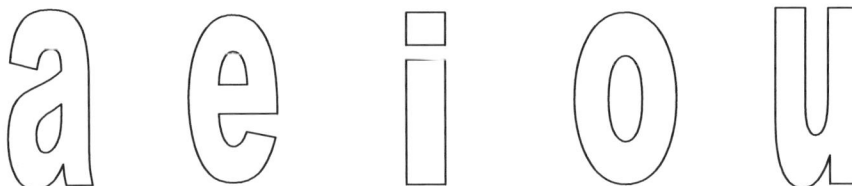

a e i o u

grey   green   bright red   yellow   blue

--✂--

another because before

similar beautiful about

23.12 Seeing Spellings

Aim: To help learners develop visualisation skills for spelling.

Materials: For each student, one A4 sheet of paper or card cut into 4:
(See B:147)

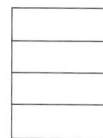

Activity:
1. Ask learners to think of a time when they were pleased with themselves because they were successful at something that was difficult. Give prompts as appropriate such as sports, school work, a business deal, a skill, making a grumpy person smile. Learners talk to their partner about this: what the achievement was, why it was difficult, what mental attitude helped them and what it felt like to succeed.

2. Tell learners that now they are going to succeed in spelling! Give out the strips of blank card. Learners choose three or four words that they want to learn. They write each one carefully (correctly!) on a separate piece of the card. If there are letters that they think they will find difficult, they overwrite these with a different colour pen. If the word is very long, they can break it into more manageable chunks.

3. They hold one word in the air, level with their forehead and slightly to the left (or to the right if they are left-handed). They look carefully at the word. They count the letters, look at the shape of the word, look at any colours they used for overwriting, etc.

4. Learners put the word on the table, face down, but look at the blank space where the word was. They try to visualise the word. They count the letters, look at the shape of the word, and look at any colours. They repeat two more times holding up the word, looking at it, putting it down and visualising it. When they are visualising it, ask "What's the third letter?" and "What's the letter before the last one?" If they are visualising well they should be able to identify these. If they can't, reassure them that it takes a bit of practice.

5. Learners write down on another piece of paper the word that they visualised. If they are not sure, they can look back up at the blank space and see if it is still 'there'. Then they check their spelling is the same as the written word on the card.

6. They repeat with the other words. After learning each word like this they check that they can remember the previous ones too.

Variations: If you think learners will be uncomfortable talking to each other about their achievements, ask them to write about them instead.

Notes: This is an NLP (Neuro-Linguistic Programming) strategy. By first focussing on a feeling of success, it is believed that this puts learners in a positive 'can do' frame of mind. When we try to remember an image many people look up and to the left (or right if they are left-handed). That is why we position the word to be visualised there.
For an interactive game that uses this method to teach the spelling of one new word a day, go to http://spellinglab.com/spelllab.htm

23.13 Hear the Spelling

Aim: To introduce learners to a range of auditory strategies for remembering the sequence of letters in a word. *(See B:144, B:145, B:160)*

Materials needed: Soft balls; cards with recently learned words on.

Activities: These are different auditory activities that help many learners remember the sound of the spelling (not the sound of the word). They are particularly useful for learning high frequency words or common letter strings. Use these activities after working on the spelling of the words.

A. Learners stand in a circle (or several circles) with one person in the middle. This person has a list of recently studied words. He or she says one word from the list and throws a soft ball to one of the learners in the circle. The person who catches it says the first letter of the word, the next learner to their left says the second letter and so on until the word is complete. If somebody says a wrong letter the person in the middle must spell the word out loud, without looking at the list, then joins the circle. The person who made the mistake is the next one in the centre of the circle. If the word is said correctly, the same person stays in the middle and says another word. This game is best used with quite confident learners.

B. Each pair has a soft ball and a pile of cards with recently-learned words on. They stand opposite each other, quite close. They turn up one card and spell the word out loud, taking turns to say a letter and throw the ball to the other person. They try to build up a rhythm. If they go wrong with the spelling, they start the word again.

C. Each learner chooses a word that they really want or need to learn. They write it and check the spelling with a dictionary, teacher or other reference. If possible, all the learners walk around the room in any direction, spelling out their word aloud. Then the teacher calls out any instructions such as these:
    •   Whisper your spelling
    •   Shout out your spelling
    •   Laugh out your spelling
    •   Rap your spelling
    •   Say it like you've been running
    •   Say it like you love it
    •   Say it like you're a mouse/ lion/monkey
    •   Say it like (name of celebrity they all know)
    If they can't spell the word now, they never will!

Notes: These can be used as warmers and fillers. Encourage learners to use the ones that seem to work for them. Some may not be culturally appropriate for all.

23.14 Grab a Vowel ⃝⃝⃝⃝

Aim: To help learners discriminate between short vowel sounds. *(See B:131, B:160)*

Materials needed: For each group of four to six students: 5 cards (preferably each a different colour) with one vowel on each, *a*, *e*, *i*, *o* and *u*.

Activity:
1. Check learners know the meaning of the words: *bag*, *beg*, *big*, *bog* (very wet, swampy land) and *bug* (insect or virus).

2. Help them with the different vowel sounds if necessary by showing the shape the mouth makes for each sound. They listen and repeat the words.

3. Give each group of four to six learners a set of five different vowel cards. They spread out the cards face up on the table in the middle of their group. Tell them that you will say one of the five words and they have to pick up the correct vowel before anyone else in the group and hold it up. So if you say *bug*, they must hold up the *U*. If the cards are different colours according to the letter you will quickly be able to see who is right. The winners return their cards to the table. Continue playing like this. Learners keep score of how many times they win.

Notes: Do not give the words in sentences. This activity aims to increase phoneme discrimination rather than understanding and spelling from context.

23.15 Feel the Spelling ⭕⭕⭕⭕

Aim: To introduce learners to a range of kinaesthetic strategies for reinforcing spelling. *(See B:118)*

Materials needed: Any of the following: a box of beads, sandpaper, carpet, spray foam.

Activities: These are different kinaesthetic activities that help many learners *feel* what the spelling is like. Particularly useful for learning high frequency words or common letter strings.

A. Write the word in the air. Try writing in different sizes. Try writing with one finger only, with a pen (or imaginary pen) in the hand, or with large arm movements.

B. Write with the finger on the desk.

C. Write with the finger on the palm of your other hand.

D. Write with the finger on somebody else's hand or on their back. The person being written on guesses the word.

E. Write with the finger in a box of beads, in foam, on sandpaper, on carpet or on any other rough surface. The tactile experience may help memory.

Notes: These can be used as warmers and fillers. Encourage learners to use the ones that seem to work for them. Activity D may not be culturally appropriate for all.

23.16 Spelling Gym   ◯◯◯◯◯

Aim: To help learners visualise word shapes. *(See B:118, B:147)*

Activity:
1. Make sure learners are familiar with letter shapes: the letters **b d f h k l t** have 'sticks' (tall letters), **g j p q y** have 'tails' (fall below the line) and the rest are 'in-line' letters: **a c e i m n o r s u v w x z**.

2. Learners stand up. Tell them they are going to spell words with their bodies. Everyone puts their hands on their own shoulders (left hand to left shoulder, right hand to right shoulder). This is 'neutral' — they must come back to this position between each letter. For a letter with a 'stick', they need to raise their hands above their heads. For a 'tail', they drop their hands to their thighs. If there is an 'in-line' letter, they cross their hands to the opposite shoulders.

3. Say a word, for example, **people**. Ask learners to close their eyes and try to 'see' the word in their heads. Then they open their eyes. Count 1, 2, 3 aloud and everybody spells the word aloud together, moving their arms for each letter. Remind learners they must come back to neutral between letters. So they take the following steps:
    - Start in neutral (left hand to left shoulder, right hand to right shoulder)
    - Say **p**   hands down to thighs, then return to neutral
    - Say **e**   hands to opposite shoulders, then return to neutral
    - Say **o**   hands to opposite shoulders, then return to neutral
    - Say **p**   hands down to thighs, then return to neutral
    - Say **l**   hands above head, then return to neutral
    - Say **e**   hands to opposite shoulders, then return to neutral.

Variations: Before learners close their eyes to visualise the word you could write it on the board, but clean the board before playing the game.
After demonstrating the first time, don't make the arm movements yourself, so learners can't just copy you.
For those who are good at it, suggest they keep their eyes closed, so they can't see what others are doing.
If you like, you could make **f** have a 'stick' and 'tail' — one hand down and one hand up. Also **i** can be a punch forward at head height (to represent the dot).

23.17 Full-body Spelling ⬭⬭⬭⬭

Aim: To make spellings and word strings memorable. *(See B:118, B:135)*

Materials needed: A floor area (about 2.5–3m²) that you can write on with chalk (such as a playground or hall). Chalk — two colours.

Activities: Draw the following on the floor with chalk. It should be about 2 metres square. The position of the letters and the direction of each one is not too important, but they should be mixed. Write the vowels (including **u**) in a different colour.

Different games can be played with this board. Most do involve some risk of a player falling over, so make necessary warnings and precautions! Note the **QU** square represents **q** or **u**. If both letters are needed, the square must be used twice.

D	H	V	P	B
W	A	L	I	T
K	R	E	G	N
F	O	S	QU	Y
X	M	C	Z	J

A. Players stand around the mat in two teams. In Team A, one player thinks of a word (but doesn't say) and steps on each of the letters in turn. Team A tries to say the word. If they get it, they get one point and a different member of the team spells out another word; if not, the first player repeats the steps. Each team has one minute to get as many words as possible. Then Team B plays. This can also be done with film titles, vocabulary from the spelling box, etc. Adjust the time limit as appropriate.

B. Team A gives Team B a word. A member of Team B steps out the word. Teams alternate turns until one team gets a word wrong.

C. One player in Team A spells a four-letter word (given by the teacher) using both hands and feet. So if the word was **cost**, the player might put one foot on **c**, one foot on **o**, one hand on **s** and the other hand on **t**. The hands and feet must be placed in the correct order of the spelling and are not moved. Now other members of Team A give another word in which only one letter is different, so for example **coat**. The player moves the hand from **s** to **a**. This continues until the player falls, puts a hand or foot on the wrong letter or the team make a mistake or can't think of a word. Then Team B starts with a new word from the teacher. No repetition of words allowed.

D. Both teams stand in separate lines opposite each other facing the board. The teacher gives a common letter string, such as **ough**. The first member of Team A steps out a word containing that string on the board. Team A say what the word was. The teacher notes it down. Then the first member of Team B spells out another word. Play continues to alternate between teams and each player spells a word in turn. The winning team is the one that spells most words. Some other useful patterns: **augh, igh, tion, wh, the**

Chapter Twenty-Four:

Discovering and Practising Patterns

24.1 Silent Letters ⭕⭕⭕⭕

Aim: To help learners spell words with silent letters. *(See B:134)*

Materials needed: One worksheet per student.

Activity:
1. Lead in to the topic of exercise.

2. Give out the worksheet. Learners read the two texts and answer the questions. You could read the texts aloud to them as they read silently. Learners might like to try the exercises (but at their own risk!). This is a very good comprehension check.

3. They try to label the picture with some of the bold words from the text. Check their answers. Drill the words, making sure they don't pronounce the silent letters.

4. Learners study the bold words. Help them to notice any patterns. Then they fold over the text and try to fill in the silent letters in Exercise 3. Drill all the words again.

Variation: In Step 4 (Exercise 3) learners write the complete word on a separate piece of paper. You could dictate these.

Key:
1. The first exercise might be good to do before and after running. The second one is useful for someone who does a lot of work at the computer.
2. Starting bottom left, moving clockwise, *knee*, *thumb*, *wrist*, *palm*, *thigh*, *calf*. They all have silent letters.
3. a. straight b. should c. knee d. slightly e. stretch f. muscles g. thigh h. calf i. palm j. right k. thumb l. wrist.

Worksheet 24.1: *Silent Letters*

1. Read the description of two exercises and decide who these would be useful for.

A
Stand and place your left leg on a step or bench. Keep this leg **straight**. You **should** bend the **knee** of the other leg **slightly**.
Gently bend forward from the hips until you feel the **stretch** in the **muscles** in the back of the **thigh**, the top of the **calf** and the back of the knee.
Stay in this position for about 8 seconds.
Repeat the stretch on the other leg.

B
Turn the **palm** of your **right** hand up, so the fingers are pointing away from you.
Put the fingers of your left hand across the fingers of the right hand. Put your left **thumb** on the back of your right hand.
Push up with your thumb and push down with your fingers so that the right hand points downwards and the elbow becomes straight. Feel the stretch in your fingers and your **wrist**.
Repeat the stretch on your other hand.

2. *Label the picture with some of the bold words from the text. What do all these words have in common (related to spelling)?*

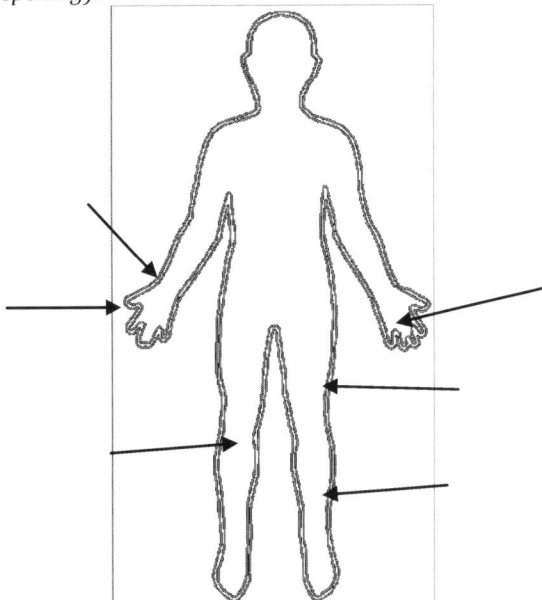

3. *Study all the bold words in the text and then fill in the gaps.*

a) strai_ _t

b) shou_d

c) _nee

d) sli_ _tly.

e) stre_ch

f) mus_les

g) thi_ _

h) ca_f

i) pa_m

j) ri_ _t

k) thum_

l) _rist

24.2 Magic 'e'   ⬭⬭⬭◯

Aim: To show how silent final *e* can lengthen a preceding vowel. *(See A:47, B:134)*

Materials needed: One worksheet per student.

Activity:

1. Lead in to the text by asking learners what they do if a friend or family member is wearing something that looks really bad.

2. Read the text to the learners or give it out and let them read it. Ask them to imagine what the last word could be. This checks comprehension. (It could be any small pet.)

3. Learners practise reading the text aloud in pairs. Monitor to check pronunciation of the words in bold.

4. Learners put the bold words from the text into two groups. They can use any criteria that they can justify.

5. Then, if they haven't already noticed, show them these two groups:

us	*mad*		*time*	*use*
Tim	*Sam*		*Pete*	*note*
hat	*pet*		*hate*	*made*
not			*same*	

6. Elicit the difference in spelling (words in the first group don't finish with *e* but those in the second group do) and pronunciation (words in the first group have a short vowel but in the second group the vowel is long). Ask why the final *e* is sometimes called the 'Magic *e*' (it makes the preceding vowel say the name of its letter). Drill the words thoroughly.

7. Learners match the words in the two lists (e.g. *us* and *use*). They practise saying the pairs of words with their partners.

8. Learners look in other texts to try to identify some more words that have a final silent *e* that makes the preceding vowel 'say its name'. Note that there are some (like *some*!) that don't follow this pattern.

Worksheet 24.2:   *Magic 'e'*

Read the conversation and decide what the final word could be.

RACHEL: How was the wedding?

MOYA: Oh, we had a great **time**. Here's a photo of **us** with **Pete** and his new wife, Susi.

RACHEL: Hey, I like **Tim**'s **hat**.

MOYA: Do you? I **hate** it. He thinks it's cool, but I told him it's **not**! He got really **mad** about it.

RACHEL: Ha ha! Poor Tim!

MOYA: Yes, and **Sam**, my son, thought the **same**. But it's no **use** — he doesn't listen to us. So when we got home, Sam took the hat, filled it with paper torn from an old **note**-book and **made** it into a nest for his **pet** _____!

Put the words in bold into two groups.

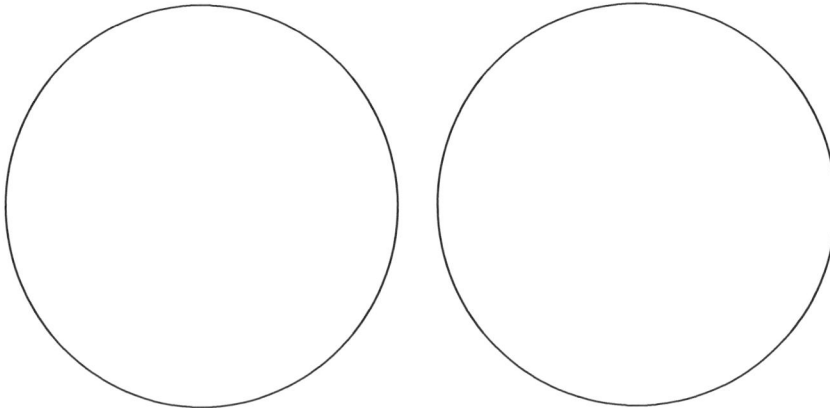

24.3 Magic 'e' Pelmanism

○○○○

Aim: To consolidate understanding of how silent final *e* can lengthen a preceding vowel.

Materials needed: One worksheet (cut into 14 separate cards) for each group of 4 learners. *(See A:47, B:134)*

Activity:

1. Students work in groups of about 4. Give each group a set of cards which they spread out face down on the table. They match pairs of words and practise pronunciation (if they haven't done activity 24.2). Then they turn the cards over and mix them up.

2. One learner turns up any card and says the word. Then he or she says the word it twins with. So if *us* is turned up, then the learner says "*us*" followed by "*use*". If *time* is turned up, the learner says "*time*" followed by "*Tim*". Then the learner turns up one more card. If it is the twin, he or she makes a sentence including both words, e.g. "The teacher told **us** not to **use** a calculator". Then the player takes the two cards. If the second card is not a twin, the player makes sure everyone has had a chance to look at both words and then turns them both back to face down in the same position. It is the next person's turn. The winner is the player with most cards when they have all been taken.

Variations: This is best used after activity 24.2.

---✂---

Worksheet 24.3: Magic 'e' Pelmanism

us	use
Tim	time
hat	hate
not	note
mad	made
Sam	same
pet	Pete

24.4 Prefix Partners   ○○○○○

Aim: To illustrate that prefixes are added to whole words. *(See A:63, B:135)*

Materials needed: One worksheet for every 12 learners, cut into separate cards.

Activity:

1. Learners to discuss what they find difficult about English spelling.

2. Give each student one card with either a prefix or a base morpheme. Learners walk around looking for their partner who has the other part of the word. When they find their partner they stand together holding their cards to make the complete word, so other students can see. Correct any that are wrong. Check they understand the meanings.

3. Learners look at all the words. Ask them:
    *   How many **s**s are there in **misspelling**?
    *   How many **f**s are there in ***prefix***?
    *   Why?
    Elicit that prefixes are added to whole words. No changes are needed. They check this against the other words.

4. Learners look carefully at the words. Tell them you are going to test them soon.

5. Collect the words and dictate them but also add some others with the same prefixes. Some of these should contain a base morpheme that starts with the same letter as the end of the prefix and some shouldn't. Some examples: ***mispronounce***, ***unnatural***, ***uncommon***, ***irrational***, ***preposition***, ***homograph***, ***revision***. Check the spelling.

6. For homework ask learners to write about what they find difficult about English spelling. They can use some of these words if appropriate.

Variations: If you have fewer than 12 learners, remove some matching morphemes. Alternatively give pairs of students all the morphemes on separate cards and get them to match them. This is also useful if it's impossible for students to move around.
If the extra words are likely to be too difficult for your learners, let them look at the base morphemes during the dictation.

Worksheet 24.4: *Prefix Partners*

mis	spelling
un	necessary
ir	regular
pre	fix
homo	phone
re	write

24.5 Word Generator

Aim: To practise forming words using prefixes. *(See A:63, B:135)*

Materials needed: One dictionary per 3 or 4 students.

Activity:

1. Divide the class into teams of three or four students. Each team needs a piece of paper.

2. Write a prefix on the board and give them one minute to write as many words as they know with that prefix. No dictionaries or other reference materials are allowed yet.

3. When the time is up, they exchange papers with another team. The other team can use a dictionary now and they check the first team's words. They give them one point for a recognisable word that exists and another point if the spelling is correct. If they are doubtful about a word, they can ask the other team for a sample sentence using the word. That team loses a point if they can't make an appropriate sentence. Be ready to referee!

4. Papers are handed back and process is repeated with another prefix. The winning team is the one with most points at the end of the game.

24.6 Confusing Prefixes

Aim: To help learners discover the differences in meaning of some homophonic or similar prefixes. *(See A:63, B:135)*

Materials needed: One worksheet per student. One dictionary per 3 or 4 students.

Activity:

1. Learners work alone to match the sentence halves. Check answers.

2. Learners work alone to choose the correct definition of each prefix. Check answers.

3. Learners work in pairs to think of more words for each prefix. They can use a dictionary if needed. They choose 5 words and write them in sentences that are related to their own lives in some way.

Key: A: 1.d 2.f 3.g 4.a 5.h 6.b 7.e 8.c.
          B: ***Anti-*** *against*; ***Ante-*** *before.*
                Dis- *negative or reversed*; ***Dys-*** *bad or wrong.*
                Hyper- *too much*; ***Hypo-*** *under, low or not enough.*
                Intra- *within*; ***Inter-*** *between.*

Variations: This could be done for homework.

Worksheet 24.6:   *Confusing Prefixes*

A. *Match the beginnings and the ends of the sentences.*

1. The anti-war protesters	a. held every Thursday.
2. Their phone was disconnected	b. people, like Einstein and John F. Kennedy.
3. The hyperactive	c. with a hypodermic needle.
4. The ante-natal clinic was	d. marched through the streets.
5. The Sales and Marketing Team had an intradepartmental	e. are vital for business executives nowadays.
6. There have been many famous dyslexic	f. because they didn't pay the bill.
7. Good intercultural communication skills	g. child just couldn't sit still in class.
8. The drugs were injected	h. competition and I won.

B. *Decide on the correct definition for the prefixes. Use the sentences above to help you.*

Anti- means *before / against.*
Ante- means *before / against.*

Dis- suggests something is *negative* or *reversed / bad* or *wrong.*
Dys- suggests something is *negative* or *reversed / bad* or *wrong.*

Hyper- means *under, low* or *not enough/too much.*
Hypo- means *under, low* or *not enough / too much.*

Intra- means *within / between.*
Inter- means *within / between.*

24.7 CVC Doubling

Aim: To illustrate that consonants double at the end of CVC words before adding vowel suffixes. *(See A:55)*

Materials needed: A map of time zones in different parts of the world would be useful. You can download one from Wikimedia Commons. Or if you have internet in the classroom, go to http://www.timeanddate.com/worldclock/converter.html

Activity:
1. Learners think of somebody they know (or a famous person) who is in a different country right now. They decide what time it is now in those countries (use the map or converter). Learners imagine what that person is doing now. Give an example yourself and write it on the board: I think my friend Ali is boiling some rice. About six learners come to the board and write their sentences. If there are any misspellings of the -ing verbs, elicit corrections and why. Ensure learners know the CVC doubling pattern *(See A:55)*.

2. Learners think of at least four other people who are in another country and they write sentences about what they imagine each one is doing. They must use a different verb in each sentence. So if they think three people are sleeping they could write that one is dreaming, one is lying in bed, etc. They check their spelling of the *-ing* verbs.

24.8 It's Good for You   ⚪⚪⚫⚪

Aim: To give practice in writing *-ing* verb forms. *(See A:55)*

Materials needed: One worksheet per student (optional).

Activity:
1. Either give learners the worksheet or dictate the end of the sentences to them (they need to start writing halfway along each line). Check dictations.

2. Learners work alone or in pairs to write the beginning of each sentence according to their own ideas. This must contain a gerund (verb + *ing*) but it can include other words too. So, for example, "Reading is good for your brain" or "Eating oily fish is good for your brain". Guide learners to check the spelling of the gerunds (especially whether to double the consonant).

3. Learners form groups of about four and discuss their ideas. If there are any they don't agree on, they write these sentences on the board for the class to discuss.

--- ✂ ---

Worksheet 24.8: It's Good for You.

1. _____   is good for your brain.

2. _____   makes you happy.

3. _____   keeps you fit.

4. _____   improves your English.

5. _____   is a good way to relax.

6. _____   helps you live longer.

7. _____   makes people more successful.

24.9 Talk About Y ⬭⬭⬭⬭ ◯◯◯◯

Aim: To help learners discover when **y** changes to **i**. *(See A:56)*

Materials needed: One worksheet per student.

Activity:
1. Write on the board "I haven't done my homework because..." and elicit reasons and excuses from learners. Give out Text A. Learners read it and decide whether they think the reasons the man gives are true or if they are just excuses.

2. Learners fill in the table in B, putting the words in bold in the text into the grey columns and the related word in the white columns. Monitor to check spelling.

3. Learners use the words in the table to help them to complete the statements in C. Check answers.

4. Ask learners to add some more words that follow these patterns to the table.

5. Learners write their own note to the teacher saying why they haven't done their homework. It can be as imaginative as they like but they should try to use at least four words from the table.

Variations: Make Exercise B easier by giving one word in each pair. Learners complete the table.
Tell learners that whenever they don't do their homework they have to write a note explaining why!

Key: B.

Singular noun	Plural noun	Verb 1 (infinitive)	Verb with inflection	Base word	Word with suffix
baby	babies	stay	stayed	beauty	beautiful
boy	boys	try	tried	happy	happiness
toy	toys	cry	crying		
		play	playing		
		worry	worrying		
		marry	married		
		cry	cries		
		study	studying		

C.
1. If a noun ends in Consonant + **y**, make the plural by changing the **y** to **i** and adding **es**.
2. If a verb ends in Consonant + **y**, before you add the inflection, **change the y to i**.
3. If a base word ends in Consonant + **y**, before you add the suffix, **change the y to i**.
4. BUT if the inflection or suffix begins with an **i**, **don't change the y to i**.
5. If a base word ends in Vowel + **y**, before you add the ending, **don't change the y to i**.

Worksheet 24.9: Talk About Y

A.

Dear Teacher,

Sorry I haven't done my homework. I **stayed** at home and I **tried** to study, but it's not quiet enough. The **babies** were **crying** and the **boys** were **playing** with noisy **toys**. Then I started **worrying** about my **beautiful** daughter. She is getting **married** pretty soon and her **happiness** is very important to me. And my wife **cries** every night because our daughter is leaving us. So you see, **studying** was impossible!

B. *Fill in the table with* **bold** *words from the text above in the grey column. Write another word in the white column.*

Singular noun	Plural noun	Verb 1 (infinitive)	Verb with inflection	Base word	Word with suffix
baby	babies	stay	stayed	beauty	beautiful

C.

Can you complete these statements? Look at the words above to help you.

1. If a noun ends in Consonant + *y*, make the plural by _____

2. If a verb ends in Consonant + *y*, before you add the inflection, _____

3. If a base word ends in Consonant + *y*, before you add the suffix, _____

4. BUT if the inflection or suffix begins with an *i*, _____

5. If a base word ends in Vowel + *y*, before you add the ending, _____

24.10 -able or -ible?

○○◐◑

Aim: To help learners know whether to use **-able** or **-ible** at the end of a word. *(See A:58, B:135)*

Materials needed: One worksheet per student.

Activity:
1. Lead in to the subject of hotels.

2. Tell learners they are going to read a review of a bad hotel. What do they think the reviewer will say?

3. Give the worksheet and learners read and see if their predictions were right.

4. Learners highlight all the words that finish with the sound /əbəl/. Ask how many they have found — it should be ten.

5. Learners copy the words into the correct columns of the table in B.

6. In the table, learners highlight the part of the word before the **-able** or **-ible**. Ask if they notice anything about these. If necessary point out that **-able** is usually added to whole words (or with perhaps small changes such as a dropped **e** or a **y** changed to **i**). **-ible**, on the other hand, is usually added to stems that are not complete words. Learners check this hypothesis with the words and any others they can think of. Remind them that this is a common pattern rather than a strict rule.

7. Learners write a review for a hotel, a service, their school, a shop, a music venue — whichever is most appropriate. They should include at least five words that end in **-able** or **-ible**.

Variations: This could be given for homework.

Key: B. -able available, unbelievable, acceptable, unbearable, uncomfortable, enjoyable.
-ible incredible, horrible, visible, inedible.

Worksheet 24.10: *-able or -ible?*

A.

Queen's Palace Hotel

★ ☆ ☆ ☆ ☆

I recently stayed at this hotel and it was incredible. Incredibly bad! There was no transport available from the airport and so we had to take a taxi which cost an unbelievable amount. The service from the receptionists was, I suppose, acceptable, but not very friendly.

When we first opened the door to our bedroom there was an unbearable smell and we insisted on moving to another room. The beds were the most uncomfortable I have ever slept in and the decoration was really horrible. Our room was supposed to have 'sea view', but the sea was only visible if you stood on a chair!

We only ate in the hotel restaurant once because the food was inedible — I wouldn't give it to my dog!

It certainly wasn't the most enjoyable holiday I've ever had!

B. *Copy the -ible and -able words into the correct boxes below.*

Words with -able	Words with -ible

24.11 World Quiz

○○○○

Aim: To raise awareness of common spellings of /wɜː/, /wɒ/ and /wɔː/ as in **work**, **watch** and **war**. *(See A:52)*

Materials needed: One worksheet per student.

Activity:
1. Learners do the quiz in pairs or teams. When you check answers, read out the statements, as it is important for learners to hear the target words. Check that their pronunciation of the target words is accurate too.

2. Learners look at the words in bold and try to put them into three groups according to their pronunciation. Then they look at the spelling and notice the pattern. Do make sure they know that not all words spelled with these patterns have these sounds.

3. Extend the activity by writing the following words on the board and asking them to fit them into the groups: **worse**, **want**, **quality**, **warm**, **worth**, **wash**, **warning**, **wallet**, **squat**.

Variations: For more advanced groups, include some words in the last stage which do not follow the pattern and ask learners to identify these, for example: **worn**, **worry**, **wax**, **wag**, **quay**.

Key:
1. The most common word in English is 'a'. FALSE. *It's 'the'.*
2. People in Japan work longer hours than anywhere else. FALSE. In South Korea *the average employee works 2,357 hours per year--that's six-and-a-half hours for every single day of their life. According to a 2008 ranking by the Organization for Economic Co-operation and Development, South Koreans work the longest hours per year, on average, out of every other OECD member.*
3. Nothing eats wasps. FALSE. Birds, other insects and even other wasps eat them.
4. A quarter of the world's population lives without electricity. TRUE.
5. The moon is slowly moving towards the Earth. FALSE. *It's moving away from it, very slowly.*
6. The world population is more than twice as big as it was in 1960. TRUE. *1960 - 3bn; 2010 - 6.7bn and growing.*
7. More people died in the First World War than in the Second World War. FALSE.
8. Twenty-five percent of the world's population watched the opening ceremony of the Beijing Olympics in 2008. FALSE. *15% (estimated)*

Worksheet 24.11:   *World Quiz*

True or False?

1. The most common **word** in English is 'a'.

2. People in Japan **work** longer hours than anywhere else.

3. Nothing eats **wasps**.

4. A **quarter** of the **world**'s population lives without electricity.

5. The moon is slowly moving **towards** the Earth.

6. The world population now is more than twice as big as it **was** in 1960.

7. More people died in the First World **War** than in the Second World War.

8. Twenty-five percent of the world's population **watched** the opening ceremony of the Beijing Olympics in 2008.

24.12 Listen to the c ⃝⃝⃝⃝⃝

Aim: To raise awareness of spelling of hard and soft **c**. *(See A:50)*

Materials needed: One worksheet per student, each cut into 2 parts.

Activity:

1. If appropriate, lead in to the subject of smoking and ask why people try to give up and what prevents them.

2. Give out the worksheets. Learners read and see if any of their ideas were mentioned. Learners discuss their reaction to the text.

3. Read the text aloud to the learners slowly and ask them to put the words in bold into the correct circle, according to whether the sound made by the **c** is soft like /s/ or hard like /k/. Learners check their answers.

4. Learners try to complete the statements according to the words in the circles.

5. Learners put away the first worksheet. Give out exercise D. They fill in the letter that follows the **c** in the text.

Key: B. Soft c: decided, Lucy, announced, cigarettes, celebrated, cents, price, cinema, places, ceilings. **Hard** *c*: Canadian, Cooper, cut, claimed, addicted, tobacco, could, come, packet, class, can, public, clothes.
C. A hard *c* is followed by *a*, *o*, *u,* a **consonant,** or is at the **end** of a word.
A soft *c* is followed by *e, i* or *y*.

Worksheet 24.12: *Listen to the c*

A.

TIME TO QUIT

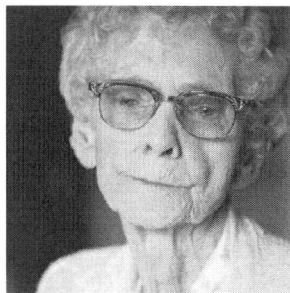

A **Canadian** woman who has smoked for 95 years has finally **decided** to give up. **Lucy Cooper announced** she would **cut** out all **cigarettes** as she **celebrated** her 105th birthday today. Mrs Cooper has always **claimed** that she is not **addicted** to **tobacco** and **could** stop at any time. Now, she says, the time has **come**. "I paid about 10 **cents** for a **packet** when I started, and look at the **price** now! We used to smoke in the **cinema** and teachers even smoked in **class**, but there aren't many **places** you **can** smoke in **public** now. The **ceilings** in my apartment are brown and my **clothes** smell. It's disgusting. I'm quitting!"

*B. Look at the words in bold. Listen carefully to the text. Put the words into the two circles below according how the **c** is pronounced.*

Soft **c** — /s/   Hard **c** — /k/

C. *What do you notice about the spelling pattern?*

- A hard **c** is followed by __, __, __, a _____, or is at the ____ of a word.

- A soft **c** is followed by __, __ or __.

Listen to the c

D. *Fill in the letter after the **c** in these words.*

A **C_nadian** woman who has smoked for 95 years has finally **dec_ded** to give up. **Lucy Cooper announc_d** she would **c_t** out all **c_garettes** as she **c_lebrated** her 105th birthday today. Mrs Cooper has always **c_aimed** that she is not **addic_ed** to **tobacc_** and **c_uld** stop at any time. Now, she says, the time has **c_me**. "I paid about 10 **c_nts** for a **pac_et** when I started, and look at the **pric_** now! We used to smoke in the **c_nema** and teachers even smoked in **c_ass**, but there aren't many **plac_s** you **c_n** smoke in **public** now. The **c_ilings** in my apartment are brown and my **c_othes** smell. I'm quitting!"

24.13 c, k, or ck?

Aim: To help learners remember whether to write **c** or **k** or **ck**. *(See A:56)*

Materials needed: One worksheet for each student, cut into two parts.

Activity:

1. Write on the board "Cat makes 400 kilometre trip" and ask learners to make predictions about the story. Give out the first part of the worksheet. They read the story to check.

2. Give out the second part of the worksheet. Learners find all the words in A containing the letter **c** and highlight them along with the following letter, like this: **cat**. Then they do the same for words containing **k**, but use a different colour.

3. Learners try to complete the statements by writing the letters **c, k** or **ck**. They look at the text to help them. They also write one sample word from the text to illustrate.

4. Learners put away Part A. of the worksheet before looking at C. They complete the same text with **c, k** or **ck**. They refer to the patterns in part B.

5. Learners check answers by looking at the original text in A.

Key: B: 1. c   2. k   3. c   4. ck   5. k   6. k.

Worksheet 24.13:   *c, k, or ck?*

A.

Cat makes 400 kilometre trip

A cat has been found more than 400 kilometres away from home. Kevin Baker thinks his cat, called Kitty, could have got into the luggage compartment of a coach and got taken to the north of England. He thought a caller from York was joking when he claimed he had found Kitty there. Luckily, the dark grey cat was wearing a collar around her neck with her name and phone number on it.

Kitty is now at home in her basket. "It's fantastic to have her back. The kids were crying and walking around looking for her. I told them not to worry but I did think she might have been killed by a car or something," said Kevin.

--✂--

B. *Find all the **c**s in the text. Highlight the **c** in each word and the letter that follows it. Do the same with **k**, but use a different colour pen.*

*Now write **c**, **k** or **ck** to complete these statements. Give example words from the text.*

1. When you hear the sound /k/, write ___ if the next letter is ***a, o, u*** or a consonant.
2. When you hear the sound /k/, write ___ if the next letter is ***e, i*** or ***y***.
3. Usually ___ is only the last letter in the word if there's an ***i*** before it. Many adjectives and nouns end like this.
4. A syllable with a short vowel sound usually ends in ___.
5. A syllable with a long vowel sound and two vowels together usually ends in ___.
6. After the letters ***n, s, r, l*** or ***oo***, we use ___ at the end of a syllable.

C. *Complete the words with **c, k** or **ck**. They all have the /k/ sound.*

_at ma__es 400 _ilometre trip

A _at has been found more than 400 _ilometres away from home.
_evin Ba_er thin_s his _at, _alled _itty, _ould have got into the luggage _ompartment of a _oach and got ta_en to the north of England. He thought a _aller from Yor_ was jo_ing when he _laimed he had found _itty there. Lu__ily the dar_ grey _at was wearing a _ollar around her ne___ with her name and phone number on it. _itty is now at home in her bas_et. "It's fantasti_ to have her ba___. The _ids were _rying and wal_ing around loo_ing for her. I told them not to worry but I did thin_ she might have been _illed by a _ar or something," said _evin.

24.14 Three-Letter Rule ⬭⬭⬭⬭

Aim: To raise awareness that content words are spelled with three letters or more.
(See A:55)

Activity:
1. Take any short text (or a paragraph from a longer text) that you have already studied. Learners highlight all the two letter words. While they are doing this, write on the board (or dictate):
   - a. All two letter words are function words. T/F
   - b. All function words are two letter words. T/F
   - c. All words with three letters or more are content words. T/F
   - d. All content words have three letters of more. T/F

   Check understanding of **content** and **function words**.

2. In pairs, learners look at the highlighted words and work out which of the four statements on the board seem true. Check answers.

3. Ask learners how this can help them with their spelling.

Key: 2. a. True, with the exception of the words **ox**, and **ax** (American English spelling). The words **go**, **be** and **do** only have two letters, because they *can* be used as function words as well as content words. There are also shortened forms (**ad**) and interjections (**oh**, **hi**).
b. False. Many function words have more than two letters: **although**, **between**, **their**.
c. False. (see b.)
d. True (see a.)
3. Knowing that content words have at least three letters helps learners with homophones, such as **to/too**, **by/buy**, **be/bee**, **so/sew**; it also helps them see a reason for double letters in words like **egg** and **add**.

Chapter Twenty-Five:

Editing and Using Reference Tools

25.1 It's Got to Be Perfect

Aim: To raise awareness of situations in which spelling must be accurate and to practise editing. *(See A:12, B:122)*

Materials needed: One worksheet per student, folded vertically so that only column A is visible.

Activity:
1. In groups or pairs learners discuss situations in which spelling needs to be very accurate. Conduct feedback with the whole class.

2. Give each student a folded worksheet. In the same groups, they look at the written items on the worksheet (Column A), identify what kind of text each one is (e.g. an email address) and discuss whether they identified that situation in their initial discussion. Conduct class feedback.

3. Learners work alone. They open the worksheet and decide which information in column B is exactly the same as in column A. They check with a partner and the class.

4. Learners write a similar activity for their classmates, using the same types of text, but using different information.

Variations: This could be a homework activity.

Key: A. 1. Email address 2. URL (web address) 3. Exam question 4. Cover letter for job application 5. User name and password for internet site 6. Order form 7. Computer game. **B.** 1. b 2. a 3. b 4. a 5. c 6. a 7. c.

Worksheet 25.1: *It's Got to Be Perfect*

A Identify these text types. If you made a mistake in these situations, what would happen?		B Which of these gives exactly the same information as column A?
1 mjpthompson1982@gmail.com	a	mipthompson1982@gmail.com
	b	*mjpthompson1982@gmail.com*
	c	mjpthompson.1982@gmail.com
2 https://quhsdns3.net~2983/cpseff52177/.html	a	**https://quhsdns3.net~2983/cpseff52177.html**
	b	http://quhsdns3.net~2983/cpseff52177.html
	c	*https://quhsdns3.net~2983/cpseff5217.html*
3 *Questions 6-10* *Listen and write TWO WORDS for each answer.* *6. What clothes should you bring on the trip?* walking boots thick socks waterproof jacket	a	*working boots / thick socks / waterproof jacket* **b** *walking boots / thick socks / waterproof jacket*
	c	walking boots / think socks / waterproof jacket
4 Dear Mr Gryzbowski, I would like to apply for the post of Engineer at Mississauga Systems as advertised on www.gizzajob.com	a	Dear Mr Gryzbowski, I would like to apply for the post of Engineer at Mississauga Systems as advertised on www.gizzajob.com
	b	Dear Mr Grzybowski, I would like to apply for the post of Engineer at Mississauga Systems as advertised on www.gizzajob.com
	c	Dear Mr Gryzbowski, I would like to apply for the post of Engine ear at Mississauga Systems as advertised on www.gizzajob.com
5 Here are your login details: User name: SDjry5qieyo Password: iUw3t4wJe	a	SDjry5qieyo / iUw3t4wJ **b** *SDjry5qiey0 / iUw3t4wJe* **c** *SDjry5qieyo / iUw3t4wJe*

6 I would like to place an order for the following:		a	150	XJ6 — 40mm — grey

Quantity	Product
150	XJ6 — 40mm — grey
225	BBP42 — 10mm — green
5	LNV2 — superfast midi

a	150	XJ6 — 40mm — grey	
	225	BBP42 — 10mm — green	
	5	LNV2 — superfast midi	
b	150	XJ6 — 40mm — green	
	225	BBP42 — 10mm — grey	
	5	LNV2 — superfast midi	
c	150	XJ6 — 40mm — grey	
	225	BPP42 — 10mm — green	
	5	LNV2 — superfat midi	

7	a	norepinephrenergic
	b	norepinephrinegic
	c	norepinephrinergic

25.2 Write First, Edit Later ⬭⬭⬭⬭

Aim: To train learners to focus on fluency before focussing on accuracy. *(See B:159)*

Materials needed: A dictionary and/or thesaurus for about every three learners. Each learner needs two different coloured pens.

Activity:

1. Think of a general topic that your learners are likely to have strong feelings about. It should also be reasonably demanding in terms of spelling needed. Some suggestions: today's news, what this town needs, favourite films, my dream.

2. Brainstorm some examples within the general subject (e.g. items in the news today) and write them on the board. Ask learners to choose one of these (or if relevant perhaps two for comparison) and tell them that they are going to write about it for 5 minutes. Set a short writing task. This will depend on the topic chosen, your learners' interest and general language level. Stress that they should express themselves as fully and honestly as possible.

3. Before they start writing give them about 3 – 5 minutes preparation time. This is time to prepare their ideas and language. They use this time to write single words or phrases that they think they will need. They can use a dictionary, thesaurus, previous notes or ask you if they don't know the spelling.

4. Learners put away all reference books and only keep out the notes they made. Ask them to spend five minutes writing. While writing, they should not ask you or anybody else. Remind them that, at this stage, you are most interested in their ideas rather than their language accuracy. If they want to say something but don't know how to spell it they should make a guess and underline the word. Stop them after five minutes. They read what they have written, correcting anything that they can with a different colour pen.

5. Learners spend another five minutes consulting each other, a dictionary, a thesaurus and you about any spellings they underlined. They write corrections with the different colour pen. Learners record their new spellings in their spelling logs if they have them. (See B:140).

6. Discuss with learners why this is a good way to write — because you say exactly what you want to say without letting unknown spellings restrict you. You also learn new spellings that you need to express yourself. Encourage learners to approach other writing tasks like this.

Variations: Of course, they can edit other language, not just spelling, in the same way in the text they have written. This strategy could be used with any writing task. To get students to write continuously, the free web tool 'Write or Die Online' is fun and very useful: http://writeordie.com/ If you pause too long in your writing, words you have written start to disappear. Cruel but motivating! Be sure to remind learners to copy their work into a word processing program as soon as the five minutes is finished or they will lose it.

25.3 The intruder   ⦾⦾⦾⦾

Aim: To help learners to notice errors in writing. *(See B:166)*

Materials needed: One worksheet per student.

Activity:

1. To lead in to the text, ask students if they have heard about any strange crimes.

2. Learners listen to you reading the text aloud (see Key) and they think of a good headline for it. Discuss their headlines and their reaction to the story, checking they understood.

3. Give out the worksheet face down and tell learners not to turn it over yet. Explain that it is the same story but there are 12 spelling errors. It's a race to find them and write the correct spellings below the text. Get them all to turn over the paper at the same time and put their hand up for you to check when they think they've found them all.

Key:
Police were called to a house yesterday to investigate a very unusual crime.

When Mr and Mrs Lee, of King's Avenue, got up on Monday morning they got a shock. The back door was open and their new television, a laptop and a handbag had all been stolen. That was bad enough, but then they were in for another shock. When 32-year-old Max Lee went to the bathroom, he found the bath was full of water and there were wet towels on the floor. Neither Mr Lee nor his wife, who live alone in the house, had had a bath. "We're shower people", said Mr Lee, "We hardly ever use the bath".

The water in the bath was still warm and they found a pair of underpants on the floor. "Not my husband's style at all", said a worried Amanda Lee. She also discovered that her shower cap was missing.

Police are looking for a clean burglar wearing a pink shower cap.

1. yesterday	5. for	9. floor
2. got	6. went	10. husband's
3. television	7. alone	11. Police
4. stolen	8. bath	12. shower

Worksheet 25.3: *The Intruder*

Find spelling mistakes in this text. Write the 12 words correctly below the text.

Police were called to a house yesterrday to investigate a very unusual crime.

When Mr and Mrs Lee, of King's Avenue, got up on Monday morning they gto a shock. The back door was open and their new televisioh, a laptop and a handbag had all been ztolen. That was bad enough, but then they were in ofr another shock. When 32-year-old Max Lee wen to the bathroom, he found the bath was full of water and there were wet towels on the floor. Neither Mr Lee nor his wife, who live al one in the house, had had a bath. "We're shower people", said Mr Lee, "We hardly ever use the bbath".

The water in the bath was still warm and they found a pair of underpants on the fhloor. "Not my hubsand's style at all", said a worried Amanda Lee. She also discovered that her shower cap was missing.

Plice are looking for a clean burglar wearing a pink shover cap.

1._____	5._____	9._____
2._____	6._____	10._____
3._____	7._____	11._____
4._____	8._____	12._____

25.4 How Do You Spell Thesaurus?   ⬭⬭⬭⬭

Aim: To show how a thesaurus can be used as a spelling reference. *(See B:149)*

Materials needed: One thesaurus between two people. The thesaurus could be in book form, a piece of software or the thesaurus built into a word processing program.

Activity: Before class, collect some words that you think your students will know, look them up in the thesaurus and find a synonym that they probably won't know. Alternatively, use the examples below.

1.   In class, show learners how to look for a word in a thesaurus if they've never used one.

2.   Write one of your difficult words on the board, with some gaps for missing letters. Write the easy word in brackets after it, like this:

    r_v_no_s (hungry)

    Learners look up ***hungry*** in the thesaurus and try to find ***ravenous***. They fill in the missing letters.

3.   Write some more gapped difficult words with easy synonyms on the board for them to look up. Stress that the object is not for them to learn these particular spellings, but to show them how they can use a thesaurus to check a spelling if they know a synonym or near synonym.

Here are some more examples you could use:
 r_v_no_s (hungry) ravenous
 in__ate (start) initiate
 _n_w (chew) gnaw
 prin_ip_ (rule) principle
 ass__ (think) assume
 rec__t (proof of payment) receipt
 an_ous (nervous) anxious

25.5 Using Spell-Checkers ⭕⭕⭕⭕

Aim: To help learners use spell-checkers effectively. *(See B:150)*

Materials needed: One worksheet per student.

Activity:
1. Lead in to the subject of studying abroad if it is appropriate.

2. Read the text aloud to learners (see Key). They decide what they think happened on the second visit that made it so different from the first one. Learners discuss in pairs and with the class (there is no right or wrong answer).

3. Give out the text and warn them that the spell-checker has marked some words that it thinks are misspellings. Learners work alone to decide which word would be the best replacement. If they don't think any of them are right, they choose *Look Up* (and write the spelling of the word if they know it). If they think the spell-checker is wrong (i.e. the word is correctly spelled) they choose *Ignore*.

Key:
A. When I was <u>eighteen</u> I went to school in England for a year. I had been to the UK two years <u>earlier</u> and had had a great time. But the second visit <u>turned</u> out to be a very <u>different</u> <u>experience</u>.
The first time I had gone to Newcastle where the <u>people</u> were really warm and <u>friendly</u>. I had <u>immediately</u> made some very good friends and we had <u>a lot</u> of fun. I was on holiday so we went on lots of <u>picnics</u> and had loads of <u>parties</u>. But going to school in London was <u>another</u> matter."

B.
1.*Look up* (eighteen) *2.* earlier 3. turned 4. different 5. *Look up* (experience) 6. people 7. friendly 8. immediately 9. a lot 10. picnics 11. parties 12. another.

Worksheet 25.5: Using Spell-Checkers

A.

When I was [1]eghttin I went to school in England for a year. I had been to the UK two years [2]hearlier and had had a great time. But the second visit [3]terned out to be a very [4]difrent [5]experients.

The first time I had gone to Newcastle where the [6]pepel were really warm and [7]frendy. I had [8]emidiatly made some very good friends and we had [9]alot of fun. I was on holiday so we went on lots of [10]bicnicks and had loads of [11]partys. But going to school in London was [12]a nother matter."

B. *If the spell-checker offered you these options which would you take? Underline the word the writer wanted if it is shown. If you think all the words offered are wrong, choose **Look up**. If you think the spelling is correct, choose **Ignore**.*

1. getting / eighty / *Look up* / *Ignore*

2. heartier / earlier / headlines / *Look up* / *Ignore*

3. termed / turned / trended / *Look up* / *Ignore*

4. different / deferent / divergent / *Look up* / *Ignore*

5. experiments / expedients / experiments' / *Look up* / *Ignore*

6. peel / papal / people / pupil / peep / *Look up* / *Ignore*

7. frenzy / trendy / ferny / friend / friendly / *Look up* / *Ignore*

8. immediately / remedially / medially / *Look up* / *Ignore*

9. allot / alto / a lot / alit / aloft / *Look up* / *Ignore*

10. bionics / picnics / bannocks / *Look up* / *Ignore*

11. parties / party's / parts / party / part's / *Look up* / *Ignore*

12. nether / mother / another / not her / other / *Look up* / *Ignore*

25.6 Forever Single   ⬭⬤⬤⬤

Aim: To raise awareness that some letters are never doubled and introduce learners to the use of concordancers for spelling. *(See B:158)*

Materials: Computers with internet.

Activity:

1. Write each letter of the alphabet, doubled, on the board: aa, bb, cc, etc. In pairs, learners decide which letters can be doubled. They try to think of one English word that contains each double letter.

2. Learners go to http://www.lextutor.ca/concordancers/concord_e.html
    In the Keyword(s) box they choose 'contains' from the dropdown menu. In the next box they type one set of double letters that they suspect might not exist in English, e.g. *jj*. They choose a corpus — 'All of the above' is the biggest. They click the 'Get Concordance' button and they will be offered a list of words that contain that string. They need to ignore names and foreign words.

3. Conduct feedback on which double letters are used in English. Also discuss with learners other uses of concordancers for spelling (to find words with particular patterns, or find which patterns are never found in particular positions).

Key: These letters are rarely (or never) doubled in native English words: *a h i j k q u w x y*. This does not apply if one of those letters is at the end of the first part of a compound word and the beginning of the second part, e.g. *hitchhike*, *withhold*, *bookkeeping*.

Chapter Twenty-Six:

Testing and Assessment

26.1 Diagnostic Test   ○○○○

Aim: To discover learners' needs regarding spelling improvement. *(See B:175)*

Materials: One test per learner.

Activity: Use any or all of the following tasks. Give learners one copy of the test each.

1. Section 1 checks for basic literacy. Use Question 6 (address), only if learners are in an English-speaking country. You may need them to bring in an official letter addressed to them to check the spelling of the address.

2. Section 2 checks spelling of some very common words which are not necessarily phonetically spelled. Read the full text (which is in the key below) to learners once, slowly but naturally. Then read it again very slowly, repeating the highlighted words as necessary. Learners fill in the gaps. Finally read the whole passage again slowly but naturally.

3. Section 3 checks whether learners can spell unknown phonetically-regular words by sound only. If appropriate, tell learners that these are the names of the players of a new football team. They all have English surnames. Say the names as many times as they need to hear them (see Key below) and learners decide which spelling is most like the sound.

4. Section 4 checks whether learners can correctly apply morphological rules in word building. Read each sentence aloud to them. They fill in the gaps, making appropriate words related to the base morphemes given at the end of the sentences.

5. Section 5 checks whether learners can see patterns and make predictions from them for other spellings. Read the text for each question and the target words. Learners write the two words, using the similar words given as reference.

Key and notes:
Section 1:   Answers will vary.

Section 2:
Both **of my** children find spelling difficult. **Their** teachers **said they were** working hard **but** my son got **two out of** 20 **on** a test last week. **One of his** friends, **who is only** a little better **than him at** spelling, **said there is** a website **about** learning spelling **that he** uses **which is very** helpful. **My** wife **says she will** work **with them for about** 30 minutes a day **on some of the** activities. **What** else **can we do**?

Section 3:

1.	Fratt /fræt/ B	Kibbing /kɪbɪŋ/ C
2.	Grabe /greɪb/ B	Strolp /strɒlp/ C
3.	Feen /fiːn/ A	Darly /dɑːliː/ C
4.	Hurb /hɜːb/ C	Gatch /gætʃ/ B
5.	Glog /glɒg/ A	Scrank /skræŋk/ A
6.	Dilk /dɪlk/ C	Dunny /dʌniː/ C

Section 4:
1. My spelling is **getting** better!
2. I was **making** a paper aeroplane when the boss walked in.
3. You can return anything that's **unneeded**.
4. Luckily, he escaped from the burning car **unhurt**.
5. Sometimes **bloggers** write very strange things.
6. He **milked** the cows by hand until last year.
7. I was surprised at the **greenness** of the grass.
8. I've **finally** finished the report.
9. I've been to three **parties** this weekend.
10. "You have three **wishes**" said the fairy.
11. The cat **scratches** at the door when she wants to come in.
12. It's the **funniest** film I've ever seen.

Section 5:
1. *could* is a modal verb. Several of the modal verbs have a similar spelling. Study the spelling of *could* carefully. Now write the words you hear.
   would, should
2. *two* has unusual spelling. Study it carefully, then try to write the four words that you hear that are related to the meaning of *two*. The spelling pattern is similar.
   twelve, twenty, twice, twin
3. *here* talks about a place. Study the spelling. Now listen to and write down two other words related to places that have a similar spelling pattern.
   there, where, nowhere
4. *hear* (the same pronunciation as *here*) is related to sound. Look carefully at the spelling. The try to write these words also related to sound.
   ear, heard, hearing
5. We often add '*ful*' to the end of a noun to make an adjective, like *wonderful*. Notice the spelling of the last part. Now write the adjectives you hear:
   careful, peaceful, hopeful

26.1   Diagnostic spelling test.

Part 1 — Words you need

Please fill in this form carefully:

1.   Your first name ....

2.   Your surname/family name ....

3.   Your country ....

4.   Your nationality ....

5.   Your job ....

6.   Your address. ....

....

Part 2 — Spelling by eye

Listen. Fill in the missing words in the text. They are very common words.

Both ____ ____ children find spelling difficult. ____ teachers ____ ____ ____ working hard

____ my son got ____ ____ ____ 20 ____ a test last week. ____ ____ ____ friends, ____ ____ ____

a little better ____ ____ ____ spelling, ____ ____ ____ a website ____ learning spelling ____

____ uses ____ ____ ____ helpful. ____ wife ____ ____ ____ work ____ ____ ____ ____ 30

minutes a day ____ ____ ____ ____ activities. ____ else ____ ____ ____?

Part 3 — Spelling by sound

Listen to the names. Which spelling is most likely?

	A	B	C			A	B	C
1	Frate	Fratt	Freat		7	Cibbing	Ckibbing	Kibbing
2	Grabb	Grabe	Gryb		8	Storlp	Strlop	Strolp
3	Feen	Fine	Hpean		9	Daly	Darely	Darly
4	Herbb	Hubb	Hurb		10	Gach	Gatch	Jach
5	Glog	Gloge	Jlog		11	Scrank	Skranc	Skrangk
6	Dikl	Dilkk	Dilk		12	Doney	Dune	Dunny

Part 4 — Prefixes and suffixes

1. My spelling is _____ better! (GET)

2. I was _____ a paper aeroplane when the boss walked in. (MAKE)

3. You can return anything that's _____. (NEED)

4. He escaped from the burning car _____. (HURT)

5. Sometimes _____ write very strange things. (BLOG)

6. He _____ the cows by hand until last year. (MILK)

7. I was surprised at the _____ of the grass. (GREEN)

8. I've _____ finished the report. (FINAL)

9. I've been to three _____ this weekend. (PARTY)

10. "You have three _____," said the fairy. (WISH)

11. The cat _____ at the door when she wants to come in. (SCRATCH)

12. It's the _____ film I've ever seen. (FUNNY)

Part 5 — Finding patterns

1. **could** is a modal verb. Several of the modal verbs have a similar spelling. Study the spelling of **could** carefully. Now write the words you hear.

   _____, _____

2. **two** has unusual spelling. Study it carefully, then try to write the four words that you hear that are related to the meaning of **two.** The spelling pattern is similar.

   _____, _____, _____, _____

3. **here** talks about a place. Study the spelling. Now listen to and write down two other words related to places that have a similar spelling pattern.

   _____, _____, _____

4. **hear** (the same pronunciation as **here**) is related to sound. Look carefully at the spelling. The try to write these words also related to sound:

   _____, _____, _____

5. We often add '**ful**' to the end of a noun to make an adjective, like **wonderful**. Notice the spelling of the last part. Now write the adjectives you hear:

   _____, _____, _____

26.2 Progress Charts

Aim: To motivate learners to track their progress on spelling tests. *(See B:177)*

Materials: One photocopy of one of the charts per learner.

Activity: When giving spelling tests, learners record their scores on one of the two charts given here. Choose one set of instructions below.

A. Give out the graph. Learners write the date of the first test in the first space on the left along the bottom axis. Then they mark a cross to represent their score on that test. Each time they do a test, they fill in their chart and will be able to see their own progress, rather than their progress in relation to others. After the first test, you could ask learners to draw a pencil line on the rest of the graph to plot the progress they are aiming for — encourage them to be realistic but optimistic!

B. Give out the target. Agree with the class or with individuals (in a very mixed ability class) what range of scores each circle represents. For example, the centre circle may be "100%" or you might decide that it's "More than 80%". Learners write this key next to the target. After each spelling test, learners write the date (or a number — 1 for the first test and so on) on the target according to their score. After about six to ten tests, give learners a new sheet and renegotiate the target values.

-- ✂ --

26.2 Progress Graph

Name:

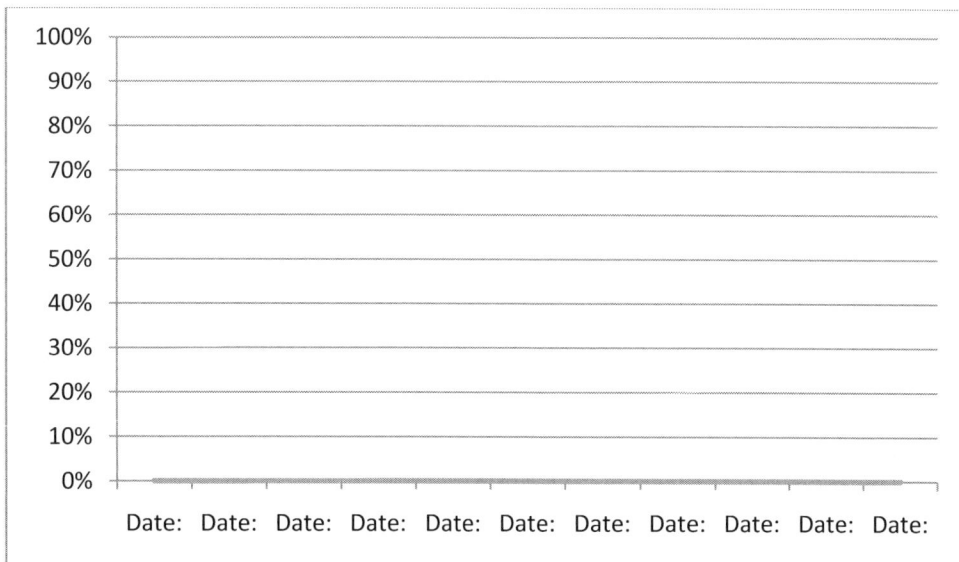

PHOTOCOPIABLE ©Johanna Stirling 2011. Teaching Spelling to English Language Learners

26.2 Progress Target

Name:

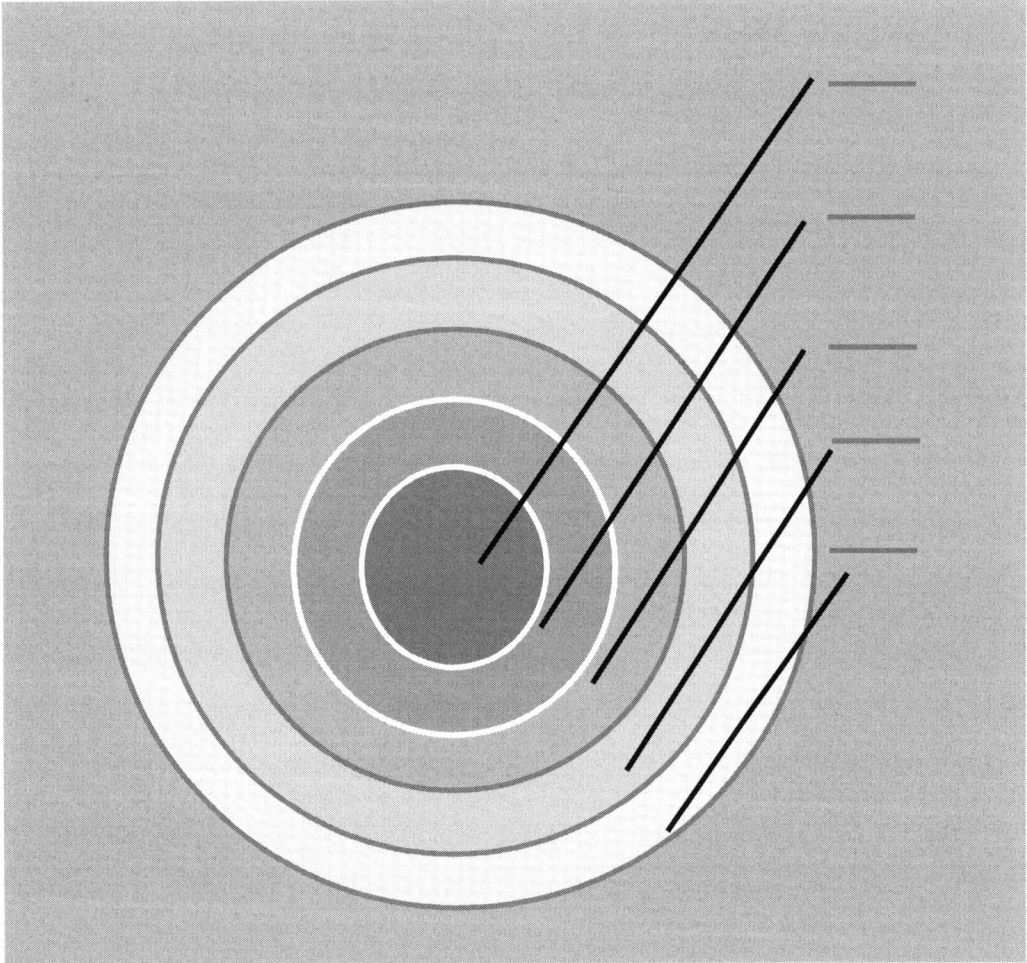

26.3 Assessment Rubric

Aim: To assess learners on their use of strategies as well as knowledge. *(See B:177)*

Materials: One photocopy per learner.

Activity:

1. Give out and explain the writing rubric to learners.

2. In their next writing task they will write the first draft, focusing on the meaning they want to express. As they are writing they highlight any words about which they are unsure. They will be marked on the range of vocabulary that they use so they should not avoid words that are difficult to spell.

3. When they have finished writing they read through their work and highlight any more spellings that they are not completely sure about.

4. Learners use reference materials or ask to check the spellings they highlighted. They write the corrected spelling above the highlighted attempt. If they are word processing, they put the highlighted word in brackets followed by the correct spelling.

5. Give learners a writing task.

6. Use the rubric when marking written work.

26.3 Writing Assessment Rubric

Criteria	5	4	3	2	1
Highlights the misspelled words.	Over 90% of misspelled words highlighted	75-90% of misspelled words highlighted	50-74% of misspelled words highlighted	25-49% of misspelled words highlighted	Less than 25% of misspelled words highlighted
Accurately corrects them in 2nd draft	Over 90% of highlighted words corrected	75-90% of highlighted words corrected	50-74% of highlighted words corrected	25-49% of highlighted words corrected	Less than 25% of highlighted words corrected
Vocabulary range	Used vocabulary considerably higher than writing level	Used vocabulary somewhat higher than writing level	Used vocabulary range appropriate to writing level	Used vocabulary somewhat lower than writing level	Used vocabulary considerably lower than writing level
Scores:					

Overall score:
General comments:

Appendix A

The hundred most common words

the	or	will	number
of	one	up	no
and	had	other	way
a	by	about	could
to	word	out	people
in	but	many	my
is	not	then	than
you	what	them	first
that	all	these	water
it	were	so	been
he	we	some	call
was	when	her	who
for	your	would	oil
on	can	make	its
are	said	like	now
as	there	him	find
with	use	into	long
his	an	time	down
they	each	has	day
I	which	look	did
at	she	two	get
be	do	more	come
this	how	write	made
have	their	go	may
from	if	see	part

Taken From: *The Reading Teachers Book of Lists, Third Edition*; by Edward Bernard Fry, Ph.D, Jacqueline E. Kress, Ed.D & Dona Lee Fountoukidis, Ed.D.

Appendix B

How the sounds of English can be spelled.

Over the next few pages you will find the different ways each of the 44 sounds in English[47] can be spelled. In fact there are a few other spellings that are rare or found in foreign words used occasionally in English — these are not included. Sometimes the choice depends on the position of the letter in the word and sometimes on other letters in the word.

To show the possible position of the letter(s) to make each sound, dashes (-) have been used. Here 'x' represents the letter or letters:

x	=	can appear anywhere in the word, beginning, middle or end.
x-	=	must be followed by another letter. It can be at the beginning or in the middle of a word, but not the end.
-x	=	must follow another letter. It can be in the middle or at the end of a word, but not at the beginning.
-x-	=	must have letters both before and after it. It cannot be at the beginning or at the end, it must be in the middle.

Where there is reference to long and short vowels, this concerns *sounds* rather than written letters *(See A:43)*.

Some of the spellings are more common and these are marked in **bold**. The others are less common.

Consonant sounds — how they can be represented

IPA	as in	Possible spellings	Example words
/p/	a**pp**le	**p**	pet, hope
		-pp- (usually after short vowel)	supper
/b/	**b**ottle	**b**	blue, baby
		-bb (usually after short vowel)	hobby
/t/	**t**able	**t**	travel, gate
		-tt (usually after short vowel)	letter
		-ed (after unvoiced consonant, V2/V3[48] regular ending)	wished
		th-	Thames, thyme
/d/	**d**og	**d**	date, made
		-dd (usually after short vowel)	ladder
		-ed (after voiced consonant, V2 / V3[49] regular ending)	owned, called

---

[47] There are of course many different English accents. This table is based on the sounds given in the International Phonetic Alphabet (IPA) for British English. However, even within Britain the sounds vary considerably.
[48] See Glossary.

/k/	kiss	**k** (usually before *e, i* or *y* or after *c* or two vowels)	kind, joke, look
		-ck (after one short vowel)	duck
		c (before *a, o, u* or consonant; only at end of word if in *-ic*)	cat, economic
		-cc-	account
		qu-	mosquito, quay
		-que (end of word only)	antique, mosque
		ch	chemist, school, stomach
		-cqu-	acquaint
		-cu-	biscuit
		-kk- (rare)	trekker
/g/	go	**g**	green, begin, bag
		-gg (usually after short vowel)	egg
		gu- (before *e, i*, or *y*)	guess, guide, guy
		-gue (at end of word)	dialogue
		gh-	ghost
/f/	fit	**f**	finger, safe
		-ff (usually after short vowel)	stuff, effort
		ph	phone, graph
		-gh	laugh
		-ppf-	sapphire
/v/	very	**v-**	vegetable
		-ve (end of word)	have
		-vv- (rare)	savvy
		f (probably the only example)	of
/s/	sand	**s**	sit, ask, books
		-ss	glass, gossip
		-se (at end of word)	nurse
		-ce (at end of word)	practice
		c- (before *e, i* or *y*)	city, nice, cycle
		-st-	listen
		sc-	science, muscle
		ps-	psychology
/z/	zoo	**z-**	zero, lazy
		-ze	breeze
		-zz (usually after short vowel)	jazz
		-s	busy, pens
		-se (at end of word)	please
		-ss-	dessert
		x-	anxiety, xenophobia
/ð/	that	**th-**	then
		-the (at end of word)	bathe
/θ/	think	**th**	Thursday, tooth
		-fth (at end of word for some speakers)	fifth
/ʃ/	shoe	**sh**	sheep, cash
		-ti-	action
		-ci-	special, suspicion
		-ssi-	discussion
		-si-	comprehension
		ch-	chef, brochure
		s- (before *u*)	sugar, insurance
		-ss- (before *u*)	tissue, issue
		-ce-	ocean
		-sci-	conscious
		-x-	anxious
		-sc-	crescendo
		sch-	schmooze

/ʒ/	vision	-si- -ge -s- -z- -t-	television beige usually, leisure seizure equation
/m/	meat	m -mm- (usually after short vowel) -mb mn	Monday, same, jam summer lamb autumn
/n/	no	n -nn (usually after short vowel) kn- gn pn- mn-	never, man funny knife gnome, sign pneumonia mnemonic
/ŋ/	sing	-ng -ngue -n- (before **k** or **x**)	thing, anger tongue thank, anxiety
/tʃ/	chair	ch -tch (at end of word, after short vowel) t- (before **u** or **ure**, for some speakers) -ti- c- -cc-	cheese, teacher, reach catch tulip, picture question cello cappuccino
/dʒ/	job	j- g- (before **e, i** or **y**) -dge (usually after short vowel) -gg- (before vowel) d- (before vowel, for some speakers)	jam, major giant, page, biology bridge suggest soldier, during
/w/	win	w- wh- o- -u- (after **s** or **q**)	water, away when, nowhere one persuade, quite
/h/	hot	h- wh-	health, perhaps who, whole
/j/	yes	y- -i-	you, royal million, onion
/l/	leg	l -ll -le (after single or double consonant)	late, feel ball, yellow people, middle
/r/	rat	r -rr (usually after short vowel) wr- rh-	red, forest berry write rhythm, diarrhoea

Vowel sounds — how they can be represented

IPA	as in	Possible spellings	Example words
/æ/	bad	**a**	hand
		ai	plait
/e/	egg	**e**	ten
		ea	bread
		a	many
		u	bury
		ai	said
		ie	friend
		ei	leisure
		eo	leopard
/ɪ/	big	**i**	little
		y	typical
		e	England
		u	busy
		ui	build
		o	women
		ie	sieve
		ei	forfeit
/ɒ/	pot	**o**	blog
		a (after *w* or *q*)	want, quality
		au	because
		o + CONSONANT + *e*	gone
		ou	cough
/ʌ/	fun	**u**	but
		o (especially before ***n, m, th*** or ***v***)	honey, mother, cover
		o + CONSONANT + *e*	come
		ou	young
		oe	does
		oo	blood
/ʊ/	book	**oo**	book, good
		u	put, full
		ou	could
/ə/	about	**a**	cinema
		er	sister, better, teacher
		re (British English)	metre, centre
		ar	grammar, calendar
		or	doctor, mirror
		our (British English)	colour
		ur	Saturday
		e	open, begin
		i	pencil
		o	button
		u	support
		ough	thorough
		ah	cheetah
/ɑ:/	car	**ar**	car, hardly
		a (in some British accents)	ask, castle, father
		al	half, almond
		are	are
		er	clerk, sergeant
		au	laugh, aunt
		ea	heart

/ɜː/	girl	ir	bird, thirty
		ur	burn, urgent
		er	verb, certain
		ear	early, heard
		or (after *w*)	word, worse
		our	journey
		ere	were
		olo	colonel
/iː/	green	ee	tree
		ea	eat
		e + CONSONANT + *e*	these, complete
		ey	money
		y (after CONSONANT)	baby
		e	me
		ie	thief
		ei	receive
		eo	people
		ay	quay
		i + CONSONANT + e	police
/ɔː/	sport	or	for, morning
		ore	more, before
		al (l)	all, walk, also
		aw	law, awful
		au	autumn, saucer
		-ar (after *w* and *q*)	war, quarter
		ough	thought
		augh	daughter
		our	four
		oar	oar, board
		oor	floor
/uː/	moon	oo	school, too
		oo + CONSONANT + *e*	choose
		u + CONSONANT + *e*	rude, include
		ew	grew
		ue	true
		ou	you, coupon
		o	do, to, who
		o + CONSONANT + *e*	whose, move
		ui	juice, suit
		oe	shoe
		eu	leukaemia, lieu
		u	truth
		ough	through
/eɪ/	name	a + CONSONANT + *e*	sale, cake
		ai	rain, daisy
		ay	say
		-et	ballet
		ey	they
		ei (sometimes followed by *gn* or *gh*)	beige, reign, eight
		ea	great
		aigh	straight
		ae	reggae

/əʊ/	home	o + CONSONANT + e	broke, hole
		oa	goal
		ow	slow, own
		o	go, sold, odour
		oe	toe
		-ou	shoulder
		-ough	although
		eau	bureau
		ol	folk
		ew	sew
		eo	yeoman
/aɪ/	hide	i + CONSONANT + e	time
		-y	try, type, clarify
		-igh	high
		i	kind, I
		-ie	lie
		-eigh	height
		-ye	eye
		-uy	buy
		ae	maestro
		ei	either (also pronounced /ɪː/)
/ɔɪ/	boy	oy	toy, enjoy, oyster
		oi	oil, toilet, avoid
/aʊ/	cow	ow	now, powder
		ou	round, out
		ough	plough
/ɪə/	ear	ear	hear, disappear
		eer	deer, engineer
		er (before another vowel)	here, cereal, zero
		ier	cashier, pier
		eir	weird
		eor	theory
		eyr-	eyrie
		-ea	idea
/eə/	chair	air	air, stairs
		are	care
		ear	wear, pear
		ere	there, where
		eir	their
		aer	aeroplane
		ayer	layer, prayer
		ayor	mayor
/ʊə/	sure	ure	pure
		our	tour
		oor (for some speakers)	poor
		eur (with a /j/ sound before it)	Euro

Bibliography

Abell, S. (1994). *Helping Adults to Spell.* London: Basic Skills Agency.

Albrow, K. (1972). *The English Writing System: notes towards a description.* London: Longman.

Barry, D. (undated). *Humourous Quotes from Dave Barry Talks Back.* Retrieved November 17, 2010, from Working Humour: http://www.workinghumor.com/quotes/dave_barry_talks.shtml#

Beason, L. (2006). *Eyes Before Ease.* New York: McGraw-Hill.

Bell, M. (2004). *Understanding English Spelling.* London: Pegasus.

Bendefy, A., & Hickmott, O. (2006). *Seeing Spells Achieving.* London: MX.

Bounds, G. (2010, October 5). *How Handwriting Trains the Brain.* Retrieved November 19, 2010, from Wall Street Journal: http://online.wsj.com/article/SB1000142405274870463150457553193275492 2518.html

Boyer, S. (2003). *Spelling and Pronunciation for English Language Learners.* Glenbrook: Boyer Educational Resources.

Brabbs, P. (2004). Magic Spell. *English Teaching Professional, 35* , 56-7.

Brooks, P., & Weeks, S. (1998). A comparison of the responses of dyslexic, slow learning and control children to different strategies for teaching spellings. *Dyslexia* , 212-222.

Cambridge University Press. (2008). *Cambridge Advanced Learner's Dictionary 3rd Edition.* Cambridge: Cambridge University Press.

Carney, E. (1994). *A Survey of English Spelling.* London: Routledge.

Carney, E. (1997). *Language Workbooks - English Spelling.* London: Routledge.

Carter, R., & McCarthy, M. (2006). *Cambridge Grammar of English: A Comprehensive Guide.* Cambridge: Cambridge University Press.

Chase, C. (1986). Essay Test Scoring: Interaction of Relevant Variables. *Journal of Educational Measurement, 23* , 33-41.

Chomsky, N. H. (1968). *The Sound Pattern of English.* New York: Harper & Row.

Chomsky, N. (1972). Phonology and Reading. In H. (. Levin, *Basic Processes in Reading* (pp. 3-18). London: Harper & Row.

Chomsky, N., & Halle, M. (1968). *The Sound Pattern of English.* London: Harper & Row.

Cook, V. (2009). *It's All in a Word.* London: Profile.

Cook, V. (n.d.). *L2 Spelling.* Retrieved November 19, 2010, from SLA: http://homepage.ntlworld.com/vivian.c/SLA/L2_spelling.htm

Cook, V. (2004). *The English Writing System.* London: Arnold.

Cook, V. (2001). *The Neglected Role of Written Language in Language Teaching. .* Retrieved November 19, 2010, from Writing Systems: http://homepage.ntlworld.com/vivian.c/Writings/Papers/RoleOfWriting.htm

Crystal, D. (1987). *The Cambridge Encyclopedia of Language.* Cambridge: Cambridge University Press.

Crystal, D. (1995). *The Cambridge Encyclopedia of the English Language.* Cambridge: Cambridge University Press.

Crystal, D. (2008). *Txtng: the gr8 db8.* Oxford: Oxford University Press.

Davis, P., & Rinvolucri, M. (1988). *Dictation: New Methods, New Possibilities.* Cambridge, UK.: Cambridge University Press.

Davis, R. (1997). *The Gift of Dyslexia.* London: Souvenir .

Department for Children, S. a. (2007, March). *Letters and Sounds: Principles and practice of high quality phonics.* Retrieved November 18, 2010, from The National Strategies: http://nationalstrategies.standards.dcsf.gov.uk/node/84969

Frith, U. (. (1980). *Cognitive Processes in Spelling.* London: Academic Press.

Gentry, J. R. (1987). *Spel ... is a four letter word.* Portsmouth, New Hampshire: Heinnemann.

Glover, G. (2004, November 29). When Spelling is Compelling. *The Scotsman* .

Hanna, P., Hanna, J., Hodges, R., & Rudorf, H. (1966). *Phoneme-grapheme corresponences as cues to spelling improvement.* Washington DC: United States Office of Education Cooperative Research.

Harmer, J. (2007). *The Practice of English Language Teaching, 4th Edition.* Harlow: Longman.

Jamieson, C., & Jamieson, J. (2003). *Manual for Testing and Teaching English Spelling.* London: Whurr.

Krashen, S. D. (1981). *Principles and Practice in Second Langage Acquisition.* London: Prentice Hall.

Learning and Skills Improvement Service. (2010). *Teaching and Learning Spelling.* Retrieved November 19, 2010, from Excellence Gateway: http://www.excellencegateway.org.uk/

Littlejohn, A. (2008). *The Tip of the Iceberg: Factors Affecting Learner Motivation.* Retrieved December 27, 2010, from AndrewLittlejohn.com: www.andrewlittlejohn.net/website/docs/iceberg.pdf

Lunsford, A. (2009, October 12). *Stanford study finds richness and complexity in students' writing.* Retrieved November 17, 2010, from Stanford University News: http://news.stanford.edu/news/2009/october12/lunsford-writing-research-101209.html

Palmer, S. (2000). *The Little Alphabet Book.* Oxford: Oxford University Press.

Peters, M. (1985). *Spelling: Caught or Taught?* London: Routeledge and Kegan Paul.

Pratley, R. (1988). *Spelling It Out.* London: BBC.

Pullen, M. (2008, May 31). *Do Spelling Tests Work?* Retrieved December 18, 2010, from The Elementary Educator: http://mrpullen.wordpress.com/2008/05/31/do-spelling-tests-work/

Quirk, C. R., Greenbaum, S., Leech, G., & J, S. (1985). *A Comprehensive Grammar of the English Language.* London: Longman.

Rochester, J. M. (2010, October 31). *Outrage at Banning Spelling tests.* Retrieved November 19, 2010, from The Washington Post: http://voices.washingtonpost.com/class-struggle/2010/10/murdering_spelling.html

Rose, S. (1993). *The Making of Memory: From Molecules to Mind.* New York: Bantam.

Rosen, M. (2006, June 6). *What's Politics Got to Do with It.* Retrieved November 19, 2010, from Michael Rosen: http://www.michaelrosen.co.uk/kingstalk.html

Schlagel, R., & Schlagel, J. (1992). The Integral Character of Spelling: teaching strategies for multiple purposes. *Language Arts* , 418-424.

Scott, C. (2000). Principles and Methods of Spelling Instruction:Application for Poor Spellers. *Topics in Language Disorders, 20 (3)* , 66-82.

Scrivener, J. (2005). *Learning Teaching, 2nd Edition.* Oxford: Macmillan.

Shaw, G. B. (1916). *Pygmalion.* New York: Brentano.

Shemesh, R., & Waller, S. (2000). *Teaching English Spelling.* Cambridge: Cambridge University Press.

Smith, F. (1982). *Writing and the Writer.* London: Heinemann Educational.

Stevick, E. (1982). *Teaching and Learning Languages.* Cambridge: Cambridge University Press.

Swan, M., & Smith, B. (. (1987). *Learner English: A teacher's guide to interference and othe problems.* Cambridge: Cambridge University Press.

Templeton, S., & Morris, D. (2001, October). *Reconceptualizing spelling development and instruction.* Retrieved November 19, 2010, from Reading Online, 5(3).: http://www.readingonline.org/articles/art_index.asp?HREF=/articles/handbook/templeton/index.html

Thake, R., & Brabben, D. (2010). *English Unlimited series.* Cambridge: Cambridge University Press.

Thornbury, S., & Watkins, P. (2007). *The CELTA Course.* Cambridge: Cambridge University Press.

Tilbury, A. e. (2010). *English Unlimited.* Cambridge: Cambridge University Press.

Timmis, I., & Islam, C. (2003, July 1). *Lexical Approach 2 - What does the lexical approach look like?* Retrieved December 14, 2010, from British Council Teaching English: http://www.teachingenglish.org.uk/think/articles/lexical-approach-2-what-does-lexical-approach-look

Torbe, M. (1977). *Teaching Spelling.* London: Ward Lock Educational.

Twain, M. (undated). *Hystorical Spelling Quotes.* Retrieved November 17, 2010, from Articles Base: http://www.articlesbase.com/self-help-articles/hystorical-spelling-quotes-133068.html#ixzz15Zu6HrLd

Underhill, A. (1994). *Sound Foundations: Learning and Teaching Pronunciation.* Oxford: Macmillan.

Venezky, R. (1999). *The American Way of Spelling.* New York: Guilford Press.

Visser, M. (1994). *The Way We Are.* New York: Viking.

Webster, N. (1884). *An American Dictionary of the English Language.* Amherst: Adams.

Webster, N. (1789). An Essay on the Necessity, Advantages, and Practicality of Reforming the Mode of Spelling and of Rendering the Orthography of Words Correspondent to Pronunciation. *Dissertations on the English Language: with notes, historical and critical.*

Weiner, E. (2010). *Early Modern English Pronunciation.* Retrieved December 4, 2010, from oed.com: http://www.oed.com/public/earlymodernenglishpronunciation

Weiner, E. (2010). *Early modern English—an overview.* Retrieved December 4, 2010, from oed.com: http://www.oed.com/public/earlymodernenglish/early-modern-englishan-overview

White, F. (2004). Cooking the Spelling Books. *EL Gazette* , 11.

Wren, S. (n.d.). *What's so irregular about exception words.* Retrieved October 12, 2009, from SEDL: http://www.sedl.org

Index

7374480R00155

Printed in Great Britain
by Amazon.co.uk, Ltd.,
Marston Gate.